THE PSYCHOTHERAPEUTIC USE OF THE TALKING, FEELING, & DOING GAME AND OTHER PROJECTIVE TECHNIQUES

by Richard A. Gardner, M.D.
Foreword by Lawrence E. Shapiro, Ph.D.

CALL 1•800•962•1141

The Psychotherapeutic Use of
The Talking, Feeling, & Doing Game
and Other Projective Techniques

by Richard A. Gardner, M.D.
Foreword by Lawrence E. Shapiro, Ph.D.

Childswork/Childsplay publishes products for mental health professionals, teachers and parents who wish to help children with their developmental, social and emotional growth. For questions, comments, or to request a free catalog describing hundreds of games, toys, books, and other counseling tools, call 1-800-962-1141.

© 2004 Childswork/Childsplay and Creative Therapeutics, Inc.
All rights reserved.
Printed in the United States of America.

ISBN 1-58815-063-1

Table of Contents

Foreword 5

The Mutual Storytelling Technique 7

   Historical Background 7

   The Basic Technique 10

   Specific Technique for Eliciting Self-Created Stories 12

   Fundamentals of Story Analysis 15

   Clinical Examples 18

   Concluding Comments 68

Dramatized Storytelling 69

   Introduction 69

   Clinical Examples 71

Mutual Storytelling Derivative Games 127

   Introduction 127

   The Board of Objects Game 130

   The Three Grab-Bag Games 140

   Scrabble for Juniors 166

   The Feel and Tell Game 179

   The Alphabet Soup Game 185

   The Pick-a-Face Game 198

   The Make-a-Picture Story Cards 204

   Concluding Comments 215

The Talking, Feeling, & Doing Game 217

   The Basic Format of The Talking, Feeling, & Doing Game......217

   Examples of Card Responses 224

   Examples of Therapist-Patient Interchanges 254

   Concluding Comments 292

References 295

Foreword

Richard A. Gardner, M.D. (1931-2003) was one of the most influential child therapists of our times. Although many writers in the field of mental health are remembered for one or two important contributions, Dr. Gardner made at least a half dozen major contributions in this area, introducing techniques used by tens of thousands of therapists in the United States and around the world. In this book, we have excerpted chapters from his seminal work, *The Psychotherapeutic Techniques of Richard A. Gardner* (1986). We have included sections that will give the reader rich clinical detail and instruction on using his most well-known tools, *The Talking, Feeling, & Doing Game* and *The Mutual Storytelling Technique* and its derivative games.

Trained in traditional child psychiatry at the Columbia-Presbyterian Medical Center and in psychoanalysis at the William A. White Psychoanalytic Institute in New York, Dr. Gardner spent his professional career striving to understand and alleviate the emotional suffering of children. But in spite of his unflagging interest in the etiology of childhood emotional problems and their treatment implications, it was his practical bent and his unique sense of fun that made him stand out as a pioneer in his field. Dr. Gardner self-published *The Talking, Feeling, & Doing Game* in 1973 and after three decades, it is still the most popular therapeutic tool used by therapists and counselors who work with children. There are many reasons why this game has withstood the test of time, but the most important is simple—children love to play it.

Dr. Gardner's explanation for designing a board game to elicit information from children was as direct as his techniques. In a 1994 interview, he modestly commented, "The children I was seeing wouldn't talk to me, so I had to do something to get them to open up." Certainly, Dr. Gardner was not alone in his frustration in working with "resistant" children. Every child therapist tries to get children to open up about their feelings, concerns, and interests, but more often than not, children verbalize very little in the initial phase of therapy, which can last several months. *The Talking, Feeling, & Doing Game* circumvented this long process. Dr. Gardner found that when children were having fun playing a game and earning chips and rewards for their responses, they would readily talk to him about both their surface concerns and their deep-rooted psychological problems.

But getting children to become interested in therapy and reveal their inner lives is only half of the therapeutic power of *The Talking, Feeling, & Doing Game*. The genius of this game is that it also allows therapists to talk to children, modeling a new way to think about the world and its vicissitudes. Throughout this book, you will read richly detailed clinical vignettes in Dr. Gardner's own words, as he helped dozens and dozens of children.

Dr. Gardner's storytelling techniques complement the therapeutic process used in *The Talking, Feeling, & Doing Game*, presenting the therapist with an ongoing source of unconscious symbolic material. Although stories had been used to gain insight into children's unconscious psychological processes since the 1940s, Dr. Gardner pioneered their use as part of the ongoing therapeutic process, treating children by responding in their own metaphoric language. This volume explains how to use *The Bag of Toys, The Bag of Things, The Make-Up-a-Story Television Program* and other clever techniques for engaging even the most inhibited child. If you are new to the intricacies of using therapeutic stories with children, you will not only find a deep understanding of the fundamentals of story analysis, but an inspiration for the way that stories can be used to help children develop an awareness of themselves and others.

For the many fans of Dr. Gardner, and I include myself at the head of the line, the candid style of this book will provide a window into the thoughts and personal style of a consummate clinician. But beyond his clinical acumen and unparalleled creativity, the book will also reveal the most basic elements that characterized Dr. Gardner's success in his lifelong commitment to the field—his original sense of humor and his profound love of children. These traits are the most important gifts that any therapist can bring to the often difficult and frustrating job of helping others, and they are ones where Dr. Richard A. Gardner was truly a master.

Lawrence E. Shapiro, Ph.D.
President, Childswork/Childsplay

I
THE MUTUAL
STORYTELLING TECHNIQUE

Originality is a return to the origin. — Antonio Gaudi

HISTORICAL BACKGROUND

The use of children's stories as a source of psychodynamic information is well known to child psychotherapists. To the best of my knowledge, this was first described in the literature (in German) by Hug-Hellmuth in 1913. (The first English translation appeared in 1921.) A fundamental problem for the child therapist has been that of how to take the information that one can derive from such stories and bring about psychotherapeutic change. Children's stories are generally easier to analyze than the dreams, free associations, and other verbal productions of adults. Often, the child's fundamental problems are exhibited clearly to the therapist, without the obscurity, distortion, and misrepresentation characteristic of the adult's fantasies and dreams.

A wide variety of psychotherapeutic techniques have been devised to use therapeutically the insights that the therapist can gain from children's stories. Some are based on the assumption, borrowed from the adult classical psychoanalytic model, that bringing into conscious awareness that which has been unconscious can in itself be therapeutic. The literature is replete with articles in which symptomatic alleviation, and even cure, quickly follows the patient's gaining insight into the underlying psychodynamic patterns. My own experience has been that very few children are interested in gaining conscious awareness of their unconscious processes in the hope that they can use such insight to alleviate their symptoms and improve their life situation. I believe that one of the reasons for this is that the average child of average intelligence is not cognitively capable of taking an analytic stance and engaging in a meaningful psychoanalytic inquiry until about the age of ten. This corresponds to Piaget's level of formal operations, the age at which the child can consciously differentiate between a symbol and the entity which it symbolizes.

Of course, brighter children are capable of doing this at early ages. But even those children are generally not interested in assuming the analytic stance and delving into the unconscious roots of their problems—unless there are significant environmentally stimulating factors. The child who grows up in a home in which both parents are introspective and analytic is more likely to think along these lines as well. Accordingly, it is only on rare occasions that I do direct analytic work with children under the age of 10 or 11. And when this occurs, it is usually a patient who, 1) is extremely bright, and 2) comes from a home in which the parents have been or are in psychoanalytic treatment themselves, and who in addition, are deeply committed to introspective approaches to dealing with life's problems. But even in adult therapy, professions of commitment to analysis notwithstanding, most of my patients are not deeply committed to psychoanalytic inquiry. And they are generally even more resistant to analyzing their resistances to such inquiry. Hence, I attempt to employ a psychoanalytic approach to the therapeutic utilization of children's stories very infrequently.

In the 1920s, Anna Freud and Melanie Klein—both influenced deeply by Hug-Hellmuth's observation—attempted to work analytically with children, and the analysis of their stories was essential to their therapeutic approaches. Although they differed significantly regarding the interpretations they gave to children's stories, they agreed that the gaining of insight into the story's underlying psychodynamic meaning was crucial to meaningful therapeutic change. Beginning in the 1930s, Conn (1939, 1941a, 1941b, 1948, 1954) and Solomon (1938, 1940, 1951, 1955) described the same frustrations this examiner experienced with regard to getting children to analyze meaningfully their self-created stories. They were quite happy to analyze those children who were receptive to such inquiries. But for those who were not, they were equally satisfied discussing the child's story at the symbolic level. They believed that therapeutic changes could be brought about by communicating with the child at the symbolic level. For example, if a child told a story about a dog biting a cat and was unreceptive to analyzing it, they found that discussions about why the dog bit the cat and what better ways there were to handle the situation could get across important messages without producing the anxiety of analytic inquiry.

During my residency training in the late 1950s I first began to suffer the frustration of children's unreceptivity to analysis. I was much more comfortable with the work of Conn and Solomon. It was from these experiences that I derived in the early 1960s the technique that I subsequently called the mutual storytelling technique. Basically, it is another way of therapeutically utilizing children's self-created stories. It stems from the observation that children enjoy not only telling stories but listening to them as well. The efficacy of the storytelling approach for imparting and transmitting important values is ancient. In fact, the transmission of such values was and still is crucial to the survival of a civilized society. Every culture has its own heritage of such stories that have been instrumental in transmitting these important messages down the generations.

It is reasonable to speculate that in the early days of civilized society attempts were made to impart directly important messages necessary for people to learn if they were to cooperate meaningfully in the social group. It was probably learned quite early that such direct confrontations, especially in the presence of others, might not be the most effective way to teach individuals in the hope that they would incorporate these messages into their psychic structures. It is reasonable to speculate that a subsequent development involved the recognition that storytelling might be a useful vehicle for incorporating such messages in a disguised, and therefore less threatening, way. After all, storytelling is an ancient tradition and, up to the twentieth century, it was probably one of the most popular forms of evening entertainment.

It was in such storytelling sessions that people would relate the events of the day and, considering the fact that external sources of entertainment were limited and infrequent, a certain amount of elaboration of events was probably welcome. Furthermore, it is reasonable to speculate that a certain amount of "expansion of the truth" was not seriously criticized because of the extra entertainment value that such elaboration provided. It is reasonable to assume further that the popularity of this form of entertainment made it an attractive vehicle for the incorporation of messages that were important to impart to individuals for immediate purposes as well as for perpetuation down the generations. It was probably appreciated that one could circumvent listeners' defensiveness regarding being told about their wrongdoings by describing the transgressions of others and the lessons they learned from their departures from acceptable patterns of behavior. The basic principle was: "Of course, none of us here would ever do such terrible things, and most of us probably wouldn't even think of such terrible things. However, it's interesting to hear about others who did these things and what they learned from them." Adding violence and sex (traditionally attractive modalities in any story) enhanced their attractiveness to listeners. Ultimately, these stories became the primary vehicle for transmitting down the generations important messages necessary for the survival of the group. In fact, I would go further and state that societies that did not have such a heritage did not survive because they did not have this important vehicle for transmitting their values to subsequent generations.

Much more recently, with the development of the written language, these stories achieved a new permanence. Our Bible is one example of such a document. The Old Testament is basically a collection of those stories that were prevalent from the period around 750 BC to 250 BC. Most consider these stories to be combinations of fact and fantasy. Each individual, of course, must make a decision regarding how much of these two elements are present. There are some who claim that everything in the Bible is completely true and others who go to the other extreme and claim that it is complete fantasy. Although people may differ regarding what they consider the fact/fantasy ratio to be, most will agree that these stories have had a profound influence on mankind and have contributed significantly to moral development and the perpetuation and survival of civilized society.

The mutual storytelling technique is in this tradition. It attempts to rectify one of the fundamental problems of storytelling as a vehicle for transmitting important messages, namely, that any story, no matter how well tailored to the needs of a particular audience, is likely to be relevant to only a small fraction of those who listen to it. After all, an audience generally consists of men and women of varying ages from childhood through old age. It is unreasonable to expect any particular story to "turn on" more than a small fraction of such a heterogeneous group. The mutual storytelling technique attempts to circumvent this drawback by using a story that is designed to be specifically relevant to a particular person at that particular time. The stories are tailor-made for the individual and therefore, they are more likely to be attended to with receptivity and incorporated into the listener's psychic structure.

THE BASIC TECHNIQUE

In this method, the therapist elicits a self-created story from the child. The therapist then surmises its psychodynamic meaning and then tells a responding story of his or her own. The therapist's story utilizes the same characters in a similar setting, but introduces healthier resolutions and adaptations of the conflicts present in the child's story. Because the therapist is speaking in the child's own language—the language of allegory—he or she has a better chance of "being heard" than if the messages were transmitted directly. The direct, confrontational mode of transmission is generally much more anxiety provoking than the symbolic. One could almost say that with this method the therapist's messages bypass the conscious and are received directly by the unconscious. The child is not burdened with psychoanalytic interpretations that are generally alien and incomprehensible to him. With this technique, one avoids direct, anxiety-provoking confrontations so reminiscent of the child's experiences with parents and teachers.

The technique is useful for children who will tell stories, but who have little interest in analyzing them (the vast majority, in my experience). It is not a therapy per se, but one technique in the therapist's armamentarium. Empirically, I have found the method to be most useful for children between the ages of five and eleven. I generally do not treat children under the age of four (I find it more efficient to counsel their parents). In addition, children under the age of five are not generally capable of formulating organized stories. In the four- to five-year age bracket, one can elicit a series of story fragments from which one might surmise an underlying psychodynamic theme which can serve as a source of information for the therapist's responding story. The upper age level at which the technique is useful is approximately eleven. At that time, children generally become appreciative of the fact that they are revealing themselves. They may rationalize noninvolvement with the technique with such justifications as, "This is baby stuff," and "I don't feel like telling stories." Lastly, the technique is contraindicated for children who are psychotic and/or who fantasize excessively. One wants more reality-oriented therapeutic approaches such as *The Talking, Feeling, & Doing Game* or else one may entrench their pathology.

Dolls, drawings, and other toys are the modalities around which stories are traditionally elicited in child psychotherapy. Unfortunately, when these facilitating stimuli are used, the child's story may be channeled in highly specific directions. They have specific forms that serve as stimuli that are contaminating to the self-created story. Although the pressure of the unconscious to create a story that serves a specific psychological purpose for the child is greater than the power of the facilitating external stimulus to contaminate the story, there is still some contamination when one uses these common vehicles for story elicitation. The tape recorder does not have these disadvantages; with it, the visual field remains free from distracting and contaminating stimuli. The tape recorder almost asks to be spoken into. Eliciting a story with it is like obtaining a dream on demand. Although there are differences between dreams and self-created stories, the story that is elicited by a tape recorder is far closer to the dream than that which is elicited by play material.

In earlier years I used an audiotape recorder. In more recent years I have used a videotape recorder. For the therapist who has this instrument available, it can enhance significantly the child's motivation to play the game. Although hearing one's story on the audiotape recorder can serve to facilitate the child's involvement in the game, watching oneself on television afterwards is a much greater motivating force. But the examiner should not conclude that these instruments are crucial. They are merely devices. Long before they were invented children enjoyed relating self-created stories, and the therapist should be able to elicit them from most children without these contrivances. They should be viewed as additional motivating facilitators and, of course, they have the additional benefit of the playback which provides reiteration of the therapeutic messages. In earlier years many children would bring their own tape recorder and simultaneously tape the stories with me, and then listen to them at home for further therapeutic exposure. Recently, I added a second videocassette recorder to my office closed-circuit television system. A child can now bring his or her own videocassette, tape the story sequences along with me, and then watch him- or herself at home.

SPECIFIC TECHNIQUE FOR ELICITING SELF-CREATED STORIES

I begin by telling the child that we are now going to play a game in which he or she will be guest of honor on a make-believe television program. In earlier years, I would ask the child if he or she would like to be the guest of honor on the program; in more recent years I seduce him or her into the game without the formal invitation. Of course, if the child strongly resists, I will not pressure or coerce. We then sit across the room from the mounted camera, and the videocassette recorder, lights, and camera are turned on. I then begin:

Therapist: Good morning, boys and girls. I would like to welcome you once again to "Dr. Gardner's Make-Up-a-Story Television Program." We invite boys and girls to this program to see how good they are at making up stories. The story must be completely made up from your own imagination. It's against the rules to tell stories about anything that really happened to you or anyone you know. It's against the rules to tell a story about things you've read about, or heard about, or seen in the movies or on television. Of course, the more adventure or excitement the story has, the more fun it will be to watch on television later. Like all stories, your story should have a beginning, a middle, and an end. And after you've made up your story, you'll tell us the lesson or the moral of your story. We all know that every good story has a lesson or a moral. Then, after you've told your story, Dr. Gardner will make up a story also. He'll try to tell one that's interesting and unusual, and then we'll talk about the lesson or the moral of his story. And now, without further delay, let me introduce to you a boy (girl) who is with us for the first time. Tell us your name, young man (woman).

I then ask the child a series of questions that can be answered by single words or brief phrases. I will ask his or her age, grade, address, name of school, and teacher. These "easy" questions reduce the child's anxiety about the more unstructured themes involved in "making up a story." I then continue:

Therapist: Now that we've heard a few things about you, we're all interested in hearing the story you've made up for us today.

Most children at this point begin with their story, although some may ask for "time out to think." Of course this request is granted. There are some children, however, for whom this pause is not enough, but will still want to try. In such instances the child is told:

Therapist: Some children, especially when it's their first time on this program, have a little trouble thinking of a story. However, I know a way to help such children think of a story. Most people don't realize that there are millions of stories in everyone's head. Did you know that there are millions of stories in your head? (Child usually responds negatively.) Yes, right here between the top of your head and your chin (I touch the top of the child's head with one finger, and the bottom of his or her chin with another finger), right between your ears (I then touch the child's two ears), inside your brain which is in the center of your head are millions of stories. And I know a way to get out one of them.

The way to do this is that we'll tell the story together. And this way, you won't have to do all the work yourself. The way it works is that I start the story and, when I point my finger at you, you say exactly what comes into your mind at the time that I point to you. You'll see then that your part of the story will start coming into your brain. Then after you've told the part of the story that comes into your mind, I'll tell another part, and then I'll point to you. Then we'll go back and forth until the story is over. Okay, here we go. (The reader will note that I again did not ask the child if he or she wished to proceed, rather I just "rolled on.")

Okay, here we go (I now speak *very slowly*). Once upon a time a long, long time ago…in a distant land…far, far away …far beyond the mountains…far beyond the deserts…far beyond the oceans…there lived a…

I then quickly point my finger at the child (jolting the child out of the semi-hypnotic state that I have tried to induce by this "introduction" which basically says nothing). It is a rare child who does not offer some associative word at that point. For example, if the word is "cat," I will then say, "And that cat…" and once again point firmly to the child, indicating that it is his or her turn to tell more of the story. I follow the next statement provided by the child with, "And then…" or "The next thing that happened was…" Or, I will repeat the last few words of the patient's last sentence, with such intonations that continuation by him or her is implied. Every statement the child makes is followed by some connective term supplied by me and indicates to the child that he or she should supply the next statement. At no point do I introduce any specific material into the story. The introduction of such specific phrases or words would defeat the purpose of catalyzing the child's production of his or her own created material and of sustaining, as needed, its continuity.

This approach is successful in eliciting stories from the vast majority of children. However, if it is unsuccessful, it is best to drop the activity in a completely casual and nonreproachful manner, such as: "Well, today doesn't seem to be your good day for storytelling. Perhaps we'll try again some other time."

While the child is telling his or her story, I jot down notes. These help me analyze the story and serve as a basis of my own. When the child completes the story, I then elicit its lesson or moral. In addition, I may ask questions about specific items in the story. My purpose here is to obtain additional details which are often helpful in understanding the story. Typical questions might be: "Is the dog in your story a boy or a girl, a man or a woman?" "Why did the horse do that?" or, "Why was the cat so angry at the squirrel?" If the child hesitates to provide a lesson or a moral, or states that there is none, I will usually reply: "What, a story without a lesson? Every good story has some lesson or moral! Every good story has something we can learn from it."

Usually, after completing my story, I will ask the child to try to figure out the moral or the lesson of my story. This helps me ascertain whether my message has been truly understood by the child. If the child is unsuccessful in coming forth with an appropriate lesson or moral to my story, I will provide it. Following the completion of my story, I generally engage the child in a discussion of its meaning to the degree that he or she is capable of gaining insight and/or referring the story's message to him- or herself. Many children, however, have little interest in such insights, and I do not press for them. I feel no pressure to do so because I believe that the important therapeutic task is to get across a principle, and that if this principle is incorporated into the psychic structure (even unconsciously), then therapeutic change can be brought about.

FUNDAMENTALS OF STORY ANALYSIS

Obviously, the therapist is in no position to create a story of his or her own unless there is some understanding of the basic meaning of the child's story. The greater the familiarity with the child, the greater the likelihood the therapist will be in the position to do this. Also, the more analytic training and experience a therapist has, the more likely he or she will be able to ascertain correctly the meaning of the child's story. I first try to ascertain which figure(s) in the child's story represent the child him- or herself and which symbolize significant individuals in the child's milieu. Two or more figures may represent various aspects of the same person's personality. There may, for example, be a "good dog" and a "bad dog" in the same story, which are best understood as conflicting forces within the same child. A horde of figures, all similar, may symbolize powerful elements in a single person. A hostile father, for example, may be symbolized by a stampede of bulls. Malevolent figures can represent the child's own repressed anger projected outward, or they may be a symbolic statement of the hostility of a significant figure. Sometimes both of these mechanisms operate simultaneously. A threatening tiger in one boy's story represented his hostile father, and the father was made more frightening by the child's own hostility, repressed and projected onto the tiger. This is one of the reasons why many children view their parents as being more malevolent than they actually are.

Besides clarifying the particular symbolic significance of each figure, it is also important for the therapist to get a general overall "feel" for the atmosphere of the story. Is the ambiance pleasant, neutral, or horrifying? Stories that take place in frozen wastelands or on isolated space stations suggest something very different from those that occur in the child's own home. The child's emotional reactions when telling the story are of great significance in understanding its meaning. An 11-year-old boy who tells me, in an emotionless tone, about the death fall of a mountain climber reveals not only his anger but also the repression of his feelings. The atypical must be separated from the stereotyped, age-appropriate elements in the story. The former may be very revealing, whereas the latter rarely are. Battles between cowboys and Indians rarely give meaningful data, but when the chief sacrifices his son to Indian gods in a prayer for victory over the white man, something has been learned about the boy's relationship with his father.

The story may lend itself to a number of different psychodynamic interpretations. It is part of the creativity of the unconscious, even in the child, that these can be fused together in the same symbols. The themes may exist simultaneously or in tandem. In selecting the theme that will be most pertinent for the child at that particular time, I am greatly assisted by the child's own lesson or moral. It will generally tell me which of the various themes is most important for the storyteller him- or herself. At times, however, the child may not be able to formulate a relevant moral or lesson. This is especially the case for younger children and/or older ones with cognitive or intellectual impairment. In such cases the therapist is deprived of a valuable source of information.

I then ask myself: "What is the main pathological manifestation in this story?" or, "What is the primary inappropriate or maladaptive resolution of the conflicts presented?" Having identified this, I then ask myself: "What would be a more mature or a healthier mode of adaptation than the one utilized by the child?" I then create a story of my own. My story generally involves the same characters, setting, and initial situation as the child's story. However, very quickly my story evolves in a different direction. The pathological modes are not utilized although they may be considered by various figures in the story. Invariably, a more appropriate or salutary resolution of the most important conflict(s) is achieved.

In my story, I attempt to provide the child with more alternatives. The communication that the child not be enslaved by his or her psychopathological behavior patterns is crucial. Therapy, if it is to be successful, must open new avenues not previously considered by the patient. It must help the patient become aware of the multiplicity of options that are available to replace the narrow, self-defeating ones that have been selected. After I have completed my story, I attempt to get the patient to try to figure out its lesson(s) or moral(s). It is preferable that the child do this, but if the child cannot, then I present it for them. (It is nowhere written that a story must have only one lesson or moral.) My lesson(s) attempts to emphasize further the healthier adaptations I have included in my story. If, while telling my story, the child exhibits deep interest or reveals marked anxiety, then I know that my story is "hitting home." I know then that I am on the right track, and that I have ascertained correctly the meaning of the story and have devised a responding story that is relevant. The anxiety may manifest itself by jitteriness or increased activity level. If the child is bored, it may mean that I am off point. However, it may also be a manifestation of anxiety, and the therapist may not know which explanation is most relevant.

Following the completion of my story and its moral, I usually try to engage the child in a discussion of our stories. For the rare child who is interested in gaining insight, we will try to analyze our stories. For the majority there may be a discussion along other lines, and these are usually at the symbolic level. In earlier years, when I used the audiotape recorder, children were sometimes interested in listening to the tape. In more recent years, since I have been utilizing the videocassette recorder, the interest in watching the program has been much greater. Playing the program makes possible a second exposure to the messages I wish to impart. And, as mentioned, I have recently purchased a second videocassette recorder—which enables the child to bring his or her own tape and replay it at home. This not only provides the opportunity for reiteration of the therapeutic messages, but also serves to entrench the therapist-patient relationship.

CLINICAL EXAMPLES
The Case of Martin: The Bear and the Bees

Martin, a seven-year-old boy, was referred because of generalized apathy, lack of involvement with peers, and disinterest in school in spite of high intelligence. His mother was an extremely angry woman who stated during the first session: "Doctor, my father died when I was two and I have no memory of him. I grew up with my mother and two older sisters. I don't know anything about men and boys. To me they're like strangers from another planet. I can't relate to them. My daughter I can relate to. We're on the same wavelength. I can understand her. Although I know nothing about men, I do know one thing about them and that is that I hate them all." Very early I found the mother to be a bitter, self-indulgent woman who used biting sarcasm as a primary mode of relating to men. She told me about a series of male therapists she had seen herself and who had seen her son, and she had only critical things to say about each of them. I could not help thinking while she was talking that my name might soon be added to the list and be mentioned with an equal degree of denigration to the next therapist. (This prophecy soon proved to be true.) The patient's father was obsessively involved in his work, was away for weeks at a time on business trips, and when home had practically no interest in his son. He had a passive-dependent relationship with his wife and served as a scapegoat for her.

In his first session, Martin told this story:

> Once upon a time there was a bear. He was trying to get some honey from a beehive. He got it from the beehive. He went home with it. The bear ate the honey.

I considered the beehive in the story to represent Martin's mother. She is the source of honey, that is, love; but this love is covered with stinging, poison-injecting, potentially painful contaminants. Seeking affection from her inevitably exposes one to her venom. In the story the bear easily acquires honey from the beehive without any interference at all by the bees. This is an atypical element in the story that is our best clue to its meaning. Typically, bees do not sit silently by while bears put their paws in their beehives and gobble up their honey.

Rather, they usually sting the bear in the obvious hope that it might retreat. The absence of this reaction on the part of the bees in Martin's story is a statement of his wish that his mother's hostility not manifest itself when he attempts to obtain love and affection from her. In short, the story reveals his wish to gain her love without being traumatized by her malevolence.

The story epitomizes well, in a few words, the mother's basic personality pattern and her relationship with the patient. It is an excellent example of how a child's first story may reveal core problems. Because the mother's psychopathology was deep-seated and because she had absolutely no interest in entering into treatment herself, I considered her prognosis for change to be extremely poor. However, even if she exhibited motivation for treatment, under the best of circumstances it would have taken many years to bring about reasonable changes. By that time Martin might be an adolescent or even an adult. I considered it antitherapeutic to tell a responding story that would provide Martin with any hope for a dramatic change in his mother's personality, either in the present or the future. Accordingly, I told Martin this story:

> Once upon a time there was a bear. This bear loved honey very much. There was a beehive nearby, but he knew that the bees were not always willing to let him have some. Sometimes they were friendly, and then they would give him a little bit. Other times they were not, and he knew then that it was wise to stay away from them or else he would get stung. When the bees were unfriendly, he would go to another part of the forest where there were maple trees which dripped sweet maple syrup. When the bees were friendly, he would go to them for honey.

In my story I attempted to accomplish two things. First, I tried to help Martin accept his mother as she really was at that time—someone who could, on occasion, provide him with some affection but who, at other times, could be punitive and denigrating of him. In my story I advise him to resign himself to the situation and to take her affection when it becomes available, but not to seek it otherwise. Second, I attempted to provide Martin with alternative sources of gratification by suggesting that there are others in the world who can compensate him somewhat for his mother's deficiency. This is an important therapeutic point. It is unrealistic to expect patients to resign themselves to giving up an important source of gratification if one does not, at the same time, offer some kind of compensatory satisfactions. Martin might not be able to have the bees' honey at times, but he certainly could have sweet maple syrup as a reasonable substitute.

The Case of Mark: The Farmer and the Stone

Mark, a nine-and-a-half-year-old boy, was referred for treatment because of disruptive and hyperactive behavior in the classroom. At home he was difficult to manage and frequently uncooperative. Particular problems existed with regard to Mark's doing his homework. He frequently refused to do it, and his parents' warnings and threats regarding the consequences of his not doing homework proved futile. He generally subscribed to the life philosophy: "I'll worry today about today and I'll worry tomorrow about tomorrow." Another dictum by which Mark lived was: "I'll cross that bridge when I come to it." His parents' concerns and warnings about the future repercussions of his inattentiveness to his schoolwork were continually of no avail.

Investigation into the background of Mark's difficulties did not reveal factors that I was certain were playing a role in his difficulties. The one factor that I considered possibly operative was the fact that his father had made significant contributions in his field, and Mark probably had the feeling that he could never reach his father's level of competence and renown. He didn't want to confront the fact that he might not achieve his father's levels of competence. This reaction, however, is inappropriate because if it were indeed justified, then all the children of distinguished contributors would end up academic failures. There are still many things to be done in this world and many ways of achieving a sense of competence. Furthermore, one need not be a super-achiever or well known to lead a gratifying life.

During his second month of treatment, Mark told a story which lends itself well to being divided into three parts. Accordingly, I will present each of the parts separately and describe what I considered to be its meaning.

Patient: Well, once there was this farmer and he liked to plant all kinds of crops, and he raised chickens and cows and horses. He liked to work out in the garden. He liked to feed the chickens and get their eggs. One day he took an egg out of underneath a chicken and the chicken bit him. And he didn't know what to do because the chicken never bit him before. So he sold the chicken to a man and this man got mad and he sold the chicken to another man. And this person that he sold the chicken to got mad and said he didn't want it. So he gave it back to him and that man gave it back to the farmer. And then that chicken died so he was kind of glad.

Generally, the protagonist of a story represents the patient. In this case, the patient depicts himself as a farmer. The other "protagonist" of the first part of the story is the chicken. The chicken lends itself well to representing a female in that it is the layer of eggs—the origin of life and a source of food. In this case, I considered the chicken to represent Mark's mother. This speculation is further supported by the fact that the chicken bites the farmer. I considered the biting to symbolize the mother's harping on Mark to do his homework. Mark would like to get rid of the chicken, that is, "get his mother off his back." But Mark, like all human beings, is ambivalent in his relationship with his mother. A part of him would like to get rid of her, and yet another part of him recognizes that to do so would be a devastating trauma. The chicken, then, goes back and forth between Mark and two prospective purchasers. Selling the chicken involves some comfort with duplicity on Mark's part in that the farmer does not inform the buyer of the chicken's alienating defect (biting) which caused him to sell it. The buyer, presumably after being bitten himself, similarly exposes the bird to a third person. The latter, equally dissatisfied, returns the chicken to the second who, in turn, gives the unwanted creature back to the original owner.

Having learned that one cannot so easily rid oneself of people who irritate us, the farmer utilizes a more expedient solution: the chicken conveniently dies. This solution, often resorted to in inferior novels, provides a quick solution to a complex problem and is generally not particularly adaptive in reality because those who hound, persecute, and otherwise make our lives miserable generally do not die so conveniently. In fact, they often appear to live longer than those who treat us benevolently.

In addition, we are not told why the chicken suddenly decides to bite the farmer. All the farmer had done was to take an egg (equals love). The farmer is portrayed as innocent, without having done anything to provoke this hostile act on the chicken's part. There is no consideration of the possibility that the farmer may have contributed to the chicken's behavior by some provocation or negligence, as is so often the case in reality. This segment of the story is also a statement of Mark's desire to solve the problem with the biting chicken (equals mother) by hostile acting out rather than civilized discussion. And now to return to the second part of Mark's story.

> So he went along with his farming and when he was planting his crops—you know corn—in his cornfields, he found like a little, whatever you want to call it, stone. And he kept it because it was kind of pretty. So when he was keeping it, he kept it in his dresser, you know. And every time when he went out to work in his crops he had the stone with him. He would put it in his pocket and every year he held it in his pocket the crops would come up just the way he wanted them to, and when he didn't have it with him something went wrong. So he always had the stone with him. And then he thought that it was a magic stone.

Here, the farmer finds a magic stone which brings him good fortune as long as he keeps it in his pocket. He need only keep the stone in his pocket and his crops will flourish; failure to do so causes them to "grow wrong." I considered this part of the story to be a manifestation of Mark's life philosophy that he need not exert any effort; things will somehow work out. He need not show any forethought or planning; somehow all will go well. He need not put in any effort to accomplish things in life, especially learning in school. He utilizes the magic stone to counteract the insecurity engendered in him by parental threats and suggests that at some level he is fearful that things will not work out. The magic stone provides him with the power to bring about a favorable outcome without any effort on his part. Again, this is a maladaptive response to his school difficulties. And now to the third and last part of Mark's story. I include here the post-story discussion which is also important if the examiner is to be certain about the meaning of a child's story:

> And then one day when he was riding along in his wagon pulled by a horse, it went across the bridge and the wheel came off, you know. And the bridge started to crack. So he grabbed the stone and put it in his pocket and then just got up and walked across to the other side. And then he took the horse to the other side with him and the bridge fell out, you know. As soon as he took it (the stone) out of his pocket the bridge fell into the river. So he had to go and tell the people about it so they could put up a sign

so nobody else could run into it. They put up a sign that said, "Bridge Out." And the townspeople paid to put up a new bridge.

And when the man found out that he lost the stone he was very unhappy and like he didn't tell anybody ever that he had the stone. So one time he was walking along in the same spot that he found the crop, he found the stone again. And he always had good luck forever on.

Therapist: Tell me something. Is it true that it was because the man had taken the stone out of his pocket that the bridge fell down?

Patient: Yes.

Therapist: And that if he had kept the stone in his pocket the bridge would not have fallen down.

Patient: Right.

Therapist: What about the wheel of his wagon? Would that have broken had he kept...

Patient: (interrupting) Well, the wheel broke and the weight of it pushed and cracked the bridge.

Therapist: I see, but it was because he didn't have the stone that the bridge fell down?

Patient: Right.

Therapist: And what's the lesson of that story?

Patient: If you've got something you believe in, you should try to hold on to it, like you know, not try to lose it. If you really believe in it don't you know, fool around with it.

Therapist: Okay.

Here, the farmer is riding a wagon. The wagon lends itself well to symbolizing an individual's feelings about his or her ability to move along life's course. It is analogous to the automobile in this regard. A man, for example, has a repetitious dream in which his automobile is just sitting there with all four tires deflated. The dream is a statement of his sense of impotency with regard to his capacity to move along life's course. A neurologically impaired girl has a dream that she is driving her father's car and each time she puts her foot on the brake, the car doesn't stop. The dream reveals her feeling that she cannot "put the brakes on" her thoughts, feelings and actions. In Mark's fantasy, the wheel of the wagon "came off." This is a statement of Mark's sense of instability. It probably reflects his awareness, at some level, that his failure to work in school is compromising his capacity to move along life's course. Furthermore, it may relate to his parents' warnings that if he does not "shape up" his future will be a bleak one.

But it is not only the wheel that comes off, the bridge itself "started to crack." This is a statement of an even more profound sense of insecurity in Mark. The supporting structure under the wagon is also weak. The wagon on the bridge symbolizes Mark's view of his capacity to move along life's course. After all, the bridge connects one point to another and facilitates such progress. If the bridge breaks, one is stopped (at least temporarily) from moving along life's path. In short, the breaking of the wagon's wheel and the falling of the bridge depict Mark's belief that his world is falling away under him. His difficulties at school and at home were interfering with his gaining a sense of competence in coping with life. In both the academic and behavioral realms he was not acquiring the talents and skills which are necessary if one is to feel confident about coping with reality. In compensation for his feelings of inadequacy in these areas, he provides himself with a magic stone which protects him from the dangerous results of his incompetence. Furthermore, the magic stone fantasy is consistent with his life philosophy that somehow things will work out.

In the post-story discussion, I questioned Mark in order to be certain that I understood completely the facts of his story. If the therapist is not completely clear about the incidents in the story, he or she is ill-equipped to analyze it. And, of course, any stories that the therapist creates that derive from an incorrect rendition of the child's story are likely to be completely off point and of little or no therapeutic value. Just as Mark's story lent itself well to being divided into three segments, I divided my responding story into three segments, each of which corresponded to one of the patient's. This was the first of the three segments of my responding story:

Therapist: Now I'll tell my story. The title of my story is "The Chicken and the Stone."

Once upon a time there was a farmer and this farmer had a chicken and this chicken would lay eggs. And one day he went over to the chicken to get an egg, and the chicken bit him. He got very angry and he thought, "I know what I'll do. I'll get rid of this chicken. I'll sell this chicken to someone else." He also thought, "Maybe it will die. Then I won't have any problems with it."

So another man came along and he said, "Would you like to buy a chicken?"

And the man said, "Well, tell me about this chicken. Is he a good chicken? Is he kind? Does he bite?"

The farmer said, "Well, he may bite."

"Look," the man said, "I don't want a biting chicken."

And the farmer didn't know what to do because there he was stuck with this chicken. He said, "Gee, I wish this chicken were dead."

The second man said, "Look, here you have a chicken that's biting. You want to get rid of him. You want him to die. Is that the only way you know how to solve a problem with a biting chicken? You know, you can't solve life's problems by killing off or selling off the people who are bothering you. You've got to work it out with them. You can't get rid of people so easily and you can't even get rid of biting chickens so easily. So I suggest that you try to figure out some way of solving this problem with the chicken."

Well, he talked to the chicken. (In my story this chicken talks.) And he found out that there were things which he was doing which were bothering that chicken and that's why the chicken bit him. And when they were able to settle that problem and he stopped doing the things which bothered the chicken, the chicken stopped biting him and then the chicken continued to lay many more eggs and he then no longer wished to get rid of the chicken to sell him and he no longer wished that the chicken were dead.

Whereas the first buyer in Mark's story gullibly buys the chicken without asking questions, in my story he inquires about the chicken's habits—especially whether he bites. I attempted thereby to communicate that buyers in reality may not easily be taken in by the seller's duplicity. I hoped to let Mark know that one doesn't easily get away with lying and in this way lessen his tendency to lie in order to achieve his ends. The farmer then tells the truth and hopefully serves as a model of honesty for the patient. Thwarted in his attempts to get rid of the malevolent chicken, the farmer expresses the wish that it die. Again, reality considerations reign and the chicken remains very much alive. At this point the buyer becomes more directly the transmitter of my healthier communications and adaptations. He advises direct inquiry into the difficulties in the farmer-chicken relationship in the service of resolving them in ways more civilized (discussion rather than hostile acting out) than those already attempted by the farmer.

Accordingly, the farmer invites the chicken to express his grievances ("In my story this chicken talks.") rather than act them out with biting. The chicken does so and the problems are resolved. Because the patient's story did not specify the nature of the chicken's source(s) of irritation, I made only general reference to them. Had I wished to get more specific I would have first asked Mark why the chicken bit the farmer. The information so gained could have served to provide me with specifics for my story. But I already had so much information to work with by the time Mark finished his complete story that I decided not to add any more material. Overloading can reduce the child's receptivity to the therapist's stories. My main message then was that if someone is hostile toward you, rather than trying to get rid of him or her by separation or death, try to work out the problem through civilized inquiry and nonviolent action.

Whereas in Mark's story the potential purchaser refuses to buy a biting chicken, and then goes his way, my purchaser conducts an inquiry and provides advice. This is a common maneuver that I utilize in the mutual storytelling technique. It is one of the ways in which I provide my therapeutic messages. I wear many guises. Sometimes a passerby stops to watch the action and then, without any invitation on the part of the protagonists, enters into a discussion with them in the course of which he dispenses advice. Sometimes, unbeknownst to the participants, a "wise old owl" has been sitting on a bough of a tree watching the activities below. Then, at some judicious point, he or she interrupts the proceedings and starts pontificating. Again, there is full attention and receptivity to everything the owl says. The protagonists "hang on every word." Sometimes I use a teenager for this purpose. The reader will do well to recognize the value of the teenager in the treatment of latency-aged children. There is no one in the world who possesses more omniscience than the teenager. He knows everything and is in no way modest about his vast knowledge of the world. The reader might be interested to learn that in the 25 years or so that I have been utilizing this technique, not once (I repeat not once) has the recipient of such gratuitous advice ever responded with a comment such as: "Listen, Buster, I would appreciate your not butting into our business. If I wanted your advice, I would have asked for it. And until that time comes, I'd appreciate your keeping your trap shut."

Now onward to the second part of my responding story which, as mentioned, directs its attention to the second segment of the child's.

Now, one day this farmer was working in his cornfields and he found a very pretty stone. It was very shiny and very pretty.

And he said, "I wonder if this is a magic stone. I'd sure like to have a magic stone. My crops haven't been doing too well lately. So he rubbed the stone and he hoped that the crops would do better. But nothing happened. The crops still were poor.

But one day he was in town and he was in a general store buying provisions and the owner of the store noticed that the farmer was rubbing the stone and holding it in his pocket. And he said, "What are you doing there?"

The farmer said, "Oh, that's my magic stone. That gives me luck."

He said, "Has it ever given you luck?"

The farmer replied, "Well, no, but I'm hoping it will make my crops better."

And the man in the store said to him, "Well, I never heard of a magic stone." He said, "What are you doing with your crops? Are you using any fertilizers and things like that?"

The farmer said, "Well, not really. I really don't believe too much in them. It's a lot of extra work putting in those fertilizers and it costs money."

And the man said, "Well, I think that the reason why your crops aren't doing well is that you're not taking care of them well enough. You're not putting in fertilizers." And he asked the farmer some other questions about what he was doing and it was clear that the farmer was not doing everything that he could. And the man in the store said, "Instead of rubbing a magic stone I suggest you get to work on your farm and start taking good care of your crops. I think there's a better likelihood that they'll do well than if you rub a magic stone."

And the farmer thought about what the man had said and he decided to try him out. So he got the fertilizer and he started to work harder on his crops, and sure enough that year he had a better crop than he had ever had before. Well, although the farmer was impressed with what the storekeeper had said, he wasn't fully sure that the stone still wasn't magic.

In my responding story, the magic stone is not effective in improving the farmer's crops. No matter how much he rubs it, the crops remain weak and malnourished. My advice to utilize more realistic and predictably effective methods is transmitted through the owner of the general store. As I am sure is obvious to the reader, this is another one of the disguises that I utilize in my responding stories. The farmer is receptive to this advice and, although it works, he still does not give up hope that his stone will perform magic. We are generally more attracted to easy and quick solutions than to difficult and complex problems, and the farmer is not immune to this human frailty. It will take a more dramatic proof of the impotency of his stone to convince him of its worthlessness in controlling natural events. (See part three of my story below.)

The above transcript does not provide the reader with information about the boy's facial expressions and gestures while I told my story. While relating the second phase of my story, the patient began to blink his eyes. I considered this to be a manifestation of the tension I was arousing in him with my statement that his fantasies of a magic solution to his problems were not going to be realized. Furthermore, he placed his right hand in a seemingly strange position, namely, as if he were holding a stone in it. His arm was flexed at the elbow and his fingers so positioned in cup-like fashion that he could very well have been holding a stone. I believe that this gesture was unconscious, and it reflected his need to "hang on" to the stone that I was symbolically taking away from him. It certainly provided me with confirmation that my story was indeed "hitting home" and touching on important issues.

I then continued and related the third part of my story:

And on his farm there was a bridge which was somewhat old and weak, and he used to look at it and say, "I wonder if I should fix it up one of these days. Nah, I'll rub my stone. It will keep it going." So he used to rub his stone every time he'd pass that bridge in order to keep the bridge solid. But one day as he was riding his wagon across the bridge a wheel broke and his wagon fell down and sure enough the bridge broke as well, even though he had had his magic stone in this pocket. And there he was in the water—his horse jumping around very scared, the wagon broken even more than it had been, the farmer sitting in the water all wet, and his wagon broken even more, and the bridge completely crushed. And there he was with the magic stone in his pocket! And as he sat there, he realized that this stone really wasn't magic. Finally it took that to make him realize and after that he decided to build a new bridge. He threw away the stone and he built a new strong bridge and that was the end of his belief in a magic stone. And do you know what the lesson of that story is?

I interrupt the transcript here before the post-story discussion which begins with the patient's response to my request that he provide the moral of my story. As is obvious, in my story, I again attempt to drive home the point that the magic stone will not work. Just as the patient's third segment is basically a restatement of his second, in that in both the magic stone is used to assuage tension (induced by his parents' threats) and perpetuate his life philosophy that all will go well even if he doesn't put in effort, my third segment is basically a restatement of my second. Here, while I related my story, the patient involved himself in even more dramatic gesturing. Specifically, at the point where I described the farmer sitting in the water, after the bridge had broken through, the patient spontaneously began to rub "water" off his thighs. He then resumed the gesture of holding the stone. However, at the point where I described the farmer's throwing the stone, the patient, without any prompting on my part, engaged in a stone-throwing maneuver. I wish to emphasize to the reader that there was no suggestion, either overt or covert, by me that the patient dramatize or in any way gesticulate the elements in my story. His spontaneous involvement in this way was confirmation that he was swept up in my story and that my message was being incorporated into his psychic structure.

As is my usual practice, rather than tell the moral myself, I generally ask the patient what he or she understands to be the lesson of my story. In this way I can often determine whether my messages have been truly understood because a correct statement of the moral requires a deep appreciation, at some level, of the story's fundamental meaning. This is the interchange that followed my question:

> *Patient:* Don't count on something else to do your work for you.
> *Therapist:* Right! That's one lesson. That's the lesson with the magic stone. What's the lesson of the part with the chicken and the egg and the biting?
> *Patient:* You should fix your own problems now if you can, or else somebody else will fix them for you.
> *Therapist:* Well, that and if you have a problem with someone it's not so easy to get rid of them.
> *Patient:* Try to figure it out.
> *Therapist:* Try to figure it out with them. You can't kill them off, you can't sell them generally. Human beings are not like chickens. You can't just sell them or kill them so easily. If you try

to, you know, you'll get into a lot of trouble. So the best thing is to try to work the problem out with the person. The end. Wait a minute. I want to ask you something. Do you want to say anything about this story?

Patient: No.

Therapist: Did you like it?

Patient: Yeah.

Therapist: Any particular part?

Patient: The part where he found the stone and it was pretty and shiny.

Therapist: Uh huh. Any other part?

Patient: No.

Therapist: Did you learn anything from this story? Did this story teach you anything?

Patient: No.

Therapist: Not at all?

Patient: Well, yeah.

Therapist: What does it teach you?

Patient: Well, you should kind of figure out your own problems and don't count on other people to do stuff for you.

Therapist: Okay. What about magic? What does it say about magic?

Patient: Magic—well, if you've got a magic stone make sure it's *really* a magic stone and then go counting on it. (laughs)

Therapist: Do you think there are such things as magic stones?

Patient: No. (laughs)

Therapist: I don't believe so either.

Patient: You can keep them as a good luck charm—as a pretty piece, but not as a magic stone.

Therapist: Do you think a good luck charm really brings good luck?

Patient: Hhmmm, not really.

Therapist: I don't think so either. No. Okay. So that's the end of the program today. Goodbye, boys and girls.

It is unrealistic for the therapist to expect that a single confrontation or story, or any other single experience in therapy, is going to bring about permanent change. Those who have conviction for time-limited therapy believe that this is possible, and they will attract patients who are gullible enough to believe this as well. If such rapid changes could indeed take place, Mark might very well say to me something along these lines: "Dr. Gardner, you're right. There's no such thing as magic. You've convinced me of that today. I can promise you that I will never again believe in magic. Now let's go on and talk about my next problem."

There are, of course, patients who say things along these lines. It is one of the more common forms of resistance and/or ingratiating oneself to the therapist. In the real world, the world in which there is no magic, the best one can hope for is to introduce an element of ambivalence regarding the patient's belief in magic. And this is what I believe occurred here. The post-story discussion reveals some discomfort on Mark's part with my message, but also some receptivity to it. In ensuing stories there were statements of negation of magic ("There's no such thing as a magic stone") which is certainly not a manifestation of "cure" of the problem. True "cure" comes when there is no mention of magic at all. Doing and undoing is not the same as never having done at all. Mark did reach the point, however, about three or four months later, in which magic did not appear in any form whatsoever in his stories. It was then, I believe, that he reached a healthier level with regard to this problem.

The Case of Evan: The Killed Guide and the Grilled-Cheese Sandwiches

Evan, an eleven-and-a-half-year-old boy, was referred because of generalized inhibition and withdrawal from peers. His personality structure was schizoid, but he was not schizophrenic. He had trouble asserting himself and showed little enthusiasm in school. His grades were quite poor, although his intelligence was above average. This was the first story Evan told in treatment:

> One day I went up with a group of people and a guide to go mountain climbing in Colorado. It was a big mountain and we were all very tired, but the view was fine. At about 1000 feet I picked up a rock and threw it down. It bounced off the stones and went all the way down. It was a dangerous climb, but we had ropes and a guide and waist chains. He would go up ahead of us on to a ledge. It was a very steep mountain. There were very few grips for our hands and feet. Then we got to the top of one of the ledges, but the guide fell off and he got killed. Then we built a fire and had grilled-cheese sandwiches.

After that it was easier to climb because the mountain wasn't so steep. However, we couldn't get to the top, so we went all the way down and went around to the other side of the mountain. We found a spot that looked good. We got another guide, but he got killed also on the way up. We got to the top and there was a pretty view. It was 5000 feet high and it took us six hours to climb it. We could see a hundred miles in every direction. We stayed up there awhile, enjoyed the view, and then we went down. It was much easier to get down.

Therapist: What's the moral of that story?

Patient: I can't think of any moral.

The most striking thing in this story was Evan's total lack of feeling for the guides who fell and were killed. He spoke of their falls with the same emotionless tone used when he described the rock that he had thrown down the mountain. The sentence describing the death of the first one is immediately followed by: "Then we built a fire and had grilled-cheese sandwiches." And the death of the second causes not a moment's hesitation or interference in the journey's progress. The story reveals severe superego deficiencies: an utter lack of sensitivity to the pains of others and an inability to place oneself in the position of someone who suffers.

This is the story I told in response:

One day a group of friends of mine and I decided to go mountain climbing. We were in Colorado and we were in the Rockies. We had a guide who was a very fine person and we all liked him very much. He had many years of experience and we felt very secure with him. He went ahead of us and we all had ropes and waist chains for protection. When we were about halfway up the mountain, he was on a ledge ahead of us and suddenly the rocks slipped from under him and, although he tried to catch on to the ledge, he slipped off and his body plummeted at least 1000 feet to the bottom of the mountain. It was a horrifying experience and we all felt completely helpless. We knew that it was sure death for him.

We were so upset that there was no question in our minds that we could not continue the trip. We were grief-stricken over this man's death, especially since he had died in the process of trying to be helpful to us in climbing this mountain. Well, we all slowly went down the mountain along the path that we had originally taken and when we got to the bottom, there we saw what we all feared and knew to be the case. There was his mangled body on the ground and it was a horrible sight. It was clear that he had probably died in the fall or died at the moment he struck the ground. Most of us cried bitterly. We then went back to the main cabin and notified the authorities. His wife was brought over and it was most painful when we had to tell her the very tragic news. The man had three children who were now left without a father as well. It was, without question, one of the most terrible experiences I have ever had.

In my story I included every ramification of the guide's death that might elicit emotional reactions. The written transcript can only convey a suggestion of the emotionalism which I tried to convey while telling my story. My hope here was to impart to Evan some sensitivity to the agony and torment which others might suffer. It would have been unreasonable to expect that this self-involved boy would, in his first session, respond significantly to an emotion-engendering story, and his overt reaction was minimal. My hope was that Evan might ultimately be reached, and this story was a step in that direction.

The Case of Todd: The Club of Mean Tigers

Todd entered treatment at the age of nine-and-a-half because of withdrawal, apathy, and shyness. His parents described him as rarely smiling and "a very unhappy boy." He never reached out for friendships, and few children found him to be a desirable or interesting playmate. He was easily scapegoated because of his fear of fighting back. With regard to this he stated, "I'm afraid I might hurt somebody real badly, so they might die." Although he is described as having been somewhat depressed since he started kindergarten, his depression increased three months prior to referral when he moved into a new neighborhood. At times he spoke of committing suicide, but there was no history of suicidal gestures or attempts.

Todd was the older of two sons and was an extremely overprotected boy. Both of his parents pampered him significantly. Although in the fourth grade, and although his school was only six blocks away from his home, he was routinely driven back and forth from school four times a day. Although the vast majority of children remained in school during the lunch break, Todd refused to do so. He wouldn't wait on line at the lunch counter, for fear he might get involved in the usual shoving, name calling, and horseplay that typically takes place in that situation. Furthermore, he feared the inevitable teasing and rambunctiousness that took place in the schoolyard when children played there after eating their lunch. His mother would drop him off at school in the morning, pick him up at the beginning of lunch break, serve him his lunch at home, return him to school at the end of lunch break, and then bring him home at the end of the day. Todd had never gone to day camp (not to mention sleep-away camp) because he had initially reacted negatively when his parents proposed the idea a few years previously. In fact there had not been one day in his life that he had been away from his parents.

Todd's father was an extremely domineering man, and his mother was passively dependent on her husband. Her overprotectiveness stemmed primarily from her submission to her husband's dictates regarding indulging Todd. (She was so passive that it would have been difficult to predict how she would have been with another husband, other than that she would have been passive to him.) I believed that an element in Todd's anger was related to the resentment he felt over his father's overbearing manner. However, he was so dependent on both of his parents that he could not dare express his hostility. I considered his pent-up hostility to be a factor in his depression. His inhibition in asserting himself served to protect him from the consequences of hostile expression that would inevitably arise were he to have been more outgoing.

During his second session, Todd drew a picture of a tiger and then told a story that I believe epitomized some of his central problems. I recognized the story as one that would lend itself well to the mutual storytelling game, and so I suggested that he show the picture on television and tell his story again on my "Dr. Gardner's Make-Up-a-Story Television Program." The patient readily agreed:

Therapist: Now our guest has just drawn a picture and he's told me a story and I thought it was such a good story that I suggested that we play the storytelling game. So first he's going to show you the picture. Put it up and show it. Okay. Now what do you want to do, what is that a picture of?

Patient: A picture of a tiger.

Therapist: Okay, now what we want you to do is tell a story about your tiger and then I'll tell a story about a tiger, too.

Patient: Okay. This tiger wants to join this club, but the club has new members.

Therapist: It has what?

Patient: It has people—the tigers are bad in the club.

Therapist: The tigers in the club are bad, yeah.

Patient: And this tiger wants to join, but he's not mean so he's thinking about it in the picture if he should join and then he says, "I'll join the club if I don't have to be mean." And then he talks to the club leader of the club and he says, "You gotta be mean to join our club." And then he says, "No, I cannot. I should be myself."

Therapist: I should be myself, yeah.

Patient: And that's all.

Therapist: And so what happens?

Patient: Everybody should be theirself.

Therapist: Okay. So does he get into the club?

Patient: No.

Therapist: Okay. And so the lesson of that story is what? Is that the end of the story? He just doesn't get into the club?

Patient: Yeah.

Therapist: Okay. And the lesson of that story is?

Patient: That you should be yourself.

Therapist: Hmm. Be yourself. You don't want to be mean. Is that it?

Patient: Yeah.

Therapist: What should you do?

Patient: Be yourself.

Therapist: Be yourself. In his case this tiger didn't want to be a member of the club unless they did what?

Patient: Unless he was mean.

Therapist: Oh, they said he couldn't be a member of the club unless he was mean?

Patient: Yes.

Therapist: And what did he say to them?

Patient: He said no.

Therapist: Did you say—I remember when you told a story before—did you say something about he told them that they should not be mean?

Patient: No.

Therapist: When you told the story before didn't you say, "I'll only join the club unless you people promise not to be mean?" Didn't you say that?

Patient: He said that if he could be nice...

Therapist: If you people in the club.

Patient: No, I said if *he* could be nice then he would join.

Therapist: Oh, you said, "I'll join your club if you let me be nice and let me not bother people." Oh, if you let him not bother people, but the others could bother people. Is that it?

Patient: Yes.

Therapist: I see. He just didn't want—he didn't want to be the one to bother people.

Patient: Yeah.

Therapist: I see. Okay. And the leader said, "You can't join the club because to join our club everybody has to bother people." Is that it?

Patient: Yeah.

I considered the club of tigers who always bother other people to symbolize Todd's view of his peers, namely, a pack of ferocious animals who were ever scapegoating and teasing him. The only way he can gain membership into their club is to become mean himself. This is something Todd is frightened of doing and so he refuses to comply with this provision of admission with the statement, "I should be myself." For Todd to be himself is to be inhibited in asserting himself. His view of his peers as mean tigers stems from Todd's timidity and fear of self-assertion and hostile expression. From his vantage point they appear ferocious. In addition, I believed that the mean tigers were made even more threatening by the projection onto them of Todd's own unconscious anger. He thereby distances himself from his anger by refusing to join the club that requires its expression as a provision for membership. His statement, "I should be myself" makes reference to his determination not to express resentment. With this understanding of Todd's story, I related mine.

Therapist: Okay, I get the idea. Okay. Now, as I've said before, the way it works on this program is that first the guest tells a story and then Dr. Gardner tells a story. And my story may start like yours, but different things happen in my story. Okay?

Patient: Okay.

Therapist: Okay, here we go. Once upon a time there was a tiger, and this tiger wanted to join a club and in this club—this was the mean club. Everybody in the club was mean. And he said, "I want to join your club, but I don't want to be mean. I don't want to bother people ever, and will you let me join your club if I don't bother people?"

And they said, "No, no, no. You can't join this club because here we bother people." So he couldn't join the club.

Anyway, he decided that he would find another club, a club where nobody bothers people. So he looked around and people said, "Well, there are other clubs that don't bother people. In fact, there are two other kinds of clubs. There's one other kind of club where everybody agrees never to bother people at all, and then there's another club where the people agree that sometimes they will bother people and sometimes they won't bother people."

So really there were three clubs. There was the original club where all the tigers always bothered people. There was a club in the middle where sometimes they would bother and sometimes they wouldn't. And then there was the other club where nobody ever bothered people. So which one of the other two clubs do you think this tiger in my story wanted to join?

Patient: He wanted to join the one where he was always nice.

Therapist: Yeah, he said, "That's the club for me, always nice." Nobody ever bothers people. He said, "That's the club for me." So he went to that club and he says, "Can I join your club?"

And they said, "Remember the rule of our club. You must never bother anybody. You must never get angry at anybody, you must never hit anybody, you must never bite anybody, and you remember that."

He said, "That's the club for me." So he joined that club and he took an oath that he would not bother people. And he said, "I swear that I will never bother people. I'll never bite people, no matter what."

Anyway, that club, the one that never bothered anyone, used to have its meetings, and one day a tiger came along while the club was having its meeting—a lion, excuse me—this is a tiger's club. It was a lion, and an elephant. And the lion and the elephant started coming around and growling and bothering the tigers in the club. And the tigers said, "Oh, please don't bother us. We mean you no harm. We're very nice. We don't bother people. Please don't bite us. Please don't bother us."

Well, that elephant and that lion weren't listening, and they started to make trouble and these tigers all ran away. They didn't want to fight. And then what happened was that the elephant and the lion got a lot of the food that the tigers had collected and a lot of their possessions and stuff. And the tigers felt very sad and depressed about it. And that used to happen from time to time because they made a promise that they would never fight, they would never bother people, they would never bite, even if people started with them. Then they used to be taken advantage of, and that made them feel very bad about themselves.

And finally the tiger decided that maybe he ought to try the second club, the club in the middle. And he went there and said, "What are your rules?"

And the club in the middle said, "Well, our rules are these. Our rules are that we're not going to start fights with other people, but if other people, if other animals start with us, we're going to fight back. So it's not that we never fight. It's not that we always fight. We're in the middle."

And this tiger said, "Maybe I'll try this club and see what happens." So he joined that club of tigers. And one day, as the middle tiger club was meeting, a couple of lions and some elephants came along and some other animals, and they started to make trouble. And the tigers in the middle club said, "Listen, we're warning you. Stay away. We didn't bother you. Don't bother us. But we can tell you this: If you bother us, you're going to be sorry."

Well, the lions and the elephants didn't listen and they started to snarl and bite, and they started to go where the middle club's food was and they started to make trouble. And these tigers in the middle club got together and they started to fight and growl and hiss and jump and claw and there was a fight. Soon the lions and the elephants who came along realized that they were going to get into a lot of trouble. They'd get bitten up and they'd get hurt and so gradually they pulled back and they ran away. And then the tigers in this middle club began talking about the importance of...what did they talk about?

Patient: Hm.

Therapist: What did they decide after everybody left, after the lions and the elephants left? What did they decide?

Patient: I don't know.

Therapist: Well, did they think that their plan was a good one?

Patient: Yeah.

Therapist: What was their plan in this club? How did they work things?

Patient: They didn't want to start trouble, but if some other animal started trouble, they would fight back.

Therapist: Right! That was their rule. That was the middle club. And so after that the animals that came around to bother them, like other tigers and elephants and other animals, realized that these guys wouldn't start up, but that they would protect their rights. They would protect themselves when there was trouble. And gradually other animals realized that that was the best of the three clubs. That was the best thing to do with animals who were always bothering people. Don't start, but if others start up, fight back. Now what about the club of the animals that never bothered people? What was the drawback of that? What was the disadvantage? What kinds of trouble did they get when they never bothered people?

Patient: And then other people would pick on them.

Therapist: Right.

Patient: And they wouldn't fight back.

Therapist: Hh hmm. So which do you think is the best of the three clubs, in your opinion?

Patient: The middle club.

Therapist: Because?

Patient: Because if they starting picking on you, you can pick on them.

Therapist: Right. Right. You defend yourself. You protect your rights. Okay, how did you like this program?

Patient: I liked it.

Therapist: Do you want to see yourself on television?

Patient: Okay.

Therapist: Do you want your parents to come up and watch?

Patient: No.

Therapist: You don't want them to. Why not?

Patient: I'm shy.

Therapist: You're shy.

Patient: Uh hmm.

Therapist: I think it would be a good idea. It's good practice for shyness to do things that you're shy about, and then you find out that it's not so terrible. That's the way to conquer shyness. Do you want to try it?

Patient: Okay.

Therapist: All right, let's call them and have them watch and you'll see that for the person who is shy, each time you do the thing that bothers you, you become less scared of that thing. Okay?

One of the purposes of therapy is to introduce options to the patient that may not have been considered or, if they have, have not been incorporated into the patient's psychic structure. In therapy one helps the patient consider the advantages and disadvantages of the various options, the pathological as well as the healthy ones. The mutual story-telling technique provides opportunities for such introductions and comparisons, and this is what I have done here. The story demonstrates symbolically the discomforts and indignities one suffers when one lives by the principle that anger expression under any circumstances is undesirable. It also demonstrates the benefits accrued to those who have a more flexible attitude about anger and use it appropriately.

The patient was deeply involved in my story and readily understood its significance. Although he expressed some hesitation about his parents' viewing the videotape, his enthusiasm more than counterbalanced this negative reaction. I believe this interchange served to catalyze his involvement in treatment.

The Case of David: The Family with Sixteen Children

David was referred at the age of nine-and-a-half by his pediatrician. Three months prior to referral, he began suffering with abdominal pains. These began about one month after starting the fourth grade and were so severe that he had not attended school during the six weeks prior to my initial consultation with him. Thorough medical evaluations by three pediatricians revealed no organic cause for his difficulties, and he was therefore referred for consultation.

David was the youngest of six children, with the older siblings ranging in age from 23 to 16. Accordingly, there was a six-and-a-half-year hiatus between David and his next oldest sibling. During the five years prior to the initial consultation, the older siblings began to leave the household, one at a time. The oldest three had already left the home and the fourth, an 18-year-old sister, was starting to apply to college. In addition, his 16-year-old brother (the fifth of the siblings) had already left the home three years previously for six months as an exchange student in Europe. The family was a tight-knit one, and these losses were painful for David.

Of pertinence to David's disorder was the fact that there was a strong history of appendicitis in the family. Four of his five older siblings had had their appendices removed and appendicitis was under serious consideration during David's hospitalization. However, absolutely no evidence for appendicitis was found. David's father was a highly successful businessman who enjoyed significant prestige in his community. The family members considered themselves paragons of what a family should he. In such an atmosphere the expression of deficiency was strongly discouraged as were crying, depressed feelings, profanity, and any other manifestations that were considered to be deviant. Lastly, David's new teacher had the reputation of being unusually strict and David found this particularly difficult to handle.

During the initial interview I concluded that David was suffering with a separation anxiety disorder. In his case it was not so much separation from his mother that was painful, but the progressive and predictable loss of his older siblings who were serving as parental surrogates. It was as if David had seven parents: mother, father, and five significantly older siblings. As they progressively left the home, he felt increasingly alone and fearful about the loss of his various protectors. The closeness of his family intensified the problem. Had there been a looser family involvement he might not have been so anxious. Furthermore, the family pattern in which everyone was required to present a facade of perfection and imperturbability made it extremely difficult for David to express the anxieties, anger, and depression he felt over these losses. Lastly, the family history of appendicitis provided a model for excused withdrawal. Others were seen to get extra attention and affection in association with this illness, and that probably served to give David the idea that he could enjoy such extra protection by the utilization of the symptom. Of course, the abdominal complaints themselves might also have been a manifestation of his tension and anxiety. During his third session, while playing the mutual storytelling game, the following interchange took place.

> *Therapist:* Good afternoon, boys and girls, ladies and gentlemen. Welcome to "Dr. Gardner's Make-Up-a-Story Television Program." We have a new guest on our program today. Tell me how old are you?
> *Patient:* Nine.
> *Therapist:* Nine years old. What grade are you in?
> *Patient:* Fourth.
> *Therapist:* Fourth grade. Okay, now, let me tell you how it works. On this program we invite boys and girls down to see how

good they are in making up stories. Now it's against the rules to tell a story about anything that really happened to you or anyone you know. The story must be completely made up from your imagination. It can't be about anything you've seen on television or read in books. Then, when you've finished telling the story, you tell the lesson or moral of the story—what we learn from the story. As you know, every good story has a lesson or a moral. And, of course, the more exciting the story is the more fun it will be to watch on television afterwards. Now, when you've finished telling the story, you tell the lesson or moral of your story. Then I'll tell a story and we'll talk about the lesson or moral of my story. Okay, you're on the air.

Patient: It can't be from a book?

Therapist: No, it can't be a story from a book. It has to be completely made up in your own imagination.

Patient: There's this man and a woman, and they lived on top of a huge rock. And they had 16 children and they couldn't find another room. They only had one room.

Therapist: Okay, so there's one room for 16 children. Uh huh.

Patient: And they were all running around and making so much noise that they didn't know what to do. So they called their friend who was really smart.

Therapist: So they couldn't handle all the kids? Is that it?

Patient: So the man said if they had any lobster pots. And they said "Yes, 16." And he asked them to get the lobster pots…

Therapist: This is the friend?

Patient: Yeah. So he took the lobster pots on his bicycle.

Therapist: He took the 16 lobster pots on his bicycle?

Patient: Yeah, to his home and then at home he got some candy and rope and then he rode back and climbed up to the house, and then when he got up to the house, he said, "Hello…." So he tied the lobster pots outside the windows. He had 16 pieces of candy and he put all the candy he had in them.

Therapist: In the lobster pots?

Patient: Yeah, and then the children ran to get their candy…and then they jumped into the lobster pots and ate the candy. And the children stayed in the lobster pots.

Therapist: The children stayed there?

Patient: These were big lobster pots. They even had dinner there.

Therapist: They even had dinner there? Who served them?

Patient: The mother and father.

Therapist: So they had more room…is that it?

Patient: Yeah.

Therapist: Uh huh. Okay. Is that the end?

Patient: That's the end.

Therapist: Lesson?

Patient: Some people will do anything just to have some privacy.

Therapist: Who's having the privacy there?

Patient: The mother and the father…they would do anything just to have some privacy.

Therapist: And what did they do to the children?

Patient: They just lived with them.

I considered this story to represent well the patient's situation with his family. Although his family consisted of six children, he symbolizes it with a family of 16 children. In either case the number is large and both figures share the numeral 6. The story enabled David to gratify his fantasy of entrapping his siblings in such a way that they could not leave the house. Each window contains a lobster pot into which a sibling can be lured with candy. There the child is trapped and cannot flee or leave. Ostensibly, the parents do this in order to provide themselves with some privacy. If that were indeed their motive, they could have allowed all the children to leave the house in such a way that there was little if any link or tie to the home. Accordingly, I considered this reason to be a rationalization. It is the opposite of what the parents really want: entrapment of the children in the home. Of course, it is not the parents who want this; it is David who attributes this desire to the parents to serve his own purposes. The story also reflects some ambivalence about closeness with his siblings. On the one hand, he wants them close enough to be seen and ever present (thus he traps them in lobster pots). On the other hand, he puts them outside the window, thereby providing him with a little distance and breathing space (a little privacy after all). With this understanding of David's story, I related mine.

Therapist: I see. Okay, now as I said, when you finish telling your story, I'll tell a story and we'll talk about the lesson and moral of my story. Now, my story will start off like your story, but different things happen in my story. Okay?

Once upon a time there was a family and this family consisted of a mother and a father and 16 children...a big family...and they lived in one room. Now everyone was getting kind of edgy... living on top of one another and things like that.

And finally they decided to consult a friend of theirs who was very wise. And they said to him, "What do you think we can do about this?"

And the father said, "I have an idea. I think maybe I ought to get lobster pots...and put candy in them and put them outside the windows and then they'll go into the lobster pots and then there will be less people around the house and I'll have more room."

And the wise friend said, "Well, look, how old are some of your children? What are their age ranges?"

He said, "Well, they range from very little ones to very big ones."

And the friend said, "Well, aren't the big ones getting ready to leave soon?...Go off on their own and become adults?"

And the father said, "Well, I think that the problem will solve itself as the older ones grow up and leave the house. I think that you want to hold onto these kids too long. If you're going to put them in lobster pots and have them hanging around the house, that tells me that you want to hold them back and keep them in the house forever and not let them grow up and become independent, self-sufficient adults."

And the man of the house realized that the wise man made sense. And he said, the man of the house said, "However, the young ones are going to miss the older ones terribly and maybe we ought to try to keep those older ones there for the young ones' sakes."

The wise friend said, "It isn't fair to the older ones. The younger ones have to accept the fact that the older ones are going to be going. They may feel lonely but you know, they have one another. And they also have other friends they can make."

And the father said, "What about the youngest one? When the other 15 leave, what's going to happen to him?"

The wise man said, "Well, he'll be old enough by then to have his own friends. He'll still have time with the older ones. He'll go and visit them and they'll come to visit him. It's not like they're lost forever. He'll still have some time with them. He'll speak to them on the phone. And then he can make his own friends. He can still be with you people, his mother and father. So it's not the end of his world that he doesn't have that many people around. So...

Patient: So they just let them grow up?

Therapist: They let them grow up and then what happened to the younger ones?

Patient: Then they...

Therapist: Are they sad?

Patient: I guess so.

Therapist: Uh huh. What happened to them? Anything happen to them?

Patient: I don't know.

It is a well-known principle in treatment that if the therapist is going to attempt to take something away from a person, he or she does well to try to find some reasonable substitute at that point. Even the suggestion that the substitutes be provided at some time in the future is generally not as effective as recommending substitutes in the present. Accordingly, although I recommended in my story that the younger ones resign themselves to the fact that the older ones inevitably are going to leave, I provide definite substitutive gratifications. I recommend that the younger ones involve themselves with one another. The patient still had one younger sibling in the home and so this recommendation was applicable. I also suggested intensified relationships with peers as another way of obtaining compensatory gratification. Last, I reminded David that one can still have frequent and meaningful contacts with older siblings even though they are living outside the home. Telephone conversations and visits are still possible and the awareness of this can help assuage the sense of loneliness one might feel after one's older siblings leave the home. At that point I attempted to engage David in a conversation to ascertain whether he appreciated on a conscious level any relationship between my story and his own situation. As mentioned, I do not consider it crucial for the treatment of the patient to have such awareness. What is important is that the message "gets through" and I am not too concerned whether it is received on the conscious or unconscious level, on the direct or the symbolic level. This is the conversation that ensued.

Therapist: Well, do you think this story I told you has anything to do with you? Has anything to do with your situation?

Patient: Ah, yes.

Therapist: In what way? How?

Patient: My brothers and sisters have gone away.

Therapist: How many brothers and sisters did you have?

Patient: Six...five.

Therapist: Five besides yourself. And what are their ages? How old is the oldest? What are their ages?

Patient: Sixteen, 19, 20, 22, and 24.

Therapist: Uh huh. How many live in the house now?

Patient: Not counting when they go to college?

Therapist: Right. If they're off at college, let's consider them out of the house.

Patient: Two.

Therapist: Two. You and...

Patient: My brother, Bart.

Therapist: Who is 16? And what year in high school is he?

Patient: Sophomore.

Therapist: Sophomore? So he still has a couple more years at home?

Patient: Uh huh.

Therapist: Uh huh. Now, how does the story I just told relate to yours?

Patient: It's like me. My brothers and sisters are going away.

Therapist: Uh huh. And how do you feel about accepting that fact?

Patient: I think I can.

Therapist: You think you can?

Patient: Yeah.

Therapist: Does it upset you a lot?

Patient: Not a lot.

Therapist: Do you think being upset about them has anything to do with your stomach? With your cramps and your going to the hospital?

Patient: No. I don't think so.

Therapist: Do you think your story has anything to do with your problems or the situation with your brothers and sisters?

Patient: No.

Therapist: I do. I think it has something to do with it. In your story, you put them in cages and keep them around the house. Isn't that right? In your story the mother and father's friend put the boys and girls in cages...lobster pots...they're kind of cages, aren't they?

Patient: Yeah.

Therapist: And they keep them around the house. They don't go anywhere. They're kind of trapped into staying around the house. I think your story says that you would like to have your brothers and sisters trapped around the house.

Patient: (appearing incredulous) Not really.

Therapist: You don't think so. Do you think your story has anything to do with you?

Patient: No.

Therapist: Do you think my story has anything to do with you?

Patient: Just a little.

Therapist: Just a little. Okay, Well, anyway, the important thing is that if brothers and sisters stay around the house too long, they don't grow up.

Patient: Yes.

Therapist: And they have to grow up and they have to leave and the other kids left behind have to make friends with others, and it isn't the end of the world.

Patient: Yeah.

Therapist: That's the main message. It's not the end of the world when your brothers and sisters leave. You still have other people...other friends. And you can still get in touch with your brothers and sisters too, and still see them. Okay, do you want to watch this for a little while?

Patient: Okay.

Therapist: Do you want to have your mother come up and see it?

Patient: Okay.

As can be seen, the patient did not gain too much insight into the relationship between his story and mine. Nor did he have much insight into the relationship between his story and his situation. There was some appreciation of some superficial similarity but basically he was unappreciative of the various relationships. He did, however, listen with interest to my story, and I believe that the message got through.

The Case of Harry: Valentine Day's Candy
from a Loving Mother

Harry entered treatment at the age of ten because of acting-out behavior in the classroom. Although very bright, he was doing poorly academically. He did not do his homework and would lie to his parents about his school assignments. He did not pay attention in the classroom; rather, he would whisper, hum, shout out, and disrupt the classroom in a variety of ways. He did not exhibit proper respect for his teachers and his principal. At home, as well, he was a severe behavior problem. He was openly defiant of his mother's and stepfather's authority and did not respond to punishment. In spite of this, Harry had an engaging quality to him. Adults, especially, found him "a pleasure to talk to." The parents of the few friends he had also found him a very likable and charming boy, and they often could not believe that he involved himself in antisocial behavior. Harry's mother was married three times. He was the product of her second marriage. He had an older sister who was born during his mother's first marriage. His father was a sales representative for a large corporation and had frequently been away from the home during the first two years of Harry's life, when his parents had still been living together. When the father was with the infant, he tended to be cool, aloof, and disinterested. Harry's mother was a secretary who began working fulltime when Harry was two months of age. He was then left to the care of a series of babysitters, most of whom were unreliable and some of whom were punitive. Unfortunately, both parents tended to ignore the signs of the babysitters' maltreatment.

When Harry was two years old, his parents separated. During the next year he and his sister lived alone with his mother. Following the separation of Harry's parents, there was a custody dispute. Both parents wanted custody, and each claimed to be the superior parent. Harry's father claimed that his wife was promiscuous and, therefore, unfit to take care of the children because she had had a transient affair during the marriage. The trial took place in a rural area in the Midwest, and the judge supported the father's position. After three months with his father, the latter returned the children to the mother with whom they were still living at the time of treatment.

When he was three, his mother's second husband moved into the home and they were married when Harry was four. This was a very stormy relationship, and Harry witnessed many violent battles between his mother and her third husband. In addition, her second husband used corporal punishment in order to discipline Harry. About two years after he moved into the house, Harry's mother's second husband deserted, and neither the mother nor Harry heard from him subsequently.

When Harry was nine, his mother's new husband moved into the house, and he was the stepfather who was involved at the time Harry began treatment. Like his predecessor, Harry's new stepfather was also extremely punitive. He used the strap primarily with the argument, "It was good enough for my father, and it's good enough for me." Harry's mother basically encouraged her husband to use the strap on Harry. When I expressed my opinion that, at ten, Harry was much too old for physical punishment and that I did not believe that corporal punishment was serving any purpose for Harry, both parents disagreed. I emphasized to them that it was my belief that they were making Harry worse, not better, and that there was no evidence that such beatings were reducing his antisocial behavior. In fact, I expressed to them my opinion that it was increasing the frequency and severity of his acting out. Again, they would not listen.

During his second month in treatment, the following interchanges took place while playing the mutual storytelling game:

> *Therapist:* Okay. And now ladies and gentlemen our guest is going to tell us his own original made up story. You're on the air!
>
> *Patient:* A man was riding his motorcycle on the street and he crashed and eventually he went to the hospital, and when he was in the hospital, his wife came to visit him. While his wife was visiting him the next day would be Valentine's Day. So she brought him on Valentine's Day lots of candy and sweets and the nurse said no candy and sweets for the patient but she did not listen. And so she gave him the candy and sweets he got even sicker.
>
> So then he had to go for an operation. The operation was successful, but the wife was not allowed in the hospital. So eventually she called the police and she told the police what happened. And she wanted to speak to her husband and she broke into the window that he was in—the room window and she took him out of the hospital and he couldn't survive on his own and she didn't get him back to the hospital on time almost. So then he had another operation that was not successful and she was not happy because he died.
>
> *Therapist:* Okay, now were you going to say something else?
>
> *Patient:* No, that is it.

Therapist: Okay, the lesson?

Patient: Lesson?

Therapist: Yeah. Every story has a lesson or a moral.

Patient: To tell you when something is told to you, to go by it. To go by the rules.

Therapist: To go by the rules! And how did this wife break the rules?

Patient: She kept on giving him things that he was not supposed to have.

Therapist: Like?

Patient: Candy and taking him out of the hospital.

Therapist: Okay, so she broke two rules?

Patient: Right!

Therapist: Why did she break those rules?

Patient: Because she wanted her husband.

Therapist: She wanted her husband...

Patient: (interrupts)...to be with her.

Therapist: She wanted him to be with her even though the doctors had said it was a bad idea?

Patient: Right, he could not handle it.

Therapist: When you say he could not handle it, what do you mean?

Patient: Like he would not even do anything else.

Therapist: You mean he did just what his wife said?

Patient: Yeah.

Therapist: I see. That is when she gave him the candy?

Patient: No, before the candy when he got even sicker.

Therapist: I see, and what was he like when she took him out of the hospital?

Patient: He was really sick, he was coughing and he was weak.

Therapist: What was the nature of his illness? What was wrong with him?

Patient: He didn't have the right type of medicine. Like he was supposed to have every so often, so he could not survive.

Therapist: I see.

I believed that the man, the protagonist of the story, represented Harry and the man's wife, Harry's mother (the only female in Harry's life). Under the guise of being benevolent she is quite malevolent. She does what she considers to be in Harry's best interests, even if what she does is directly opposed to the doctor's orders. Harry is too weak and passive to say no and suffers the consequences of her "benevolence." He eats the candy and knows that it will make him sicker—and this is exactly what happens. He allows himself to be taken out of the hospital—seemingly because of his mother's love and her desire not to be separated from him—and he gets sicker, and ultimately dies.

The story demonstrates well what Harry Stack Sullivan referred to as the "malevolent transformation." This phenomenon is seen in individuals who grow up in homes where a parent professes love and affection; however, whenever such love is dispensed, it most frequently results in pain to the child. Somehow the affectionate maneuver results in a painful experience—always under the guise that love is still being provided. For example, a mother while professing strongly her love and affection will so vigorously hug the child that significant pain is produced. Under such circumstances the child comes to associate professions of love with physical and/or psychological pain. This produces a fear of those who display affection because there is ever the anticipation that the pain will be soon forthcoming. Here, Harry's mother expresses her affection by giving a box of Valentine's Day candy. A more direct and undisguised symbol of love would be hard to find. However, for Harry it is poison because his physical condition is such that sweets are specifically detrimental. Then his mother takes him out of the hospital against the doctor's advice—again because of her love and her strong desire to be close with him. And he almost dies because of her "affection."

This story also had implications for Harry's therapy. The doctors might very well represent this examiner. Harry's mother and stepfather were both beating him with a strap under the guise of affection. It is another example of the malevolent transformation in that Harry could not but experience pain in association with their allegedly well-meaning attempts to help him become a law-abiding citizen. The story also has some prophetic elements in that it implies that if Harry continues to get such "love," it may kill him.

With this understanding of Harry's story, I continued.

Therapist: Okay, now it's my turn to tell a story. Remember I said that I would tell a story? My story may start like your story but different things happen very quickly. Okay, here we go.

Once upon a time there was a man, and he was sick in the hospital and the doctor said to him that he was absolutely not to have sweet things like candy and things like that.

Patient: Oh, too bad, I like that...(mumbles)...

Therapist: Now, what did you say? Too bad what?

Patient: Too bad. I'm glad I'm not him because I like candy.

Therapist: Well anyway, this man knew that it was important to obey the doctor's orders. Anyway, one day his wife came in, and it was Valentine's Day, and she said "I love you very much dear. Oh my dear husband, I love you very much. You are really my love, and I brought you this big box of Valentine's chocolates."

And he said, "Well, they sure look good, but the doctor said no sweets, no way." And she said, "Just go ahead and eat them."

And he said, "No, no. It's a bad idea. If I eat those sweets I may get even sicker." And he just absolutely refused to eat them, and she realized that he meant what he said and in no way would he eat those candies.

He also said, "If you want to get me something else as a present, something that would not harm me, I would be very happy."

Patient: How about some ice cream?

Therapist: No ice cream! The same thing. It's also sweet. What do you think she came up with?

Patient: A Valentine's card.

Therapist: A Valentine's card, right. Anything else?

Patient: A new car.

Therapist: Well, that is some Valentine's present! How about something more reasonable? Something that costs more than a Valentine's card and less than a car?

Patient: A kiss.

Therapist: A kiss is good. She gave him a big kiss! And he really liked that. He said, "That's very nice."

Patient: Did she get him candy then?

Therapist: No, no. She realized that he was right and that he shouldn't eat the candy. Anyway, the next day she said, "I don't like that hospital. I don't like my husband in that hospital because they don't let me do the things that I want, and I'm going to get him out of the hospital." So she came and tried to get him out. She wanted him to get signed out against doctor's advice, and he absolutely refused. So she said, "I love you very much, and I want you at home."

And he said, "If you love me very much, you'll listen to the things that I want. Right now I want to be with you, but I must stay at this hospital and get better. If you really loved me as much as you say, you would *listen* to what I want and would also do many of the things I want. If you want to spend some time at home, okay. But if you want to spend some time at the hospital with me, okay. *But I will not go home now.*

Well, after he said that she started to raise a real fuss. She had a tantrum and a fit. And she started screaming, "But I love you so much I want you home!"

Then the doctors and the nurses said, "If you don't cut out that screaming, we'll call the police. You can't have him home and you can't steal him out of the hospital."

And the man didn't want to go with her, and he said, "Right, I have to be in this hospital 'til I'm better." Well, she realized that once again he wasn't going to do what she said just because she said it, and then he said, "If you really love me, you'll listen to the things I want and try to do some of those things, not just the things you want." So she realized that maybe he had a point. So what do you think happened then?

Patient: You said, "They called the police when she set foot in the door."

Therapist: No, no, they didn't have to. They threatened her. They said, "If you don't stop these fits and all this screaming and everything, we will call the police." But you see they didn't have to because she listened to reason.

Patient: I see, and she stopped screaming.

Therapist: Yes, well now what was happening was she was sad about it, but she realized that what her husband said made sense, that it was certainly true that he had to stay in the hospital. (Patient making sounds.) What's the matter?

Patient: Nothing.

Therapist: What were those noises?

Patient: My stomach.

Therapist: Your stomach. Okay. Do you want to settle down? Do you want to hear the rest of the story?

Patient: Yeah.

Therapist: Anyway, she realized that what he said made sense. She realized that he needed to be in the hospital and that getting him out of the hospital early, before the doctors said his time was up, was a bad idea. So what do you think then happened?

Patient: Was his time up?

Therapist: In the hospital?

Patient: Yes.

Therapist: Well, not at the time she wanted him out. But what happened after that?

Patient: He stayed there and he got lonely.

Therapist: And then what happened?

Patient: Then he signed out.

Therapist: No, no. He did not sign out. He did not break the rules. He listened to the doctors, and he finally got better, went home, and then he and his wife had much more time with one another. And do you think she changed after that?

Patient: Yes.

Therapist: She began to realize that he had a point. And what was the big problem his wife had in my story?

Patient: Not listening.

Therapist: Not listening to what?

Patient: The rules, just like mine.

Therapist: The rules, but something else she did not listen to.

Patient: Her husband. She wanted her own way.

Therapist: Right, and not listening to what her husband wanted to do. And what should you do with other people?

Patient: Take their thoughts into consideration.

Therapist: Right, take their thoughts and feelings into consideration. You have to compromise. Anyway, that is what happened. They went home. What do you think the lessons of my stories are? Try to figure them out.

Patient: To tell you to listen and you've got to take other people's thoughts into consideration.

Therapist: Right!

Patient: And you have to go by the rules.

Therapist: Very good. You got the lessons. Take into consideration other people's feelings and then compromise. Sometimes you do what they want, sometimes they do what you want. Right?

Patient: Right.

Therapist: And then follow the rules if you think they are important ones and good ones like the rules the doctor makes about getting better. Okay, well, ladies and gentlemen, this is the end of our program today. Do you want to watch this?

Patient: Yeah.

Therapist: Okay, let's turn this off now.

On a few occasions I interrupted my story to ask for the patient's input. The patient's suggestions regarding presents that would be preferable to Valentine chocolates were for the most part reasonable (with the exception of the car). In addition, I periodically interrupted my story to be sure that the patient understood my main points.

Whereas in the patient's story the man is passive (and conspicuously so), in my story he takes an active role in protecting himself from his wife's (symbolizing mother) misguided and coercive benevolence. It is a statement to the patient that, even though he was ten, he was not completely helpless to protect himself from some (but certainly not all) of the indignities he suffers in his home. My story also attempted to help Harry appreciate the basic malevolence behind some of his mother's professions of benevolence. Such clarification can lessen the likelihood that the patient will become involved in pathological interactions. His stomach churning noises were, I believe, a concomitant of the anxiety my message was creating. It is a statement also of the fact that my story was "hitting home."

The Case of Frank: The Nutcracker and the Three Peanuts

The last patient I will present exhibited typical manifestations of the Oedipus complex. In order for the reader to appreciate better the way in which I dealt with this boy's oedipal story, I will present first my views of the Oedipus complex.

Freud's Theory of the Oedipus Complex. Freud described the Oedipus complex as a normal childhood psychological phenomenon in which the boy or girl, between the ages of three and five, exhibits sexual-possessive fantasies toward the opposite-sexed parent and simultaneously views the same-sexed parent as a rival. The boy anticipates that his father will castrate him for his incestuous designs on his mother and the girl is said to fantasize that she once did indeed have a penis but lost it or it was cut off. Freud's theory of the Oedipus complex was derived from the analysis of adults—most of whom Freud considered neurotic and some of whom we would today consider psychotic. To the best of my knowledge, Freud only published one article on the treatment of a child, the case of Little Hans (1909), and...even here Freud was not the therapist. Rather, the boy's father treated him with Freud serving as the supervisor. In the three-and-a-half month course of treatment, Freud saw the boy only once. Freud believed that Hans' treatment confirmed his theories of infantile sexuality and the

Oedipus and castration complexes. Furthermore, Freud believed that sexual attraction toward the opposite-sexed parent and jealous rivalry against the same-sexed parent universally appeared in children between the ages of about three and five.

Freud's Theory of the Resolution of the Oedipus Complex. Freud believed that the healthy child resolves the Oedipus complex at about five years of age and then enters into a six-year period of relative sexual quiescence—the latency period. According to Freud, the resolution of the Oedipus complex comes about partly via natural developmental processes. He compared oedipal resolution to the loss of the milk teeth and the growth of the permanent teeth. In addition, he believed that natural psychobiological processes also contributed to the resolution, specifically that the boy's fear that his father would castrate him contributed to the development of his superego and subsequent suppression and repression of sexual fantasies toward the mother (S. Freud 1924). Freud held that the therapist's role in helping children alleviate oedipal problems was to foster resignation that the boy cannot gratify his sexual-possessive cravings toward his mother. However, he is consoled with the hope that someday he will get a suitable substitute, someone "as wonderful, beautiful, etc." as his mother. In short, the boy is asked to forestall gratification in this area for many years. Last, Freud believed that the failure to resolve the Oepidus complex successfully was a central contributing factor in all neuroses.

The Author's View of the Oedipus Complex. My own experience over the 28 years that I have worked intensively with children is that only a small fraction, less than two percent, exhibit oedipal problems. The remainder have difficulties that are unrelated (or only remotely related) to oedipal difficulties. And when oedipal problems are present, there are usually specific factors in the family constellation that are directly contributing to the development of such. They do not arise naturally, as Freud would have us believe, but are the result of very specific family patterns that are conducive to the development of such symptomatology.

To elaborate, I believe there is a biological sexual instinct that attracts every human being to members of the opposite sex. From birth to puberty this drive is not particularly strong. Although weak and poorly formulated during the prepubertal period, it nevertheless exhibits itself through behavior that I consider manifestations of oedipal interest. A normal boy may speak on occasion of wishing to marry his mother and get rid of his father. These comments may even have a mildly sexual component such as "and then Mommy and I will sleep in bed together." I believe that the possessive, more than the genital-sexual, interest predominates here. The child is primarily interested in a little more affection and attention undiluted by the rival.

In a setting where the child is not receiving the affection, nurture, support, interest, guidance, protection, and generalized physical gratifications (such as stroking, warmth, and rocking) necessary for healthy growth and development, he or she may become obsessed with obtaining such satisfactions and develop one or more of a wide variety of symptoms that are attempts to deal with such frustrations. One possible constellation of symptoms are the kinds of sexual urges, preoccupations, and fantasies that Freud referred to as oedipal. The instinctive sexual urges, which are normally mild and relatively dormant, have the *potential* for intensive expression even as early as birth. Getting little gratification from the parents, the child may develop a host of fantasies in which frustrated love is requited and the rival is removed. Such fantasies follow the principle that the more one is deprived, the more one craves and the more jealous one becomes of those who have what one desires. Such manifestations can appropriately be called oedipal problems in the classical sense. The foundation for the development of neurosis is formed not, as Freud would say, through the failure to resolve successfully one's sexual frustrations regarding the parent of the opposite sex but through the failure to come to terms with the more basic deprivations from which the child is suffering.

Furthermore, I believe other specific factors must also be operative in order that ocdipal paradigm symptomatology be selected. It is not simply the aforementioned deprivations. There must be other factors that channel the adaptation in the oedipal direction. I believe that the most common of these for the boy are sexual seductivity by the mother and/or castration threats (or the equivalent) by the father. It is important for the reader to note that the oedipal paradigm includes two phenomena: 1) sexual attraction toward the opposite-sexed parent, and 2) fear of retaliation by the same-sexed parent. Although the latter is considered to be caused by the former, this is not necessarily the case. A boy, for example, might be threatened with castration without there necessarily being any kind of sexual seductivity on his mother's part. A boy, for example, might be threatened that his penis will be cut off if he plays with it, and this threat might be made in a situation where there is no seductivity on the mother's part (this is what I believe took place in little Hans' case [Gardner 1972b]). Or there might be maternal seductivity without any retaliatory threats by the father. When either one or both of these processes are operative—on a preexisting foundation of parental deprivation—then, I believe, there is the greatest likelihood that symptoms will arise that can justifiably be referred to as oedipal. Of course, one might ascribe "unconscious" oedipal factors to a wide variety of other symptoms, but I am confining myself here to the phenomenological definition, one based on observable or accurately reported symptoms.

My discussion focuses here primarily on boys. I do not believe that this reflects any bias on my part; rather, it reflects the fact that Freud himself elaborated much more on oedipal manifestations in the boy and had great difficulty applying oedipal theory to girls. (It is beyond the purpose of this book to speculate on the reasons for this.) It is also important to differentiate between *sexual seductivity* and *sex abuse*. Oedipal problems may arise when there is sexual seductivity, but not when there has been sex abuse. When there is sexual titillation, the child develops cravings that cannot be gratified, and symptoms may then emerge which are designed to deal with these frustrations and deprivations. In sex abuse, there is no sexual frustration and an entirely different constellation of symptoms may emerge, such as symptoms related to distrust, fear of disclosure of the sexual activity, and generalized fear of involvement with adults who are of the same sex as the abusing parent.

The Author's Approach to the Alleviation of Oedipal Problems. Freud used the term *resolution* to refer to the passing of the Oedipus complex between the ages of five-and-a-half and six. I prefer to use the term *alleviation* because I do not believe that oedipal involvements and interests are ever completely resolved. At best, oedipal problems can be alleviated. In fact, I generally go further and use the term *alleviation* to refer to the therapeutic aim of just about all psychogenic symptomatology. Considering the present state of our knowledge (perhaps the word ignorance would be preferable here), it is premature to use such strong words such as *resolution* and *cure*.

My therapeutic approach to the alleviation of oedipal problems reflects my concept of the Oedipus complex itself. The problems to be alleviated relate to the general problem of emotional deprivation and, if present, parental seduction and/or threats of castration. I attempt to ascertain whether there has been parental seduction. If so, I inform the parents of my opinion that their behavior is seductive and strongly recommend that they refrain from such activities. At times they are consciously aware of the process and, at other times, they are not. In the latter situation, it may be very difficult to impress upon them the seductive elements in their behavior. I also try to learn whether there have been castration threats, overt or covert. Again, if present, I do everything to discourage them. (The case of Frank [below] is a good example of this aspect of the treatment of oedipal problems.)

When addressing myself to the deprivational element I consider the improvement in the parent-child relationship crucial to the alleviation of oedipal problems in children. An attempt is made to improve the boy's relationship with his mother so that he will obtain the gratifications that are due in childhood and will be less obsessed with gaining them in neurotic ways. A similar approach is used with girls exhibiting oedipal problems in their relationships with their fathers. In addition, such children are helped to accept the fact that they cannot completely possess either of their parents and that the affection and attention of each of them must be shared with other members of the family. This sharing concept is an important one to impart. The child must be helped to appreciate that no one can possess another person completely: The father shares the mother with the children; the mother shares the father with the children; and the child has no choice but to share the mother and father with the siblings. In the context of such sharing, children must be reassured that, although they may not get as much as they might want, they will still get something. In addition, they must be helped to gain gratifications from others during the present time. Whatever deficiencies may exist in the parent-child relationship can be compensated for to some degree by satisfactions in other relationships. It is a well-known therapeutic principle that if one is going to take something away from a patient, one does well to provide substitute gratifications at that time, that is, gratifications which are healthier and more adaptive. My approach does not involve suggesting to the child that he wait. To wait for his possessive gratifications may appear to consume an endless number of years. Rather, he has the potential to gain some of these satisfactions in the present and he is given the hope that as he grows older he will have greater autonomy to acquire the more exclusive type of possessive relationship enjoyed by his father. The clinical example I will now present demonstrates how I utilize these principles in treatment.

The Case of Frank. Frank, a seven-and-a-half-year-old boy, was referred for psychotherapy because of generalized immature behavior and poor school performance. Both his teacher and his parents described him as being silly to the point where he rarely took things seriously. He was ever trying to avoid responsibility and typically took the path of least resistance. Most often he would deny responsibility for any unacceptable behavior and was always blaming others. Not taking schoolwork seriously and rarely doing homework, his grades were suffering. He played well with younger children but did not get along with children his own age because of his low frustration tolerance, impulsivity, and inability to place himself in other children's situations to the degree appropriate for his age.

Although there was nothing in the presenting symptoms to suggest that Frank was suffering with oedipal problems, many of the stories he told centered on the theme of rivalry with the father figure for possessive control of the mother figure. In addition, castration anticipations and fears, symbolically presented, were common. As mentioned, when I do see oedipal problems, there are generally specific factors in the family situation that are conducive to the development of this typical reaction pattern. Frank's family situation is an excellent example. His father, an obstetrician, was away for significant periods from the time of his birth right up until Frank began treatment. In the early years this was associated with his residency training and in later years with the building of his practice. Frank and his two younger brothers were left alone with his mother. Although she was by no means seductive, the long periods of being alone with his mother provided Frank with opportunities for intimacy (physical and social, but not sexual) that other boys do not usually have. His father exhibited slightly effeminate gestures, but there were no signs of homosexuality.

Frank was born with undescended testicles which required frequent examination. Often, it was his father who conducted the examinations and reported his findings to the consulting urologist. In addition, at the age of three, an inguinal hernia was found and this, too, was periodically examined by Frank's father. Frank's appreciation that his father's work as an obstetrician and gynecologist involved extensive manipulation of the genital region of people who lacked external genitalia was conducive, I believe, to Frank's viewing his father as a "castrator." Frank's father did, indeed, operate on women in the genital region and it is easy to see how Frank could have viewed his father as having castration potential.

We see, then, three factors in Frank's family situation that were conducive to the development of oedipal problems:

1. The long absences of Frank's father from the home allowed Frank an unusual degree of intimacy with and possessive gratification from his mother.
2. The father's occupation as an obstetrician and gynecologist—an occupation in which the father literally performed operations on the genitalia of people who already lacked a penis and testes—contributed to the father being viewed as a potential castrator.
3. The frequent examination by his father of Frank's own genitalia also could have induced castration anxieties in that such examination was indeed performed to assess Frank's readiness for surgery in that area.

On the Rorschach test, Frank often saw as female those blots traditionally seen by boys as male. In addition, there was some evidence for identification with the stereotyped passive female. This, I believe, was the result of the long contact alone with his mother, depriving Frank of opportunities for more masculine identification models. In addition, the somewhat definite, albeit slight, effeminate gestures of his father probably played some role in this feminine identification problem. However, the Rorschach and TAT did not reveal a complete absence of masculine identification. Rather, a sex-role confusion was evident. Oedipal themes were also apparent. On one TAT card, Frank related this story:

Now his father dies...he and his mother went to the funeral and after to the Greek hall to eat something. He got shrimp cocktail and she ate the same. Then they went home and got into bed and thought about their husband and father. His mother had him before she married his father and so he loves his mother more than his father.

This was the story Frank told during the third month of treatment:

Patient: Once there was three little peanuts and a nutcracker lived down the block. And every day when they went outside, the nutcracker would try to crack them open. So they said they'd have to move from their mother's house because the nutcracker lived right down the block. So they moved. So they found a house that was sold to them and they had a new house. They had a mansion. But the nutcracker moved right across the street from them.

Therapist: Wow.

Patient: And every time they went out in the street to play again, the nutcracker would come out and try to crack them open. So one day the nutcracker came to the door and looked in the window and saw them playing cards. So he shut the window real fast. And then right there was a metal monster eater and he just loved nutcrackers. He gobbled the nutcracker up and there was never a nutcracker again. The end.

Therapist: What did he do?

Patient: He liked metal and especially nutcrackers. He ate the nutcracker whole and there was a happy ending and they never were aware of the nutcracker again. So that's the end of the story. The end. Good-bye.

Therapist: Okay. And the lesson of that story?

Patient: Ah, think smart and you'll be smart.

Therapist: And what was the smart thinking here?

Patient: Uh, they put a metal monster eater right underneath the window.

The three peanuts, as the protagonists of the story, symbolize the patient and his two younger brothers. The nutcracker, who lives down the block, represents Frank's father. He is already out of the home and Frank has gratified his oedipal wishes to possess his mother completely. However, the nutcracker, castrator that he is, is obsessed with the notion of cracking the three peanuts. Their attempts to elude him prove unsuccessful as he pursues them to their new home. Interestingly, it is a mansion—implying that Frank has the wherewithal to live with his mother in "high style." The problem of the nutcracker's relentless pursuit is solved by the peanuts' engaging the services of a "metal monster eater" who "just loved nutcrackers." The story ends with his gobbling up the nutcracker and "there was never a nutcracker again. The end." Finally, "there was a happy ending and they never were aware of the nutcracker again." Now all is well with the world. Frank gains complete possession of his mother and his father is not only removed from the house but is completely obliterated assuaging, thereby, Frank's castration fears.

It was with this understanding of Frank's story that I told mine:

Therapist: Okay. Now it's time for me to tell my story. Now my story may start like your story, but different things happen very quickly. Once upon a time there were three peanuts. And these peanuts lived in a neighborhood where they lived with their mother.

Patient: Yeah.

Therapist: They also lived with their father.

Patient: Yeah, uh huh.

Therapist: (looking at patient) In my story, the father is a nutcracker! (At this point, the patient looks up toward the therapist, somewhat incredulously.)

Therapist: That's my story.

Patient: Uh, huh.

Therapist: And the three peanuts are very upset because they think that their father wants to crack them. So they said to him one day, "Are you going to try to crack us? Are you going to try to crack us open?" (Patient now rolling his knee socks down.) And the father said, "No, but at times you boys get me angry and I sometimes feel mad at you. But I don't have any desire to crack you or crumble you up or get rid of you that way." (Patient now rolling his knee socks up.)

Patient: Or throw you out of the window or throw you on the concrete floor or make you smashed. (Patient now laughs nervously.)

Therapist: "No, I'm not going to do that."

Patient: (in a reassured tone) Uh, huh.

Therapist: He said, "However, you boys sometimes get me angry." They said, "Yeah, we know that we sometimes get you angry." And (turning toward the patient) do you know when the boys would sometimes get the father angry?

Patient: When?

Therapist: What kinds of things do you think they did that would get the father angry?

Patient: (now bends over, puts his elbows on his knees, and supports his chin in his cupped hands) Let's see now. They would do things that the father didn't tell them to do? (Patient now resumes his original position of facing the examiner.)

Therapist: Like what?

Patient: Like, when he wanted them to clean his car and they wouldn't do it.

Therapist: Yeah, that would be the kind of thing that would get him angry. One of the things that would get him angry was when they would want the mother all to themselves, and they wouldn't want him to spend any time with the mother. You know, that would get him angry sometimes, when they would say, "We don't want you around. We don't want you to be with Mommy all the time. We don't want you to be with her." Things like that. He said, "That's the kind of thing that gets me angry." (Patient now tying his shoelaces.) And they said, "Well, that's the kind of thing that makes us think you want to get rid of us. That you want to kill us. That you want to get rid of us. That you want to crack us up and get rid of us, and then have Mommy all to yourself." You see the father and the three boys were kind of rivals. (Therapist now turns to patient.) Do you know what *rival* means?

Patient: Uh huh.

Therapist: What does *rival* mean?

Patient: I don't know.

Therapist: They were kind of fighting for the mother to have time with her. Each wanted the mother all to themselves. The father wanted the mother a lot of times and the boys wanted her. The boys wanted to have her to take care of them, to teach them things, and to read books with them, and things. (Patient now stops tying his shoelaces and interlocks the fingers of one hand with the other.) And the father said, "I get angry at you when you want her all to yourself." And they said, "And we get angry at you, because we don't want you around. We want her all to ourselves." They were kind of fighting for her. So what do you think happened?

Patient: (now resting hands in his lap) I think the father got so mad that he cracked them open.

Therapist: (shaking his head negatively) No way! No. What they decided to do was...they realized that the father shouldn't have the mother all to himself, because the boys were still part of the family. And that the boys shouldn't have the mother all to themselves because the father was still part of the family. So they decided to compromise. And they decided that they will share the mother. That sometimes the boys will have time with the mother (patient now takes his hand out of his lap and slaps his thighs) and sometimes with the father. (Patient now puts his hands on his thighs.) Now this still made the boys feel a little bit sad, because they didn't have their mother all they wanted to. (Patient now whistling and flapping the palms of his hands on his thighs.) So what did they do then?

Patient: They had a whole day with the mother and didn't let the father have...no...they had a whole week with the father. (Patient now moving his hands toward his groin area.) No (patient now rubbing his penis), and had a whole week with the mother (still rubbing his penis) and then the father had a whole week with the mother.

Therapist: That was one way. Sharing. That's one thing they can do. (Patient still rubbing himself.) And another thing that made the boys feel better was to spend time with their friends. When they weren't with their...

Patient: ...mother...

Therapist: ...mother, they could spend time with their friends. And also, another thing (patient still rubbing his penis), was they knew that when they grew up they would have (patient now grasps his penis with his left hand and pulls up his shirt with his right hand) a lady. Each one would get married. Or live with somebody, or have a girlfriend. Something like that. (Patient now pulls his pants forward, at the belt level, with his left hand and puts his right hand inside and starts stroking his penis.) And then they would not feel so jealous of the father, you know. (Patient now pulls his right hand out of his pants and strokes his penis from the outside.) Because they would have...

Patient: (slapping his both hands now on his thighs with an air of certainty)...a lady of their own.

Therapist: ...a lady of their own. (Both the patient and the therapist's statement, "a lady of their own" was said simultaneously. It was clear that the patient knew exactly what words the therapist was going to say and so they both made the exact statement simultaneously.) Right!

Patient: (laughing with a sigh of relief) Uh huh. (Patient again moves both hands toward the groin and rubs the penis area.)

Therapist: And that's exactly what happened. (Patient still rubbing penis.) And what do you think the lessons of that story are?

Patient: Uh. (Patient still holding penis and laughing nervously.)

Therapist: What are the lessons?

Patient: Let me see. (Patient now removes hands from groin and puts them on top of his head.) Share.

Therapist: Share.

Patient: Share with other people.

Therapist: Right. And is there any other lesson?

Patient: (hands now clasped behind his head)...and you'll get along together.

Therapist: Share, and you'll get along together. Any other lesson?

Patient: (hands on top of head, nodding negatively) No.

Therapist: There's another lesson. What you can't have in one place, you can have in another. Like they couldn't have the mother all the time, but they could have friends: boys and girls that they played with in the street or in the home...

Patient: (interrupting) Did they have a busy street?

Therapist: Yeah. There were a lot of kids around.

Patient: Were there a lot of cars? (The patient then removes his hands from his head and imitates moving cars with buzzing sounds.)

Therapist: Yeah. But they had quiet streets too in that area. If there weren't friends in their neighborhood, they would go elsewhere. And also, if you can't have something now there's always the hope that you can get it in the future. You know?

Patient: Yeah. (Patient now playing with his wristwatch.)

Therapist: And then they could have a girl all their own. Anything you want to say?

Patient: No.

Therapist: Do you like this game?

Patient: (while clasping his hands) Yeah.

Therapist: Do you want to watch this?

Patient: (with an excited expression on his face, while still clapping his hands) Yeah!

Therapist: Okay. Let's watch this. Do you want to have your mother come in and see it?

Patient: (still excited) Yeah.

Therapist: Let's do that. (Both arise.)

When creating responding stories, the therapist often has a conflict. If the therapist retains the original symbol used by the child, pathological elements may have to be retained. For example, if the child uses a worm or pig to symbolize him- or herself, the utilization of these in the therapist's story implies agreement that the child warrants being symbolized by such loathsome animals. In contrast, to dispense with such symbols entirely may rob the therapist of rich symbolism that significantly enhances the impact of the therapeutic communications. I generally will retain the symbol and make sure, in the course of my responding story, to emphasize the healthy element associated with it and to de-emphasize, ignore, or directly negate the unhealthy aspects of the symbol. In my responding story here I purposely retained the nutcracker symbol because I considered the advantages to far outweigh the disadvantages. However, after informing the patient that the father was a nutcracker, I quickly emphasized the point that he has the *potential* for castration but that he does not use his power. Rather, I focused on behavior manifested by the peanuts that might cause the father to be angry and studiously avoided any possibility that the anger could reach such proportions that castration, symbolic or otherwise, could possibly occur.

In addition, at the beginning of my story, I make it quite clear that *the father lives with the peanuts*. This is in contradistinction to the father in Frank's story who has already been ejected from the household. In my story the problem with the father is worked out through discussion rather than acting out. In Frank's story the father is already removed and the father is a castrator. In mine, the father is present, is not a castrator, and engages in meaningful communication to discuss problems with his peanut sons.

The main point that I make in my responding story is that it is not a question of *either* the father or the peanuts having full possession of the mother. Rather, they can share. Sometimes the peanuts spend time with the mother, sometimes the father spends time with the mother, and sometimes all of them spend time with her. And, when the father is with the mother, the peanuts can still spend time with others in their neighborhood to compensate for their loss. In addition, they are provided with the hope that when they get older they will have more opportunity for greater possession of an appropriate female peanut.

According to Freud, the Oedipus complex naturally passes like the milk teeth that give way to the permanent teeth. In addition, fears of the father castrating the child contribute to the development of the superego which suppresses and represses the boy's possessive, sexual longings for the mother. Lastly, the boy is consoled with the fact that someday he will have a female of his own. Most therapists agree that it is very difficult to take something away from patients without offering something in return. In Freud's formulation, the boy is consoled with the knowledge that someday he will have a female of his own.

For the child of five, this future is like a million years away and is not likely to serve well as a meaningful consolation.

In the kind of oedipal resolution I propose, the boy is not asked to give up entirely his present desires for possessive involvement with his mother. Rather, he is advised to share her with his father. It is certainly easier to share a prized possession than to give it up entirely. In addition, the boy is given the consolation that there are opportunities with others at the present time. Last, he is also told about future possibilities.

In the course of telling my responding story, the patient continuously rubbed his genital area and pulled his pants tightly against his penis. It became apparent that he had an erection and that the prospect of possessive opportunities with a female were sexually titillating. Frank's response was clear evidence that my story was indeed dealing with issues that were most important for him and that my message was a most meaningful one. The vignette is an excellent demonstration of a situation in which the therapist knows that his responding story is indeed being received with interest and receptivity and that it is touching on important psychological issues.

The reader who is interested in more detailed discussions of my views on the etiology and treatment of oedipal problems may wish to refer to other publications of mine in this area (Gardner, 1968, 1973c, 1983a).

CONCLUDING COMMENTS

I have described the basic rationale of the mutual storytelling technique. I do not claim to have invented a new method of treatment. The principle is an ancient one, and many therapists have no doubt utilized the method. I believe that my main contribution lies in having written articles on the subject and having formulated more specific criteria for analyzing and creating stories. The utilization of the method in the treatment of a wide variety of psychiatric disorders of childhood is discussed in a number of other publications of mine (Gardner, 1968; 1969; 1970b,c; 1971c; 1972c,d; 1973d; 1974b,c,d; 1975a,b; 1976; 1979a,b; 1980a; 1981a; 1983a). A comprehensive description of the details of utilizing the technique (with regard to story analysis and the therapist's story creations) is provided in my full-length text on the subject (Gardner, 1971a).

2
DRAMATIZED STORYTELLING

Give a man a mask and he'll tell you the truth. — Ancient Greek aphorism

All the world's a stage
And all the men and women merely players.
They have their exits and their entrances
And each man in his time plays many parts. — William Shakespeare

INTRODUCTION

Children call us "talking doctors." Many of us do not fully appreciate the significance of this epithet, especially with regard to its implication that our therapeutic approach is a relatively narrow one. Let us compare, for example, the following experiences with respect to our involvement in a play. First, we can read the play. Such an experience is purely visual with regard to the reading as well as the visual fantasies that the reading material may engender within us. Compare this to attending a theatrical performance of the play. Here, in addition to seeing the performance, we hear it as well. Auditory stimuli have been added to the visual. With two sensory modalities of communication acting simultaneously, there is a greater likelihood that the play will affect us. Imagine, then being an actual participant in the play as an actor or actress. Now, added to the visual and auditory sensory modalities are the kinesthetic, tactile, and possibly even the gustatory and olfactory. With these additional modalities of sensory input, it is even more likely that the play will have an impact. However, no matter how skilled and experienced the actor may be, his or her emotions are feigned. No matter how much both the actor and the audience may be swept up by the part, all recognize that everything is basically being dictated by the script: it is not real, it's only a play. Compare now play-acting in which there is an actual living experience in which emotional reactions are elicited by real events. Here the linkage between the emotions and the aforementioned sensory modalities is deep and genuine. Nothing is playacted. Rather, the individual is having an experience. And it is the experience that has the greatest effect on us. To the degree that we provide our patients with experiences—as opposed to relatively sterile insights—to that degree we improve our chances of helping them.

Because the therapeutic situation may not allow us to provide our patients with as many natural and uncontrived experiences as we would like, we do best to provide them with every possible encounter that comes as close to them as we can. Although playacting does not have as much "clout" as an actual experience, it may be a superior form of interaction and communication than merely talking—and this is especially true for the child. Just as the mutual storytelling technique was developed from the observation that children naturally enjoy both telling and listening to stories, the idea of dramatizing them arose from the observation that children would often automatically (and at times without conscious awareness) gesticulate, impersonate, intone, and enact in other ways while telling their stories. I found that when I introduced such theatrics myself the child became more involved in my stories and receptive to their messages.

Whereas originally I introduced the dramatic elements *en passant*, that is, in the process of telling my story (just as the children tended to do), I subsequently formalized the process by inviting the child to reenact our stories as plays following our telling them: "I've got a great idea! Let's make up plays about our stories. Who do you want to be? The wolf or the fox?" At times I would invite the mother and even siblings to join us. (We often face the problem of having a shortage of available actors.) We see here another way in which mothers can be useful in the child's treatment. (A little encouragement may be necessary at times to help some mothers overcome their "stage fright.") Of course therapists themselves must be free enough to involve themselves in the various antics that are required for a successful "performance." They must have the freedom to roll on the floor, imitate various animals, "ham it up," etc. They have to be able to be director, choreographer, writer, and actor—practically all at the same time. They may have to assume a number of different roles in the same play, and quickly shift from part to part. Such role shifts do not seem to bother most children nor reduce their involvement or enjoyment. Nor do they seem to be bothered by the therapist's "stage whispers," so often necessary to keep the play running smoothly.

Younger children, especially those in the four- to six-year age group, who may not be inclined to tell well-organized stories, will often improve in their ability to relate them when the dramatic element is introduced. Others, who may have been initially unreceptive to or too inhibited to freely tell stories, may do so after the enjoyable dramatic elements are utilized. The experience becomes more fun and the child tends to forget his or her reservations. In this younger group, as well, the strict adherence to the pattern of the child's first telling a story and then the therapist's telling his or hers may not be possible or desirable. A looser arrangement of interweaving stories and plays back and forth may be more practical and effective.

Children generally enjoy television (a statement which I'm sure comes as no surprise to the reader). Even more, children enjoy seeing themselves on television (something a child rarely has the opportunity to do). Therapists who have available a camera and videocassette recorder can provide children with an immensely beneficial therapeutic modality. Making a videocassette recording of a therapeutic experience increases significantly the likelihood that children will expose themselves to reiteration of the therapeutic communications. In the 1960s, when I first developed the mutual storytelling technique, the child and I would often listen to the audiotape recording of the mutually told stories. In the late 1960s, I began encouraging children to bring to the sessions their own audiocassette recorders (a practice initiated by a child) and to listen to these stories at home afterwards.

Around 1970, I purchased a closed-circuit television system and began making videotapes of our stories, both the standard interchanges as well as those that were dramatized. Around 1980, I purchased a standard home videocassette system and camera. This enabled me to lend the videotape to those children who had such an instrument at home. In the last few years, I have added a second videocassette recorder and invite the child to bring his or her tape to the office. This enables the child to watch at home the various therapeutic interchanges that we tape. Of these, probably the most valuable are those in which dramatizations occur because this ensures even more that the child will listen to the tape and profit from what is contained therein.

CLINICAL EXAMPLES
The Case of Adam: Can a Dead Frog
Be Brought Back to Life?

Adam, an eight-year-old boy with a neurologically based learning disability, exhibited significant social difficulties. It was very difficult for him to place himself in another person's position and this caused him much pain and rejection in social situations. Intellectual impairment (his IQ was about 85) and difficulty in conceptualizing and abstracting resulted in his failing to appreciate and learn many of the subtleties of social interaction. Many of these appear to be learned almost automatically by normal children. Children with minimal brain dysfunction may find this their most crippling problem and it behooves the therapist to appreciate this when working with such children. In Adam's case it was the primary focus of his treatment.

In session one day, his mother reported that on the previous day Adam had pulled off the leg of a frog that he had caught in his backyard. I immediately responded with disgust: "Ych, that sounds terrible!" Although I knew that my response was going to lower Adam's self-respect at that point, I felt it was the price that had to be paid for a little superego development. I then asked Adam if he would like to play a game in which I am a frog and he is a boy who wants to pull off my leg. He hesitantly agreed. I lay on the floor and invited him to try to pull off my leg. My moans were immediate: "Ooooh, that hurts! Please stop. Please, my leg is going to come off. Ahhhh—" I asked the patient what the boy then did. He replied that he stopped because he didn't want to hurt the frog any longer. "That's right," I replied. "When the boy realized how much he was hurting the frog, he stopped pulling its leg." I then asked Adam if he would like to play a game in which the boy doesn't stop after the frog screams out and he pulls off the leg and the frog dies. He agreed. This time, in spite of my blood-curdling cries, the boy pulled off the frog's leg. "Now my leg is off and I'm dead," I mumbled as I lay stiffly on the floor. "Try to bring me back to life," I whispered to the patient as if giving stage directions (a maneuver commonly required in such plays). In spite of the patient's attempts to revive me (these included poking, pulling, artificial respiration, and a little feigned mouth-to-mouth resuscitation), I remained stiff and prostrate, all the while mumbling, "Even that doesn't help. When you're dead, you can never be brought back to life." The game ended (as such games usually do) with questions: "How does a frog feel when someone tries to pull off its leg?" "What can happen to a frog if someone pulls off its leg?" "Can a dead frog be brought back to life?"

One might argue that the above approach is a little too strong and that it might create intense feelings of self-loathing in the child. I can only reply that I do not believe that this has been my experience. Whatever transient lowering of self-esteem the child may suffer in such a game (and I grant that he or she certainly may) is more than compensated for by the ultimate enhancement of self-worth that results from heightened sensitivity to the pains of others and his or her ceasing to inflict unnecessary and wanton pain on others. Last, if such a game is indeed too ego-debasing to the child, he or she can usually be relied upon to refuse to play it or to discontinue it if it gets too "hot." It is grandiose of the therapist to consider knowing beforehand whether a healthy communication is going to be devastating to a patient. I tend to try it out and respect the patient's defenses when they exhibit themselves.

The reader should appreciate that I am fully aware that this child's cruel act related to hostility that was being redirected from other sources onto the frog. One cannot focus simultaneously on many of the multiple factors, which usually contribute to a pathological act. Here I chose to direct my attention to the egocentrism issue (the child's inability to project himself into the situation of another living thing) and his ignorance of certain aspects of social reality.

The Case of Frank: Gonga Wants Too Much More

Frank's situation demonstrates how a child's feelings about a competent sibling can contribute to the development of an antisocial behavior disorder that interferes with academic functioning. Frank was 11 when I first saw him. He had been referred by his school psychologist because of antisocial behavior. The parents claimed that Frank's antisocial behavior began when he was three years old, about the time of the birth of his only brother. He became restless, distractible, and exhibited frequent temper tantrums. He was evaluated by a child neurologist who diagnosed him as "hyperactive," and at the age of four, he was placed on methylphenidate—on which medication he remained for over six years.

When he began the first grade, things deteriorated significantly. He would not concentrate on his schoolwork. Rather, he would engage in various types of horseplay in the classroom, tell jokes, laugh at the teacher, make faces, thump on his desk, and disrupt the class in a variety of ways. Frank was considered to be very bright, but not surprisingly, received very low grades and did not learn very much. He was always trying to avoid school responsibilities and rarely did meaningful homework. This behavior continued and he was finally placed in a special educational class in the third grade, where he still was when I first saw him when he was at the fifth-grade level.

Peer difficulties were also described. He sought friendships but was not sought by peers. He insisted upon having his own way and had temper tantrums when thwarted by friends. He did not respect the rights of others and exhibited little ability to put himself in other children's situations. He taunted other children and became excessively argumentative. He would cheat while playing games and generally "didn't know when to stop." He often felt cheated or gypped and tended to blame others when there were difficulties.

At home, as well, Frank had many problems. He did not respect parental authority and exhibited impulsivity and low frustration tolerance. He had temper outbursts, and on occasion, would physically abuse his younger brother. He did not seem to learn from punishments that were dispensed in the attempt to control Frank's antisocial behavior.

Frank's parents were very proper, well-to-do, upper-middle-class people for whom everything seemed to be going smoothly. The father, an attorney, was in a law firm that had been started by his grandfather. I viewed them as somewhat "uptight" people but did not consider this enough to explain Frank's severe antisocial behavior. His younger brother was getting along quite well and was viewed by the family as being a "wonderful boy" who excelled in academics, sports, and social relationships. The fact that he was so stable suggested that Frank's parents could not have been significantly deficient in their parenting role—even considering the fact that Frank was their first-born and they might have been more tense with him than his younger brother.

During the first three months of Frank's treatment, I really could not say why he was so angry. At the beginning of the session when his mother and/or father were present, he would be obstructive, use profanities toward them, and at times make himself thoroughly obnoxious. However, although initially resistant to involve himself in the therapeutic activities, I was able to engage him in a meaningful way. The vignette presented here demonstrates how dramatizations enhanced the therapeutic efficacy of doll play. Among the dolls and puppets I have in my office is a small gorilla whose name is Gonga. In the show, he used this doll as well as a monkey doll that he called Chip. He then drew an announcement sign for the program: *Gonga Never Listens*. Prior to the program he requested that I sit on the sidelines and not be within the view of the camera. The dolls were placed on a bridge table, and during most of the performance, the patient hid himself either behind or under the bridge table so that only the puppets were in direct view of the camera.

Therapist: Good afternoon, boys and girls, ladies and gentlemen. Today is Saturday, the 27th of February, 1982, and I'm happy to welcome you once again to Dr. Gardner's program. Our guest today is going to present a show. Now will you please tell us the name of the show?

Patient: Gonga Never Listens. (Holds up sign: GONGA NEVER LISTENS.)

Therapist: Okay, before I turn this off and get ready for the show, is there anything else you want to say?

Patient: This cartoon show is animated.

Therapist: This animated cartoon will be shown in just one minute. We'll be right back.

And now ladies and gentlemen, we are back with you with our show. Our guest has requested that I not be in the picture at this point so I will sit on the sidelines. Okay? You're on the air!

Patient: Hello, my name is Gonga. (Patient holds up gorilla doll named Gonga.) And here is my friend, Chip Monkey. (Patient holds up monkey doll.) The show is named *Gonga Never Listens* because that's exactly what I do. I never listen. So here's one of my stories of what I have done. Okay.

Patient: (as Gonga) (Patient turns on tape recorder he has brought to the session and plays loud rock music.) I really love that tape recorder. I want to buy it from the store. I'm going to go in there and ask that guy how much it is.

Patient: (as man) Yes, what do you want?

Patient: (as Gonga) I want to know how much that tape recorder is.

Patient: (as man) $97.

Patient: (as Gonga) And how much is the tape above?

Patient: (as man) $9.50.

Patient: (as Gonga) Boy, how am I going to get that much money?

Patient: (as man) I hope you do because that's a very fine model. I only have three of them left.

Patient: (as Chip Monkey) How are you going to get that money?

Patient: (as Gonga) I'll find a way.

Patient: (Whispers in therapist's ear.)

Therapist: Now our guest has asked me to play the part of the mother. I'll be the mother's voice and he's told me what lines

I say. Okay.

Patient: (as Gonga) Mommy, at the record shop today I saw a very neat tape recorder. It's really neat and it's only $97.50.

Therapist: (as mother) $97.50!!!!!!! Are you asking me for the money?

Patient: (as Gonga) Yes, I am, but I'll help out with $7 of it.

Therapist: (as mother) No, you can't have it. If you want to get one of those, you've got to earn the money yourself. You've got to save up from your allowance and you've got to do work.

Patient: (as Gonga) But how can I earn enough money for that?

Therapist: (as mother) It'll take a long time, but there are things you can do.

Patient: (as Gonga) But they only have three of the tape recorders left!!! (Gonga waves hands during conversation.)

Therapist: (as mother) Well, you know it's never the case that there are no more. The store may only have three left, but the person who manufactures that tape recorder has thousands that they send all over, and I'm sure that that store can get you more. And when you earn enough money, then you can buy it. I'll tell you what I will do, though. If you earn $87.50, I'll give you $10 as a present. Because if you earn the $87.50, that shows me that you have worked very hard and then I'll give you the extra $10.

Patient: (as Gonga) Gee, that's great. Thanks, mom.

Therapist: (as mother) Well, I'm very happy to do that in order to help you work harder and you'll really feel good after you've earned that $87.50, and then you'll get that tape recorder. You'll see.

Patient: (as Gonga) Okay, Goodbye. I'm going up to my room.

Therapist: (as mother) Okay.

Patient: (as Gonga) With Chip Monkey. I'm taking him up to my room too.

Therapist: Okay. Now what happens?

As can be seen, I drive a somewhat hard bargain with Gonga regarding the purchase of the coveted tape recorder. I will give him $10, but he must earn the remaining $87.50. Again, I introduce the old work ethic. Although Gonga seems highly committed to the proposition (talk is cheap and it is only a story) it would have been nice if the patient were a fraction as committed as he professed. We then continued.

Patient: The next day, they were playing *The Talking, Feeling, & Doing Game.* (Sets up *The Talking, Feeling, & Doing Game* on the table.)

Patient: (as Gonga) Boy, I really like this *Talking, Feeling, & Doing Game.* I'm glad that Dr. Gardner let me use it.

Patient: (as Chip Monkey) I like it too. Considering I'm losing, it's still a pretty funny game.

Patient: (as Gonga) Well, I'm going to win this game because I'm ahead of everybody...naturally...

Patient: (as Turtle) Don't brag, Gonga.

Patient: (as Gonga) Don't tell me what to do. It's my turn.

Therapist: Do you think Turtle sort of likes Gonga when he brags or is he sort of turned off by Gonga?

Patient: Yeah, turned off.

Therapist: But not enough to stop playing the game. He just thinks he's a drag to play with.

Patient: (as Gonga) (Continues to play *The Talking, Feeling, & Doing Game.*) Boy, let me check this card!

Therapist: What does Gonga's card say?

Patient: (as Gonga) "Scratch your backside"...that's something I'm really good at doing... (Gonga scratches backside.)

Therapist: Okay.

Patient: (as Turtle) It's disgusting, Gonga.

Patient: (as Gonga) But that's what the card told me to do.

Therapist: Yes, but you don't do that in front of other people.

Patient: (as Gonga) I know that. Well, I'll move my piece. (Moves piece and purposely knocks Chip Monkey's piece off the table.) Your piece (speaking to Chip Monkey) is always in the way.

Patient: (as Chip Monkey) Don't knock my piece on the floor, Gonga.

Patient: (as Gonga) Chip Monkey, you can get it yourself.

Patient: (as Chip Monkey) Boy, Gonga has been really mean today. (Begins to have a side conversation with Turtle.)

Patient: (as Turtle) I'm not playing everything down here. I know.

Patient: (as Chip Monkey) Do you want to go home?

Patient: (as Turtle) No, I still like this game.

Patient: (as Chip Monkey) Well, if he bothers me one more time, I think I'll leave.

Patient: (as Turtle) Well, maybe me too.

Patient: (as Gonga) So I go 12 spaces, 1-2-3-4-5-6-7-8-9-10-11-12. I landed on "Go back one." No! (Patient slams down hard on the table.) A stupid game! I'm going to my room.

Therapist: Why'd he get so angry? What happened?

Patient: Because he had to go back one.

Therapist: Boy, he really has a temper! So what did the turtle think of that when Gonga messed up the whole game just because he had to go backward one space?

Patient: (as Turtle) Let's go home, Chippy.

Patient: (as Chippy) Yeah.

Therapist: The turtle didn't want to play with him anymore?

Patient: No.

Therapist: I don't blame him.

Patient: Cut.

Therapist: Okay. Cut. (Patient puts away *The Talking, Feeling, & Doing Game*.)

Patient: (Later, after Gonga has gotten over his tantrum) "Boy, was I a dum-dum! Well, I don't care about him. Well, I'm going to call Chippy and see if he still wants to play. (Dials phone.) 652-1301. (Bring-g-g-, B-r-rring...)

Patient: (as Gonga) Hello, may I speak to Chippy?

Patient: (as Chippy) This is Chippy.

Patient: (as Gonga) Oh, hi, Chippy. This is Gonga. Do you want to play? (Sound of phone hanging up and dial tone.)

Patient: (as Gonga) I wonder why he hung up on me?

Therapist: Why do you think he hung up?

Patient: Because he was mad at Gonga.

Therapist: Mad at him for what?

Patient: Getting sore, having a tantrum, and knocking his piece on the floor.

Therapist: So what did Gonga do then?

Patient: She went to her room.

Therapist: She went to her room? Is Gonga a he or a she?

Patient: A he.

Therapist: So he went to his room and did what?

Patient: Sulked.

Therapist: And then what happened?

Patient: He decided to come hack down and call Chippy again.

Therapist: Call Chippy again. Okay. So go ahead and call Chip Monkey.

Patient: (as Gonga) I can't because Chippy just hung up.

Therapist: That was the first time. Try a second time and see what happens. Maybe if Gonga says that he's really sorry and he means it, maybe Chippy will listen to him.

Patient: (as Gonga) I'll try one more time. (Dials) 652-0210. (Ring-ring.) Hello. Can I speak to Chippy? Okay. Hello, Chippy?

Patient: (as Chip Monkey) What do you want, Gonga?

Patient: (as Gonga) I'm really sorry about when I threw a temper tantrum.

Patient: (as Chip Monkey) I'll bet you are.

Patient: (as Gonga) Wait. Don't hang up. I'm sorry. You can come back and play with me if you want to.

Patient: (as Chippy) Well, if you won't get so mad over things.

Patient: (as Gonga) Okay. Goodbye. (Hangs up.) I want to play more of *The Talking, Feeling, & Doing Game*. I'm going to call Turtle.

Therapist: Okay, he calls Turtle.

Patient: (as Gonga) 652-0352. (Ring-ring, ring.) Hello. Hello, Turtle? Can you play?

Patient: (as Turtle) Who is this?

Patient: (as Gonga) It's Gonga.

Patient: (as Turtle) Gonga, why did you get so mad?

Patient: (as Gonga) Well, I get mad at things like that. You know I can never listen.

Patient: (as Turtle) Well, only if you aren't so mean to me and Chippy. Okay, I'll call Chippy.

Patient: (as Gonga) I've already done that.

Patient: (as Turtle) He came?

Patient: (as Gonga) Yes.

Patient: (as Turtle) Okay, I'll be right over. Goodbye.

Patient: I've got to put this telephone away.

Therapist: Mmm. Okay, so they forgave him?

Patient: Yup.

Therapist: So what happened then?

Patient: I can't...they're coming.

Patient: (as Turtle) I want to play some more of that game?

Therapist: Okay. Why don't you set it up again on the TV and start playing it? Shall I help you?

Patient: Cut it so they can't see you.

Therapist: You don't want me in it, huh?

Patient: So they can't see me either.

Therapist: I'll cut it.

Patient: (as Gonga) Boy, oh boy, let me get my dice. Boy, am I doing good at this game! Let's see my card. (Picks card.) That card's no good.

Therapist: What does it say?

Patient: (as Gonga) (Puts "bad" card back and takes another.) That's not...that's good. "Good luck! You get an extra turn."

Therapist: No, no, he's not playing fair.

Patient: (as Chip Monkey) Wait, Gonga, you can't do that.

Patient: (as Gonga) Why not?

Patient: (as Chippy) Because you're cheating!!

Patient: (as Gonga) I can do what I want to!

Patient: (as Chippy) Gonga, you never listen!

Patient: (as Gonga) Well, I'll do what I want to.

Patient: (as Turtle) Well, you're not going to do what you did last time.

Patient: (as Gonga) Okay, jerks. (Picks previously discarded "best" card.) "Jump up and down three times."

Therapist: So Gonga decided to follow the rules now. Huh?

Patient: Uh-huh.

Therapist: What would the guys have done?

Patient: They would have left him.

Therapist: Do you think they would have played with him again this time?

Patient: No.

Therapist: Yeah, he probably realized that.

Patient: (as Gonga) Well, I did that. I jumped. Now it's your turn, Chippy.

Using the puppets as players of *The Talking, Feeling, & Doing Game* (a play within a play), Frank exhibits some working through here. A part of him, as represented by Gonga, is the primitive, impulsive individual who acts out his anger. The other parts, as played by Turtle and Chip Monkey, represent the civilized superego aspects of his personality. In the end of this segment, Gonga becomes somewhat civilized and suppresses his infantile behavior so as not to alienate his friends.

The question must be considered here as to what the therapeutic significance of all this is. It is clear that Frank knows the "right" answers. Gonga knows well what is the "wrong" thing to do and his friends know well what is the "right" thing to do. This knowledge is really Frank's. If Frank knows what's right, why is he still doing what's wrong? The answer relates to the fact that, without resolution of the fundamental problems that are generating the anger in the first place, it is likely that there will be some acting out, or at least, anger expression in some other way. Here Frank is attempting consciously to suppress the angry impulses in order to protect himself from the alienation of his friends. He is gratifying this desire via his play fantasy.

I believe that something else is being accomplished here as well. The reiterative process serves to entrench the dictates in the superego. Each time the principle or caveat is repeated, it becomes incorporated into the psychic structure. The hope is that such incorporation will ultimately be strong enough to modify behavior even though the fundamental problems have not been dealt with. The superficiality of this process notwithstanding, it is still contributory to therapeutic change. At this point, the play turns back to an as yet uncompleted theme: the purchase of the tape recorder.

> *Patient:* (as Chip Monkey) Gonga, remember when you wanted to get that tape recorder?
> *Patient:* (as Gonga) Yeah.
> *Patient:* (as Chip Monkey) Well, they only have one left.
> *Patient:* (as Gonga) They do?
> *Patient:* (as Chip Monkey) Yeah.
> *Patient:* (as Gonga) Well, I'm going to get that.
> *Therapist:* How's he going to get that?
> *Patient:* He's going to get it any way he can.
> *Therapist:* And what way is that?
> *Patient:* He'll do anything he can to get it.
> *Therapist:* Like what, for instance?
> *Patient:* Work as hard as he could. Steal it.
> *Therapist:* Steal it?
> *Patient:* He's crazy. Gonga doesn't listen.
> *Therapist:* Oh, I see. He's going to steal it...
> *Patient:* (as Gonga) I might steal it.
> *Patient:* (as Chip Monkey) You're crazy, Gonga!!
> *Patient:* (as Gonga) Well, who cares. I'm not going to get into trouble.
> *Patient:* (as Chip Monkey) You'll get caught and you'll be in the pen. You'll get sent to jail.

Patient: (as Gonga) Well, I don't care. It's getting late. You guys ought to go home.

Patient: (as Turtle and Chip Monkey) Well, thanks for inviting us. Bye!

Therapist: Well, what happened now with the tape recorder?

Patient: We'll see.

Therapist: We'll see what happened!!

The interchange between Chippy and Gonga is somewhat reminiscent of Jimmy Cricket and Pinocchio. Pinocchio, the "bad boy," is in perpetual conflict with Jimmy Cricket who clearly serves as his conscience. In this part of the story, the primitive impulses win out over social dictates.

Patient: (Holds Gonga in the center of the camera field.) "Gonga's Dream." Where am I? (Sounds of "alien" people coming on stage with Gonga.) Who are you people?

Patient: (as People) You are in the land of "Don't Listen"…

Patient: (as Gonga) "Don't Listen"??? What is this, some kind of joke? Where am I? You move out of the way. (Pushes "alien.")

Patient: (as Alien) Gonga, don't touch me or I'll zap you.

Patient: (as Gonga) Don't touch me. I'll punch you across the room.

Patient: (as Alien) Boy, some specimen this is!

Patient: (as Gonga) What are you calling me a specimen for?

Therapist: They're calling Gonga a specimen?

Patient: Yeah.

Therapist: Okay, go ahead.

Patient: (as Gonga) I wouldn't talk so much about you guys either…

Therapist: Why are they calling him a specimen?

Patient: These guys are from another planet…

Therapist: Yeah, listen, we have to stop very soon so get to the end of the story.

Patient: (as Gonga) Well, what are you people?

Patient: (as People) We're moon people…

Patient: (as Gonga) Moon people…what's that? I'm not going to listen to anything you say.

Therapist: So what do they say when he says that?

Patient: (as Moon people) Strange specimen!

Patient: (as Gonga) I'm not listening...(Tries to put fingers in ears.) Hey, my hands won't go into my ears....

Patient: (as Moon people) That's right. We have secret powers.

Patient: (as Gonga): Well, I don't know, but I'm getting out of here. I can't move either...

Patient: (as Moon people) Yeah, that's why. Well, we are here to talk to you about the tape recorder.

Patient: (as Gonga) Tape recorder...Oh, rats, well I'm going to get that any way I can...I may have to steal it.

Patient: (as Moon people) Steal it????

Patient: (as Gonga) Oh yeah. You guys haven't been listening to anything I said...

Patient: (as Moon people) Yeah...

Patient: (as Gonga) Well, I don't care what you think...I think you're crazy.

Patient: (as Moon people) Well, we don't think you're crazy. We think you never listen. We're trying to teach you a lesson.

Patient: (as Gonga) How?

Patient: (as Moon people) By getting you with all our creepers.

Therapist: They're going to teach Gonga a lesson for not listening. What are they going to do to him?

Patient: You'll see.

Patient: (as Gonga) Hey, where'd you guys go? Hey, you look scary...(Gonga attacked repeatedly by creepy crawlers, little monsters, and a variety of weird creatures.)

Therapist: What are they doing to Gonga?

Patient: Trying to scare him.

Therapist: Why are they trying to scare him?

Patient: So they can teach him a lesson.

Therapist: What's the lesson they're trying to teach?

Patient: To listen.

Patient: (as Gonga) Help! Get that spider off me!!! Help me! I'll listen all the time. (Screams as creatures attack him.) And then Gonga woke up from the dream screaming.

Therapist: So did Gonga learn a lesson?

Patient: Yeah.

Psychodynamically, the same process is occurring here as described previously with the rejection of Gonga by his two friends. We see here an excellent demonstration of intrapsychic conflict. There is a conflict between the patient's superego (as represented by the punitive creatures) and his primitive impulses (as represented by Gonga, who is the one who threatens to steal the tape recorder). By this process, the patient is attempting to entrench and strengthen his superego dictates.

> *Therapist:* I have one question. Why did Gonga not listen in the first place?
> *Patient:* Because he wanted everything his way.
> *Therapist:* Why was that?
> *Patient:* Because he was a snob.
> *Therapist:* Because he was a snob? How did he get to be a snob?
> *Patient:* Well, he just wants everything in the world.
> *Therapist:* He just wants everything in the world.
> *Patient:* It's a she.
> *Therapist:* Okay, I've been a little confused on that point. Okay. How'd she get to be that way? How'd it happen that she wants everything in the world? Why is she so different from others who do listen?
> *Patient:* She wanted everybody to do what she wanted them to do.
> *Therapist:* Yeah, but how did she get that way? How did it happen?

I decided not to analyze the reasons why the patient was switching Gonga's sex. Rather, I decided to persist with the inquiry regarding how Gonga got to be so selfish and why she wouldn't listen. One answer had been provided: "Well, he just wants everything in the world." Although this is not a deeply significant comment, it does provide some insight into the feelings of deprivation with which the patient was suffering. I suspected that the change in sex at this point related to Frank's desire to provide further disguise. I say this because of the very important information that was soon to follow. Now, to return to the transcript at the point where the patient is responding to my question: "Yeah, but how did she get that way? How did it happen?"

> *Patient:* Well, a long time ago when she was really young, she had this little brother, and he was getting so much attention that Gonga went crazy. She wanted everything. She wanted all the attention.

I hope the reader shares the excitement I felt at this point. I considered this last statement to represent a real "breakthrough" in Frank's treatment. For the first time, I learned about an important psychodynamic factor in Frank's antisocial behavior. Using Gonga as the vehicle for expressing his thoughts, Frank is essentially telling us that his anger began a long time ago at the time of the birth of his brother. At that time, he suffered a loss of attention that was so painful that he "went crazy." In addition, it tells us something about his insatiable demand to have his own way: "She wanted everything." The revelation demonstrated well the old Greek aphorism: *Give a man a mask and he'll tell you the truth.*

In the ensuing interchange, I made an attempt to get Frank to consider an alternative to dealing with the problem of lost attention following the birth of a younger brother. His way of dealing with this situation involved antisocial acting out, insatiable demands for attention, and indulgence of his whims.

Therapist: So what finally happened to her?

Patient: She turned into wanting everybody to do everything for her. When they did something for her, she would give them a lot of grief.

Therapist: Okay, so how'd it finally end up for her?

Patient: The dream taught her a lesson.

Therapist: Oh...well, what would have been a better thing for Gonga to do after the birth of her brother?

Patient: Try to help.

Therapist: How? In what way?

Patient: Like feeding it...by looking after the baby.

Therapist: Well, what about the fact that the baby got so much attention? What would have been a better thing for Gonga to do about that? Rather than wanting everything her own way, what would have been a better thing? Instead of wanting everything her own way and getting very angry and not listening, what would have been a better way once the baby's there and the mother and father are giving the baby attention, what should you [sic] have done? To get away from what she did?

Patient: Not ignore it.

Therapist: The thing is what would have been a better way for Gonga to have dealt with the new baby rather than want everything to herself and never listen?

Patient: To help.

Therapist: To help is one thing but there's another thing I'm thinking of.

Patient: To stay out of the baby's way.

Therapist: Well, I would say another thing. To *share* the parents' attention. Can you elaborate on that? What does that mean to *share* the parents' attention?

Patient: To let the baby have someone and Gonga have someone. Not let Gonga have it all.

Therapist: Right! That's the key thing…to share! So that Gonga would have some attention and the baby would have some attention. Because when Gonga was being so selfish and mean and wanting everything himself, what happened to him? Did he get attention from the parents?

Patient: No.

Therapist: He got a kind of attention, but…

Patient: (interrupts) Bad attention.

Therapist: Bad attention rather than good attention. So he was worse off. So what did he finally decide to do?

Patient: Stop after the dream.

Therapist: And what did he do?

Patient: He became better.

Therapist: And what kind of attention did he then get from his parents?

Patient: Good attention. He worked really hard and got the $80…$87…

Therapist: $87…and the mother kept her promise and gave him the $10. Okay. Do you want the actors to introduce themselves now that the show is over? (Patient stands, bows.) Shall I come over and I'll be the person who was the voice? I'll take a bow, okay. So long, everybody. Okay, do you want to watch this? Okay, but we don't have enough time to watch it all. We'll watch a little of this now.

Frank's first solutions were not, in my opinion, likely to be efficacious. He suggested trying to help take care of the baby by feeding it. One could argue that via this mechanism he would gratify vicariously his own desires to be an infant and thereby regain in fantasy some of his parents' lost attention. It also might have provided some compensatory enhancement as he assumed the position of the adult who feeds the child. Perhaps, there is an "identification with the aggressor" element here in that feeding the baby is clearly a parental function. Although this mechanism may have provided some compensation, I did not consider it a high-priority solution. In addition, I did not consider it warranted attempting to help Frank analyze this suggestion. I do not think that he was capable of doing so, and I felt that our time would be better spent continuing along other lines.

His next suggestion was that the baby be ignored entirely. Basically, this suggestion involved the utilization of denial mechanisms. These are rarely judicious and are just the opposite of what one attempts to do in the treatment of most people.

His next solution was to "stay out of the baby's way." I believe that this is another statement of the denial mechanism and avoids dealing directly with the problem.

I believed that at that point the patient exhausted all possible solutions that he could think of. Therefore, I introduced mine: for Gonga to *share* his parents' affection with his brother. This is an important point in the treatment of such problems. The patient has to be helped to appreciate that getting parental attention is not an all-or-none situation. He may not be able to get all the attention he wants, but he does not have to settle for no attention at all either. I utilize a similar approach in the treatment of oedipal problems (discussed in Chapter One). The boy is helped to appreciate that although he cannot get all of mother's affection, it does not mean that he will end up with none of it. He can share her with father in certain areas.

The reader may have noted that at one point I used the word "you" when I was referring to Gonga. This often happens in discussions in which the symbolic material is being used as a thin disguise for the patient's own behavior. Sometimes the patient may interrupt and remind me that we are not talking about him or her. At other times, the patient may actually switch into a discussion of the issues in such a way that he or she is aware that the conversation is self-directed. Here, Frank made no mention of the slip and might have missed it entirely.

The story ends with the patient's appreciation of the difference between "bad attention" and "good attention." Lastly, Gonga decides to earn the $87 rather than steal it. Again, a healthy resolution. One cannot expect dramatic behavioral change following such an interchange, but my experience has been that sessions such as this do contribute to a reduction of antisocial behavior and other psychogenic problems.

Five days later we once again played *The Talking, Feeling, & Doing Game*. Prior to the program he drew a sign for the announcement: "Gonga Wants Too Much." This was held close enough to the camera to serve as a general title of the program.

Therapist: Our guest today is going to put on another show called, as you can see on the screen, "Gonga Wants Too Much." We'll be back with you in just a minute. Do you want to say anything at this point?

Patient: No, thank you.

Therapist: Before our program starts, I'd like to introduce our guest. Here he is. (Patient waves.) Do you want to introduce Gonga to us also?

Patient: Here's Gonga.

Therapist: Put him on the screen. Here he is. (Patient holds up Gonga.) Hi, Gonga. Okay, let's turn this off and we'll be right back with you. (At the patient's request, the therapist and patient set up a table with Gonga, Chippy, Turtle and *The Talking, Feeling, & Doing Game*.)

Patient: Hi, and here are Gonga's friends, Chippy. (Holds up Chip Monkey.)

Therapist: Hi, Chippy.

Patient: (Holds up Turtle.) The Turtle.

Therapist: Hi, Turtle. That's it? Just those two friends? Okay.

Patient: And now we must start the show.

Patient: (as Gonga) (Patient now under the table.) Hello. My name is Gonga, and this is another one of my great stories. This is Chippy. (Holds Chip Monkey above table and says "Hi" in a high voice, as if speaking for Chip Monkey.) And this is Turtle. (Holds Turtle above table and says, "Hi, there" in high voice, as if speaking for Turtle.) As you all know, this is my best show yet…We're really working on this one. This one is called "Gonga Never Listens." Okay.

Therapist: Our guest has asked me to play *The Talking, Feeling, & Doing Game* with Gonga. Okay? So how do you want to proceed now? What should we do? Shall I roll the dice for Gonga or do you want to roll the dice for Gonga?

Patient: (as Gonga) Um…you can do it.

Therapist: I'll roll the dice for Gonga. Okay, Gonga got a seven 1-2-3-4-5-6-7. Do you want to read Gonga's card or should I?

Patient: (as Gonga) I'll read it.

Therapist: You'll read it. Here's Gonga's card. What's it say?

Patient: (as Gonga) "What is the worst problem a person can have?"

Therapist: Okay, Gonga, what is the worst problem a person can have, Gonga?

Patient: (as Gonga) Ummm, let's see. I'd say that the worst problem a person can have is probably a bad handicap.

Therapist: A bad handicap. For example, what kind of handicap, Gonga?

Patient: (as Gonga) No legs.

Therapist: No legs.

Patient: (as Gonga) No arms, or deaf, or blind, or dumb.

Therapist: I see, those are pretty bad handicaps. Which of all those would you say is the worst?

Patient: (as Gonga) No legs.

Therapist: No legs. Why would you say that?

Patient: (as Gonga) Or blindness.

Therapist: Or blindness. Why would you say that?

Patient: (as Gonga) Because you need your eyes for a lot of things. Or no hands, because you need your hands for a lot of things, too. And your eyes you need...you can't do many things without your eyes.

Therapist: Uh huh. You know there are some people, Gonga, who have eyes that are good...You test their eyes with an eye chart, and they're fine. However, they don't want to see things that they do that are causing all kinds of trouble. And that's a kind of trouble. And that's a kind of blindness, also. Did you ever hear about that?

Patient: (as Gonga) No.

Therapist: Never heard about that?

Patient: (as Gonga) No.

Therapist: Are you serious?

Patient: (as Gonga) Yeah.

Therapist: That's called psychological blindness. Do you understand what I'm talking about?

Patient: (as Gonga) No, not really.

Therapist: You don't really...try to figure out what I'm...

Patient: (as Gonga) They don't see because they don't want to?

Therapist: Right! They don't want to. Why? Why don't they

want to?

Patient: (as Gonga) They're afraid of what they might see.

Therapist: Right! And what do you think would happen if they were to look at the thing?

Patient: (as Gonga) They would get scared.

Therapist: Yeah, but do you think it would be better or worse for them to look at it and not be psychologically blind?

Patient: (as Gonga) Better.

Therapist: Why do you say that?

Patient: (as Gonga) Well, because then you can do more things.

Therapist: Right! If you make believe there's no problem, then you can't solve it. Did you ever read that book, *Stories About the Real World*?

Patient: (as Gonga) Ummmmm. *Stories About the Real World*...which one is that? Is that the one with "Mack and the Beanstalk"?

Therapist: No, that's a different book. That's a book of fairy tales, called *Modern Fairy Tales*. *Stories About the Real World* has one story in it called "Oliver and the Ostrich." Remember that one?

Patient: (as Gonga) The ones I read were *Dorothy and the Lizard of Oz* and "Mack and the Beanstalk" and yeah, the one with "Oliver and the Ostrich" and "The Million Dollar Lie."

Therapist: Right. What did we learn from "Oliver and the Ostrich"? What did we learn from that?

Patient: (as Gonga) He didn't want to hear. He made believe there was nothing wrong, but there really was something wrong.

Therapist: Right! What was the trouble?

Patient: (as Gonga) He was failing in school.

Therapist: Right! Now how does the ostrich fit into that?

Patient: (as Gonga) Well, he thought that the ostrich would poke his head underneath the sand and make believe nothing was there. But really the ostrich would fight as hard as he could...

Therapist: The ostrich does what?

Patient: (as Gonga) He'd fight as hard as he could.

Therapist: Fight...but if the animal who attacked him was too big, what would he do?

Patient: (as Gonga) He would run.

Therapist: Yeah, but does he ever hide his head in the sand?

Patient: (as Gonga) No.

Therapist: Do human beings do that?

Patient: (as Gonga) Well, maybe.

Therapist: Really, or do they act as if their heads are in the...

Patient: (as Gonga, interrupts) They act. They never really hide in the sand.

Therapist: Right! That's called psychological blindness. Tell me something. Do you do anything...

Patient: (as Gonga, interrupts) What you can't see can't hurt you.

Therapist: Yeah, but what you can't see can hurt you. If the ostrich has his head in the sand, he can't see anything, but can he get hurt?

Patient: (as Gonga) Yes.

Therapist: So, is it true that what you can't see can't hurt you?

Patient: (as Gonga) No.

Therapist: It's not true. Tell me something, do you do anything that's like that...when you make believe that there's no problem when there really is?

Patient: (as Gonga) Oh, yeah.

Therapist: Yeah? How do you do it?

Patient: (as Gonga) At school.

Therapist: How do you do it at school?

Patient: (as Gonga) Well, I don't listen too much.

Therapist: Uh huh. You don't listen.

Patient: (as Gonga) Especially in social studies.

Therapist: Why especially in social studies?

Patient: (as Gonga) Because social studies is so boring.

Therapist: So what do you do in social studies?

Patient: (as Gonga) Talk about the great explorers.

Therapist: Yeah, but what do you do when everybody's talking about the great explorers.

Patient: (as Gonga) Play with my fingers...(mumbles).

Therapist: Pardon me?

Patient: (as Gonga) Play with my fingers sometimes.

Therapist: Uh huh. Why do you do that?

Patient: (as Gonga) Because there's nothing else to do.

Therapist: Uh huh. Anything else?

Patient: (as Gonga) No.

Therapist: Any other reasons why?

Patient: (as Gonga) No, not really.

Therapist: Do you make believe that there's no problem for you there?

Patient: (as Gonga) Sort of.

Therapist: Do you think there's a problem that you play with your fingers?

Patient: (as Gonga) Yes.

Therapist: Why do you think you do that?

Patient: (as Gonga) Because I don't want to listen.

Therapist: How come?

Patient: (as Gonga) Because it's sort of boring to listen.

Therapist: Well, so okay. Let's say it is a little boring. What's so terrible about a little boredom...hmmm?

Patient: (as Gonga) Yeah, well, nothing's so terrible about a little boredom.

Therapist: There's nothing wrong with a little bit of boredom?

Patient: (as Gonga) No.

Therapist: You say it's boring; therefore, you're not going to listen. It sounds to me like you have the idea that anything that's unpleasant you shouldn't do. Is that right?

Patient: (as Gonga) Well, sort of.

Therapist: But, you know, do you think there's any problem with that way of handling things—that if it's unpleasant you're not going to do it.

Patient: (as Gonga) No.

Therapist: There's nothing wrong with that?

Patient: (as Gonga) No.

Therapist: I see. I disagree. I think that there are times in life you have to do things that are unpleasant because if you don't, you get into even worse trouble. What do you think about that?

Patient: (as Gonga) Well, it's sort of true.

Therapist: I mean everybody can't like every subject in school, and if you decide if you don't like one subject, you're not going to do it or you're not going to push through a little boredom, then you're going to get into a lot of trouble. You fail. So, at times, you have to do things you don't like. What do you think about that?

Patient: (as Gonga) Well, that's okay.

Therapist: That's okay? Have I changed your mind on the subject?

Patient: (as Gonga) Yeah.

Therapist: Are you sure?

Patient: (as Gonga) Yeah.

Therapist: Okay, but what are you going to do now when you go to school.

Patient: (as Gonga) I'm going to listen.

Therapist: Well, people don't usually change that fast—I hope you're right—I hope you will listen, but I hope that you'll someday appreciate what I'm saying. Maybe you will now, but people usually take some time to change, and just saying that you're going to listen isn't enough.

By this point, the reader has probably forgotten that this discussion began with the patient's card regarding what is the worst thing that can happen to someone. I used his response about going blind as one of the worst things to embark on a discussion of "psychological blindness," utilization of the denial mechanism. There was some receptivity on Frank's part to accepting the fact that he utilizes denial and "makes believe" that there is no problem when there really is. I also used the opportunity to make reference to my story, "Oliver and the Ostrich" from my book *Stories About the Real World* (1972a) which deals with the same issue via a discussion of the ostrich. Basically, in the story the child learns that ostriches do not stick their heads in the sand when there is trouble ("they would never do such a stupid thing"). Rather, they scrutinize the danger and decide whether to fight or flee (like all the other animals, except the human being).

In the ensuing discussion we touched upon the patient's failure to take seriously his school assignments and other obligations. I believed that Frank, like many children who feel deprived, subscribed strongly to the pleasure principle. Specifically, he had the feeling that he had gotten very little pleasure in life, and he therefore was not going to tolerate any discomforts or frustrations. In Frank's case, the deprivation related to the birth of his brother and the attendant attention that the latter received. In this vignette he appeared to be resolving to tolerate the discomfort of occasional classroom boredom in order to avoid the discomforts of failure, which he agreed is worse than boredom. However, the facility with which he promised to reform was unconvincing and I described my incredulity. At this point, I resumed my conversation with Gonga. The reader should recall that the patient was still under the table during the course of this conversation and that I was continuously speaking with "Gonga," the doll that he was holding above the table in my view.

Therapist: Let me ask you one other question.

Patient: (as Gonga) Yeah?

Therapist: Why do you think, Gonga, you don't want to accept anything that's unpleasant? Why do you go around just doing just what you like? Why do you say, "I don't like to do it, I'm not going to do it...I'm not going to do what I don't like," when most other people mix it. You know, they have some things they like, some things they don't like and they accept the fact that there are times they have to do things they don't like.

Patient: (as Gonga) I give up!

Therapist: You give up? You haven't any idea why you do it?

Patient: (as Gonga) No.

Therapist: Just try to guess. Why do you do that?

Patient: (as Gonga) Can you say it again?

Therapist: Okay. You go around with the idea that if it's unpleasant you say: "I don't like it, I'm not going to do it." Do you do that, Gonga?

Patient: Yeah, sometimes.

Therapist: Give me an example of how you do that. When you don't like something, you just don't do it.

Patient: (as Gonga) When Chippy and I play *The Talking, Feeling, & Doing Game* at home, when I cheat, he tells me, "Don't cheat or else I'm going to go home." Then I do what I want.

Therapist: You play *The Talking, Feeling, & Doing Game* at home?

Patient: (as Gonga) You let me borrow it.

Therapist: I didn't let you borrow it. I don't lend the game to kids to play at home. Is Gonga making that up? Is that it? No, say it, it's all right.

Patient: (as Gonga) You really did...let's say you really did let Gonga borrow it...

Therapist: Oh, you're making believe that I let Gonga borrow it. Because I usually don't let people borrow that game. It's not a game for home. Oh, so you're saying that Gonga is saying I lent it. But I'd like you to make up something that's real...that really happened...that Gonga...that really happened to Gonga...not a made-up thing.

Patient: We play a regular game.

Therapist: You play a regular game...then what does Gonga do?

Patient: (as Gonga) And I cheat, and Chippy says he'll go

home and he won't play with me.

Therapist: So you cheat.

Patient: (as Gonga) I don't listen to him.

Therapist: You don't listen to him...you just cheat. Why do you cheat?

Patient: (as Gonga) Because I want to win all the time.

Therapist: Uh huh, you want to feel good all the time.

Patient: (as Gonga) Because I want too much.

Therapist: You want too much...uh huh...you don't want to hear no for an answer, huh?

Patient: (as Gonga) That's right.

Therapist: Uh huh. How come? How come you don't want to hear no for an answer?

Patient: (as Gonga) Because I just like to have a lot of stuff.

Therapist: You just like to have a lot of stuff. And you just want to feel good all the time, huh?

Patient: (as Gonga) Yeah.

Therapist: And you never want to feel bad?

Patient: (as Gonga) Yeah.

Therapist: Why is that?

Patient: (as Gonga) Because I don't like feeling bad.

Therapist: Okay, and what did I say before about bad feelings in life?

Patient: (as Gonga) That you have to face them.

Therapist: Yeah, at times you have to have bad feelings. Besides, you have to do things you don't like. What do you think about that?

Patient: (as Gonga) I think it's true.

Therapist: And if you don't, what will happen?

Patient: (as Gonga) You'll get in trouble.

Therapist: Yeah. You'll feel even worse than you did if you just had a few sad feelings.

Patient: (as Gonga) Yeah.

Therapist: Now, why haven't you learned that lesson? Most kids, Gonga, learn that lesson. They know that they've got to do things at times they don't want to do, because they know that if they don't, they'll feel even worse and they'll get left back, or they'll be punished, or they'll be sent to the principal's office, or they'll be grounded, or things like that. Why haven't you learned that lesson yet, Gonga? Why do you think that is?

Patient: (as Gonga) I give up.

Therapist: Do you want my guess?

Patient: (as Gonga) Yeah.

Therapist: My guess is...

Patient: (as Gonga) That I don't want to...

Therapist: But why don't you want to?

Patient: (as Gonga) I don't know.

Therapist: There are many reasons, but I have a guess about one of the reasons.

Patient: (as Gonga) What?

Therapist: My guess is that a long time ago...like you said at the end of the last program...when you were very little, and your brother was born, and before that time, you were like "king of the world." You were the only kid. You were the first grandchild. Everybody doted on you; everybody thought how great you were, and you were really sitting there on the throne. And then, boom, whammo, along came your brother.

Patient: (no longer as Gonga) My dumb old (mumbles) brother...

Therapist: What did you say? Your dumb little brother?

Patient: Dumb.

Therapist: Dumb, okay. So I say this: You got so mad that you said, "I'm very angry at everybody, because they give him all that attention." That's one thing. And another thing you said was, "I'm not going to suffer any more pain. I'm going to do what I want, when I want, and I've got enough pain with everybody giving him attention. No more pain for me." You see, you say two things: "No more pain for me; I'm just going to get pleasure," and "I'm going to get attention by being bad." What do you think about that?

Patient: That's being greedy.

Therapist: That's being greedy? What did I say? Tell me the two things I said that happened to you when your brother was born.

Patient: When my brother was born, I didn't like it. After my brother was born, everybody paid attention to him and not to me. Then I wanted it all so I took over...

Therapist: You wanted what?

Patient: All the attention.

Therapist: So how do you get the attention now?

Patient: By being bad.

Therapist: That's one thing you do. And what else are you doing since your brother was born? You get the attention by being bad and what else did I say you do?

Patient: I don't listen.

Therapist: Yeah, but what happens when you don't listen?

Patient: Well...

Therapist: I said that not listening was the same as being bad. I said something else about pleasure. What did I say about that?

Patient: I wanted it all.

Therapist: You wanted it all — why?

Patient: Because I was greedy.

Therapist: Uh huh. And why do you say that you were greedy?

Patient: Because my little brother was born.

Therapist: And...

Patient: And I wanted all the good things.

Patient: Yeah.

Therapist: You wanted only pleasure, no pain.

Patient: Yeah.

Therapist: Now, what's this got to do with playing with your fingers in social studies class? Can you link that up?

Patient: No.

Therapist: In social studies, it's boring, right?

Patient: Right.

Therapist: So, that's pain, right? So what do you do? What's the pleasure?

Patient: Playing with my fingers.

Therapist: Right. Do you think that's true?

Patient: Yes.

Therapist: Do you think it has something to do with your brother being born?

Patient: Yeah.

Therapist: How would you link it up? — just so I'm sure you understand.

Patient: I get all pleasure. When my brother was born, I wanted all pleasure and no pain and in social studies I wanted all pleasure and no pain.

Therapist: Right! But what'll happen to you if you live a life in which you only get pleasure and avoid pain.

Patient: You'll be a snob.

Therapist: Anything else? Snob doesn't tell me much...

Patient: Be greedy.

Therapist: Yeah. Any other thing that'll happen?

Patient: When you want something and you get it, you'll get a lot of grief.

Therapist: You'll get a lot of grief?

Patient: Yeah.

Therapist: Why will you get a lot of grief?

Patient: Ummmmm. Because…well, I don't know!

Therapist: Well, if you don't do your social studies and you just sit there avoiding the pain and the boredom of social studies and just getting the pleasure of playing with your fingers, what's going to happen?

Patient: You can do that all the time.

Therapist: And what'll happen with your social studies?

Patient: You won't learn.

Therapist: And what'll the teacher do?

Patient: Get you in trouble.

Therapist: Yeah, you won't learn anything, so you'll be kind of dumb or ignorant, right? And you'll also get in trouble. So, in my opinion, it's probably worth it to push through the boredom and learn what you have to from the teacher, and then enjoy some of the other subjects more.

Patient: Okay.

Therapist: What was the last thing I said, just so I'm sure you understand it, Gonga?

Patient: (as Gonga) I would get in trouble and I would be in trouble instead of learning.

Therapist: Yeah. And what causes more trouble? Which is more painful? The boredom of school or the trouble of failing and getting in trouble with the teacher and not learning and being ignorant, being dumb.

Patient: (as Gonga) The second.

Therapist: You say it so I'm sure you understand it. Which is more trouble? Say it, I want to make sure you understand.

Patient: (as Gonga) Getting in trouble with the teacher and failing in school and not being able to learn…

Therapist: …is more trouble than…

Patient: (as Gonga)…boredom.

Therapist: Right, right. By the way, you get a chip for that. That was your question.

I attempted here to help the patient gain some insight into the relationship between his antisocial behavior and the birth of his brother. I had the feeling that some inroads were made here, but I certainly can't say that he responded with the kind of strong emotional response one sees in patients (especially adults) when the therapist has "hit home." Although the insight was at a minimal level, I believe it was nevertheless there.

The reader may have noticed that at the point where I began speaking about the birth of the brother the patient dropped the Gonga disguise and began talking about himself. Near the end of the interchange, I purposely returned him to the Gonga role in order to "preserve anonymity" and thereby assure a freer flow of revelation.

After being awarded the chip, the patient requested that Gonga and I discontinue playing *The Talking, Feeling, & Doing Game* and go on to another activity. The reader may note that only one card had been drawn between the outset and the time we went on to another activity.

> *Therapist:* Our guest now has decided that we stop *The Talking, Feeling, & Doing Game* and now he's going to put on a little play about Gonga and his friends and the fire truck. Okay, you're on the air!
>
> *Patient:* (as Chip Monkey and Turtle) Boy, look at that. That's really neat. I love that. Hey, wow, look at that neat thing with the little sprays.
>
> *Therapist:* What are they looking at?
>
> *Patient:* The fire engine.
>
> *Patient:* (as Gonga) Hi, guys. (Gonga knocks Chip Monkey.) Oops, sorry, Chippy.
>
> *Therapist:* So Chippy and Turtle are looking at that fire engine and think it's really neat. Okay, go ahead.
>
> *Patient:* (as Gonga) Boy, that's really…Neato…Boy, it's neat.
>
> *Therapist:* Gonga thinks it's neat, too, huh?
>
> *Patient:* (as store manager) Hey, kid, don't touch.
>
> *Patient:* (as Gonga) Shut up. Boy, wow. I really want this…look at those pieces…
>
> *Therapist:* He really wants it.
>
> *Patient:* Those little pieces, those little sprays on the fire engine, everything it's got…
>
> *Patient:* (as store manager) Kid, you're not supposed to touch it.
>
> *Patient:* (as Gonga) Shut up, mister.
>
> *Patient:* (as store manager) Okay, out of my store.

Patient: (as Chip Monkey) Gonga!!

Patient: (as Gonga) Who cares about that dumb old guy anyway!!

Therapist: The guy kicked Gonga out of the store because he touched the fire engine?

Patient: Yeah.

Therapist: Okay, and then what did Gonga say?

Patient: Shut up.

Therapist: Who'd he say shut up to?

Patient: The guy.

Therapist: The owner of the store?

Patient: Yeah.

Therapist: And then what happened?

Patient: He left.

Therapist: Gonga left. Okay, now what happens?

Patient: (Whispers to therapist.)

Therapist: You want a cut, okay. Gonga is now home and our guest wants me to play the role of Gonga's father and has told me what to say. Okay, go ahead, you begin.

Patient: (as Gonga) Daddy...

Therapist: (as Gonga's father) Yes, Gonga, what is it?

Patient: (as Gonga) There's this fire engine at the store, and I want it very bad. Can I have it?

Therapist: (as Gonga's father) Well, how much does it cost?

Patient: (as Gonga) $36.

Therapist: (as Gonga's father) $36?

Patient: (as Gonga) Well, it's because it's remote control.

Therapist: (as Gonga's father) Well, that's a very expensive toy, Gonga, and that's a lot of money for a toy. I'll tell you what I'll do. I'll be happy to give you part of the money, but you're going to have to save up from your allowance and your earnings in order to pay for most of it. I'll pay for $10 of it, and you've got to pay the other $26.

Patient: (as Gonga) No, I want the whole thing!! (Gonga jumping up and down, imitating a temper tantrum.)

Therapist: (as Gonga's father) I'm sorry, Gonga...I'm sorry you just can't have everything you want when you want it, and you just can't have every toy you want and that's the answer.

Patient: (as Gonga) Get you...(mumbles)...

Therapist: (as Gonga's father) What was that?

Patient: (as Gonga) No, I want it now. (Gonga has another temper tantrum.)

Therapist: (as Gonga's father) Now look, Gonga. If you're going to continue with those tantrums, I'm going to have to send you to your room because I just don't like the noise of those tantrums. So either you're going to stop the tantrums or off to your room.

Patient: (as Gonga) If I'm good, can I have it tomorrow?

Therapist: (as Gonga's father) Well, I'll tell you...

Patient: (as Gonga) And then pay you back...

Therapist: (as Gonga's father) You want to borrow the money?

Patient: (as Gonga) Yeah.

Therapist: (as Gonga's father) Well, I won't lend you all the money. I'll lend you part of the money, but you'll have a debt. The total amount that you owe for that is $26. Now, how much money do you have right now in your bank?

Patient: (as Gonga) $11.

Therapist: (as Gonga's father) $11. Okay, so how much do you want me to lend you?

Patient: (as Gonga) Could you lend me...

Therapist: (as Gonga's father) Well, we're running out of time, so I'll lend you $15. Fifteen dollars and $11 is $26, and I'll give you $10 toward it. That's $36. But remember you owe me $15 that you have to earn, right?

Patient: (as Gonga) Yeah.

Therapist: (as Gonga's father) Okay, so here's the $15 and you can buy it.

Patient: (as Gonga) Okay. (Patient whispers in therapist's ear.)

Therapist: (as Gonga's father) Our guest now has asked me to play the part of the storekeeper. Okay?

Therapist: I'm going to play the part of the storekeeper. Okay. Hiya, Gonga.

Patient: (as Gonga) I want that. (Gonga points to fire engine.)

Therapist: (as storekeeper) Okay. You got $36?

Patient: (as Gonga) Yeah, right here.

Therapist: (as storekeeper) Okay. Give me the money. Ten, 20, 30, 35, 36 dollars. Here you are, my good friend.

Patient: (as Gonga) Thanks.

Therapist: (as storekeeper) Now you have a remote control fire engine. Tell me, how did you get this money?

Patient: (as Gonga) My father lent it to me but I had $11.

Therapist: (as storekeeper) Uh huh. So your father lent you some money.

Patient: (as Gonga) Yeah.

Therapist: (as storekeeper) Okay. He lent you money. How much did he lend you?

Patient: (as Gonga) Ummmm. Fifteen dollars.

Therapist: (as storekeeper) Okay. And that makes $26. Where'd you get the other $10?

Patient: (as Gonga) Ummm. He gave it to me.

Therapist: (as storekeeper) That was pretty nice of him. I guess you're going to have to work now to earn the $15 to give him back the money, right?

Patient: (as Gonga) Yeah.

Therapist: (as storekeeper) Good for you. That'll give you a really good feeling when you work off that debt. And then you'll have that all yourself when you know that you worked for it.

Patient: (as Gonga) Okay, thanks.

Therapist: (as storekeeper) Okay. I hope you enjoy that fire engine.

Patient: (as Gonga) Okay. Bye.

Therapist: (as storekeeper) Bye. Okay. Now we're coming to the very last part of the show. Go ahead.

Patient: (as Gonga) Boy, am I sure glad I earned all that money, and I paid back my debt and I got that money from my father by doing the paper route, mowing lawns, and raking leaves.

Therapist: (as storekeeper) Uh huh.

Patient: (as Gonga) Boy, do I feel good about myself.

Therapist: (as storekeeper) Uh huh. You really feel good about yourself?

Patient: (as Gonga) Yeah.

Therapist: (as storekeeper) Uh huh. Okay. Now how's it working out with that remote fire engine?

Patient: (as Gonga) Great!

Therapist: (as storekeeper) Are you really enjoying it?

Patient: (as Gonga) Yeah, watch this. You just press the button and it goes.

Therapist: Okay, before we close, I'd like to hear from you,

Gonga, what are the lessons of this story? All the different lessons we can learn from this story, which is quite a long one. See if you can figure them out.

Patient: (as Gonga) Umm. Don't be greedy...

Therapist: Because...

Patient: (as Gonga) It will never bring you good.

Therapist: Why will it never bring you good?

Patient: (as Gonga) Because it's not good to be greedy and nobody will pay attention to you.

Therapist: Well, yeah, they won't like you if you're greedy. They may pay attention if you make yourself a nuisance, you know?

Patient: (as Gonga) Yeah.

Therapist: Okay. Go on, why isn't it good?

Patient: (as Gonga) Ummm. Because it's not good for you.

Therapist: How come?

Patient: (as Gonga) Well, when you grow up, you'll keep wanting stuff.

Therapist: And...

Patient: (as Gonga) You'll turn into a snob.

Therapist: What is a snob as you see it? What do you mean by snob?

Patient: (as Gonga) A jerk.

Therapist: Be more specific.

Patient: (as Gonga) You want too much.

Therapist: And then what'll happen if you want too much?

Patient: (as Gonga) When you get it, you'll get grief.

Therapist: Why will you get grief?

Patient: (as Gonga) You'll *give* grief.

Therapist: Why will you give grief?

Patient: (as Gonga) Because once you get your way...

Therapist: How do you give grief when you get your way?

Patient: (as Gonga) You misbehave.

Therapist: Uh huh. Okay. And any other lessons?

Patient: (as Gonga) Things aren't always as bad as they really are.

Therapist: Say that again.

Patient: (as Gonga) Well, we were playing *The Talking, Feeling, & Doing Game.*

Therapist: What did you learn from that?

Patient: (as Gonga) Let's see. Ummm. I think...

Therapist: What did we learn in that game?

Patient: (as Gonga) We learned that…umm…that getting in trouble and pain is much worse than boredom pain.

Therapist: Right, right! And what did we learn about how sometimes you have to take a little pain? Huh?

Patient: (as Gonga) Yeah.

Therapist: To avoid bigger pain.

Patient: (as Gonga) Yeah.

Therapist: Uh huh. And that's part of life, right? And what'd we learn about you and your brother? That's the last thing before we close. What did we learn about you and your brother?

Patient: (as Gonga) Ummm. We learned that…you can't …you mean about me and my brother?

Therapist: Yeah, what did we learn about you and your brother?

Patient: (as Gonga, crawling on floor around table.) We learned that you can't have all the attention all the time.

Therapist: Right. That we share.

Patient: (as Gonga) Yeah.

Therapist: And what did we learn about what you're doing? After your brother was born, to get attention, what do you do?

Patient: (as Gonga) Get into trouble.

Therapist: And that gives you attention. What did we learn about your feelings about pleasure and pain after your brother was born?

Patient: (as Gonga) That I wanted bad pain.

Therapist: You wanted what?

Patient: (as Gonga) Umm…I don't know.

Therapist: You wanted…how did you feel about getting pleasure and pain after your brother was born? What did you want?

Patient: (as Gonga) Just pleasure.

Therapist: Right, right. Okay, do you want to come up and say goodbye to everybody, to show your face now? Okay. This is our guest. (Patient stands up and bows.) He's been the guy…he's been the voice that you've been hearing. Okay. So long everybody. And now, ladies and gentlemen, we just want to announce that this is the end. (Patient holds up sign which says *The End*.) We hope you enjoyed this show. Goodbye, everybody. Do you want to say goodbye?

Patient: So long.

Therapist: So long. Bye.

Within the few weeks following this session there was a definite reduction in Frank's antisocial behavior. He was much more compliant in school and cooperative at home. I believe that these sessions played a role in the behavioral change. I do not believe that this was simply related to the insight he gained about the relationship between his antisocial behavior and the birth of his brother. I believe that he gained some appreciation of the fact that his antisocial behavior caused him more pain than the discomforts associated with doing what is socially acceptable and desirable. In addition, I believe he gained some solace from the concept of sharing. He could not have his parents as much as he wanted, but he could have them to some degree. Unfortunately, this patient's therapy had to be interrupted because his father was required to relocate for business purposes. Arrangements were made for him to continue therapy with a psychiatrist near his new home. A follow-up conversation six months later revealed that Frank continued to improve.

The Case of George: This Damn Magic Wand Is No Good

This eight-year-old boy suffered with a neurologically based learning disability. He was quite immature in many ways and was over-protected by his mother. His view of the world of magic was very much like that of the five year old and his magic-cure expectations were strong. Near the end of his second month in treatment he told this story.

Patient: The name that I'm gonna have—I'm gonna have two names of the story each.

Therapist: Go ahead.

Patient: One name is gonna be "Little Ducklings" and the second name is gonna be "One of the Ducklings Turns into a Grown Man." There's only gonna be one duckling.

Therapist: Okay.

Patient: There's the mother, the father, the brother.

Therapist: Okay. Now do you want to start the first story? Go ahead.

Patient: I said there's going to be two names and that's the story.

Therapist: Oh, just one story with two names?

Patient: Yeah.

Therapist: Okay. Start the story.

Patient: And two lessons.

Therapist: And two lessons. Okay. This is a story, one story with two names and two lessons. Go ahead. Let's hear.

Patient: Once there's a duckling. He said, "Ooh, how did I get changed into a duckling? I was a person all my life. How—how could this happen? How did this happen? I must even act like a duck now so a fairy godmother will come and save me. Quack, quack, quack, quack." But no fairy godmother came. So he said, "Quack, quack, quack, quack, quack" and he was begging for his fairy godmother.

Therapist: Okay, then what happened?

Patient: Then he said, "Quack, quack. Oh, I wish a fairy godmother would come. Quack, quack, quack, quack." And he was quacking so hard that he flew over to the water and fell in.

Therapist: Okay. Then what happened? This is a very good story.

Patient: Then he said, "Caw, caw, quack, quack, coo, coo, quack, quack," and he was...(mumbles)...up.

Therapist: And he was what?

Patient: Burning up.

Therapist: He was burning up. Why was he burning up?

Patient: Because he said, "Quack, quack, quack, quack, quack!" Like that.

Therapist: Okay. Then what happened?

Patient: Then he said, "Quack, quack, quack." (Patient speaking in singsong manner.) "Oh, I wish a fairy godmother, a fairy godmother." That's a little song the duckling made up.

Therapist: Okay. Go ahead.

Patient: (sings again) "Oh, I wish a fairy godmother would come and get me out, would come and get me out, would come and get me out." And he was going, "Quack, quack, quack, quack, quack!" And then he turned into a horse!

Therapist: He turned into a horse! Yeah. Go ahead.

Patient: Then he said, "Boy, what happened with me? I was a duckling before. I used to go heeee, heeee. I hope a fairy godmother comes this time. Heeeeewwwwww quack, quack." And then he changed back into a duck because he went "quack, quack" by accident.

Therapist: Uh huh. Then what happened?

Patient: And then the fairy godmother *really* came and said, "Huh! What, what. I thought I heard somebody calling me. I don't see anybody. Hmmm. Must be my magic wand...(mumbles)...by accident.

Therapist: Wait a minute. The fairy godmother said, "What, I thought I heard somebody calling me," and then she said what about a wand?

Patient: And then she said, "Hhhmmm! My magic wand probably made him disappear." But the duck was really in the pond under the water.

Therapist: (interrupts) She thought that her magic wand made the duck disappear. That's why she didn't see him in the pond. Go ahead.

Patient: "Ooh, oh, oh, oh, I tricked her."

Therapist: Wait a minute. I don't understand that. Who's talking now?

Patient: The duck.

Therapist: And what did he say?

Patient: "Ooh, I tricked that fairy godmother by accident. I'll go get her. Fairy godmother, quack, quack. I'm a duckling. Change me back into a person." But the fairy godmother was in the clouds.

Therapist: So what happened then?

Patient: Then he was there again and when the fairy godmother came again she saw him turned into a horse. And she said, "Hey, what happened, horse? You were quacking before. Don't you know how to make a horse sound? A horse goes, 'Heeehawww, heeehawww.' You went 'quack, quack, quack' and clapping your hands. I'm not gonna help you. Keep this magic wand and try yourself." And then the fairy godmother went away.

Therapist: And then what happened? (Pause) So the fairy godmother went away and wouldn't change him into a person?

Patient: No, because she was so mad at him. He didn't know how to make a horse sound. He changed before the fairy godmother came there.

Therapist: Oh, the fairy godmother was mad because he changed from a duck into a horse?

Patient: Yeah, and she heard him quacking.

Therapist: Oh, she heard him quacking and then he turned into a horse. Okay, and then what finally happened? So the fairy godmother got angry at him and went away. Then what finally happened?

Patient: Then the magic wand worked on him and that's the end.

Therapist: It worked on him. And what happened when the magic wand worked on him?

Patient: It flew back…it was um…it flew back to the fairy godmother.

Therapist: What happened to the duck or horse?

Patient: He turned back into a boy before it went…

Therapist: (interrupts) Oh, he turned back into a boy. Oh, I see. Okay. And the lesson of that story?

Patient: Two lessons, remember?

Therapist: What are the two lessons?

Patient: Never…(long pause).

Therapist: Never what?

Patient: Never be mad at a duck!

Therapist: Never be mad at a duck? And the other lesson?

Patient: Don't think there's no such thing as fairy godmothers. There's, there's a lesson that goes with that also. And the third lesson is: Don't believe in fairy godmothers because there's no such thing and if you heard a duck quacking and it changed into a horse it was really the duck and don't be mad at it.

Therapist: I see.

Patient: That's the lessons.

Therapist: Okay. Now it's my chance to tell a story.

This story is typical of that told by many children with neurologically based learning disabilities. It is somewhat disorganized and the patient does not concern himself with whether his listener understands what is going on in it. Frequent questioning is required if the therapist is to surmise the story's psychodynamic meaning. In analyzing such a story it is best to think about main issues and general trends and not get bogged down in minutiae. The main event in this story is that a boy is turned into a duck and in that state he has the power to change himself into a horse. Finally, after a few somewhat confusing experiences with the fairy godmother, he is turned back into a boy. George had a speech defect for which he had received some therapy. In addition, his lower lip protruded somewhat and occasionally saliva dripped from it. (Characteristically, his mother was ever at hand to catch the saliva and it was not until I recommended it that she taught George how to use a handkerchief and to think about his tendency to salivate.) His depicting himself as a duck related, I believe, to his speech deficit as well as to his protruding lip. The horse, with his odd vocalization, also lends itself well to symbolizing the patient and his speech defect.

The story also depicts some hostile interchanges between the duck-horse and the fairy godmother: the duck tricks the fairy godmother by making a quacking sound and then changing into a horse; the duck hides from the fairy godmother so that she cannot find him; and the fairy godmother throws her wand at the horse. To play a trick on someone is a common childhood way of expressing hostility. In this case, the tricks involve hiding from the fairy godmother and fooling her by back-and-forth transformations between a horse and a duck. I suspected that the fairy godmother might have symbolized me (the magic curer) and that the hostility might have related to anger over my not having provided George with a magic cure—but I was not certain.

The story, then, contains two themes: a desire for magic transformation from infrahuman to human status and the expression of hostility (probably toward the therapist). His first lesson: "Don't think there's no such thing as fairy godmothers. There's, there's a lesson that goes with that also." This lesson makes reference to a previous story in which I promulgated the notion that there is no such thing as a fairy godmother. This idea apparently produced such anxiety that he had to negate it with a lesson in this subsequent story. He then continued. "And the third lesson is: Don't believe in fairy godmothers because there's no such thing and if you heard a duck quacking and it changed into a horse it was really a duck and don't be mad at it." Here we see apparent acceptance of my message that there is no such thing as a fairy godmother. Clearly the patient is ambivalent regarding this idea. However, one can't expect immediate receptivity regarding a patient's giving up such an attractive symptom and a phase of ambivalence is a step toward its elimination. Furthermore, the third lesson also makes reference to the hostility issue by advising the listener (me?) not to be mad at a quacking duck that changes into a horse. The request suggests that the patient anticipates that I will be angry at him for his tricks.

I decided not to attempt to create a story that would simultaneously incorporate both the hostility and magic themes. It is generally judicious of the therapist to select one of the themes from the patient's story and use only that for his or her responding story. To try to do more may not only be too much for the child to handle, but the therapist's ability to create a unified story with more than one theme is not as great as the capacity of the child's unconscious to do this. I decided to choose the magic transformation theme rather than the anger. First,

I was more certain of its meaning. Second, I reasoned that if I could help the patient reduce his dependency on magic he would rely more on realistic solutions to his problems. Because that goal had a greater likelihood of success, he would then be less likely to be angry at me.

Another problem that I faced in formulating a responding story was that of what to do with the duck. As described, the duck lent itself well as a symbol of the patient because of his speech problem and his salivating, protruding lip. To portray the patient as a duck in my story might entrench this pathological personification and might thereby be antitherapeutic. However, to depict the patient as a boy would then rob me of the opportunity to deal with the magic transformation issue in a manner that was close to the patient's representation of the problem. If the therapist's story gets too remote from the patient's, it becomes less therapeutically effective.

In addition, the child's ability to create a fantasy that most efficiently and effectively synthesizes the symbols is far greater than that of the therapist. I believe that we lack the ingenuity not only of our child-patient's unconscious, but of our own unconscious as well. We ourselves cannot consciously create a dream as rich and as efficient as that which can be created by our own unconscious. The efficiency and ingenuity of our unconscious processes to utilize simile, metaphor, allegory, and efficient and innovative symbol fusion far surpasses that of our conscious mind. Therefore, I do not try to reconcile all elements of my story nor do I strive for one-hundred percent consistency. In this case I chose to be a little inconsistent (and even possibly a little antitherapeutic) in order to preserve the duck symbol for the larger purposes of my story, that is, to present a story that focused on the patient's magic cure delusion.

Also, using another symbol would remove us from the scene of the patient's metaphor. This shift would lessen the likelihood of the patient and I then moving along the same psychological track and would lessen thereby his receptivity to my story. However, when I retain the undesirable symbol I am quick to modify it or introduce qualifications that reduce its psychologically detrimental import. When introducing the duck I was quick to point out that the duck was a regular, "plain," and "nice" duck and that his only defect was that he had a speech problem. As will be seen in the transcript, the patient was relieved by this circumscription of his deficits. It wasn't that the duck was totally loathsome; rather he suffered only with an isolated defect. In short, I considered the advantages of retaining the duck symbol to far outweigh the disadvantages and told this story in response.

Therapist: Once upon a time there was a duck and he was just a duck. He was a real duck. He never was a person.

Patient: What's the name of the story?

Therapist: The name of my story is: "The Duck and the Fairy Godmother." Okay? No, excuse me. I'm going to change the name: "The Duck and the Old Lady." Okay?

Patient: (laughs)

Therapist: "The Duck and the Old Lady" is the name of my story. Once upon a time there was a duck. And he was just a duck, a plain duck. He was a very nice duck but he thought it would be better not to be a duck. He thought it would be best to be a person. So he used to go around saying, "Quack, quack, quack, quack, quack quack," hoping he would find a fairy godmother. And he would sing a song and the song would go. How did the song go?

Patient: (in singsong manner) "Quack, quack, quack, quack, quack, quack."

Therapist: He'd go, "Quack, quack. I wish I saw a fairy godmother." He'd go, "Quack, quack, quack, quack, quack, quack, quack. Fairy godmother! Where's the fairy godmother?" No fairy godmother came.

Patient: Talk slow. The duck talks so fast, I can't hear you.

Therapist: He would say, "Quack, quack, quack."

Patient: (joins in) "Where's my fairy godmother?"

Therapist: "Where's my fairy godmother?"

Patient: And he was shaking his hands...(mumbles)...

Therapist: But he couldn't find any fairy godmother. Then one day he saw an old lady. She was walking by the river.

Patient: Did that old lady...Was that old lady really a wicked witch?

Therapist: No.

Patient: Or a good witch?

Therapist: No, she was just an old lady, but this old lady...

Patient: (interrupts) Did she have a wand?

Therapist: This old lady used to think that she was a fairy godmother. She thought that maybe there was such a thing as a fairy godmother and she thought...

Patient: (interrupts) You told...you told this the other day except it didn't have a duck in it.

Therapist: No. This is a different story. Do you want to hear my story?

Patient: Yes, but the other day you told it about the old woman.

Therapist: Yeah, but this is a different story about an old woman. Okay? Do you want to hear this one?

Patient: Yes.

Therapist: So the duck went over to her and he said, "Quack, quack, quack, quack. Fairy godmother, will you change me into a person?" And she thought that she had magic powers so she said, "Okay." (Therapist waving imaginary stick over patient's head.) And she had a wand...she had a stick and she said to the duck, "Magic...magic duck...duck, quack three times and I'll change you into a person. Quack three times." Okay, you make believe you're the duck.

Patient: (while therapist rotates imaginary stick over his head) "Quack, quack, quack."

Therapist: And she waved it around and do you know what happened?

Patient: What?

Therapist: The duck still remained a duck!

Patient: (laughs)

Therapist: And she said, "Say quack again. Say quack harder."

Patient: (yells) Quack!

Therapist: Harder!

Patient: (yells louder) Quack!

Therapist: Harder!

Patient: (yells again) Quack!

Therapist: Harder!

Patient: (screams) Quack!

Therapist: And he still stayed a duck. And she got very angry ..."Ooh, this magic wand! (striking the imaginary wand against a table) I'm hitting this magic wand. This magic wand (makes angry sounds) is no good! We'll try it again! Now you say quack again three times. Go ahead. Magic wand...

Patient: (while therapist is waving wand again over patient's head) "Quack, quack, quack."

Therapist: And he still remained a duck. And she got very ..."This damn magic wand!" (Therapist angrily breaks the imaginary wand over his knee.) And she took it and threw it away. (flings the wand away) She said, "Wait, I'll get another magic wand." She came back with another one and she said, "I'm going to say a new thing (waving wand over patient's head). Abracadabra, hocus, pocus, turn this boy (sic: therapist's error) into a person. He's a duck!" What happened?

Patient: He still remained a duck?

Therapist: Right! And she said, "I can't stand these magic wands. Umph!" And she took it and she broke it on her knee (breaks wand on knee) and she threw it away! (throws wand away) She was very mad. As she was standing there, a man came along and he saw her.

Patient: Who was that man?

Therapist: (jumping up and down) And she was jumping up and down screaming and crying, and this man said to her—who was this man? He was just a man walking by, an old man. And he said, "What are you so mad about, old lady?"

She said, "My magic wands don't work. I want to turn this duck into a boy, into a person.

And the man said, "There's no such thing as a magic wand."

And she said, "You know, I'm beginning to see that."

Patient: (interrupts) In the other story there was a woman with a magic wand like that, but there was no man; there was an owl. There was no duck.

Therapist: Right. In the other story there was a wise old owl. Right.

Patient: And the boy.

Therapist: What's that?

Patient: And in the other story there was a boy who wanted to be turned into a duck, I think.

Therapist: Well, it was a different story, but let's talk about this one. Anyway, so this man said, "There's no such thing as magic wands."

And the old lady said, "You know, I'm beginning to see that. I thought that I would like to be a fairy godmother and do this duck a favor and turn him into a boy."

And the man said, "Well, why would you want to turn him into a boy? He's a perfectly fine duck!"

And the duck said, "No, I'm not! No, I'm not!"

And the man said, "Why? What's wrong with you?"

He said, "I don't speak too well."

Patient: (with sigh of relief) He doesn't speak too well.

Therapist: Yeah. And he said, "That's the reason why you

want to turn into a person? You can learn to speak well."

And the duck said, "No, I can't! No, I can't!"

What did the man say?

Patient: "Yep, you could."

Therapist: And what did the man say as to how he could learn to speak well?

Patient: By going to a speech teacher.

Therapist: Right! So what do you think the duck did?

Patient: Go to a duck speech teacher.

Therapist: He went to a duck speech teacher. He left the old lady who he realized could not really change him into a person. He was a duck. And he went to the speech teacher and then after that, it was very hard and it took a long time, but after that what happened?

Patient: He, he, he...oy, yoy yoy...he...(mumbles)...

Therapist: He what?

Patient: He, he...

Therapist: What happened after that?

Patient: He...

Therapist: (interrupts) Forget something?

Patient: He...uh...

Therapist: What happened after he went to the speech teacher?

Patient: He...(long pause)

Therapist: Come on, you can...

Patient: (interrupts) He could talk well.

Therapist: Right! Very good! He could talk well. He practiced very hard and then after that did he keep wishing then he would be a person?

Patient: No.

Therapist: He was happy he was a duck. And the lesson of that story is what? What are the lessons of that story? Can you figure them out?

Patient: How many...(mumbles)...

Therapist: The first lesson. What's the first lesson?

Patient: Uno (Spanish: *one*) lesson is...

Therapist: (interrupts) Uno lesson.

Patient: Never think you can change your magic wand into a person or a duck.

Therapist: Right. There's no such thing as magic. There's no such thing as a magic wand. Okay. Come over here. What's the second lesson?

Patient: Number dos (Spanish: *two*) lesson is never cry—
eey, yie, yie.

Therapist: Never cry. That's not a lesson. Sometimes people
cry. That's perfectly all right. All right. Let me tell you the second
lesson. The second lesson of that story is: If you are a duck and
you have some trouble speaking, the best thing you can do is to what?

Patient: Is to go to a duck speech teacher or a regular speech
teacher.

Therapist: Right. And practice hard and after that you'll be
able to speak well.

Patient: The end.

Therapist: The end.

Patient: Could we stay here all day until I want to go home,
until I get tired?

Therapist: Well, we'll stay a little while longer.

Patient: Goody!

Therapist: Right. Do you want to watch this program?

Patient: (running to turn on TV monitor) Goodbye!

Therapist: Goodbye, everybody.

The purpose of my story is obvious. I attempted to impart the
notion that there are no such things as magic cures and that a more
practical and predictably effective course toward overcoming one's
handicaps is through constructive action. The written transcript cannot
completely convey all the theatrical elements that I introduced in order
to enhance the patient's interest in my story and encourage receptivity to my therapeutic messages. The therapist who is able to "ham it
up" in this manner provides the patient with a valuable therapeutic
adjunct. The child was swept up by my wild gestures and readily par-
ticipated in the little play. His statement at the end: "Could we stay
here all day until I want to go home, until I get tired?" confirms quite
well the kind of enthusiasm that such dramatizations can evoke.

When I started my story I was not completely clear about exactly
how I was going to develop it. I did know, however, that it was going
to center on a denial of the efficacy of magic. When a child asks me
to tell the title of a story I generally provide one that epitomizes the
story's primary theme or message. In this case, the patient's question
caught me a little bit off guard because I had not yet precisely formulated my story. Accordingly, I gave the title "The Duck and the Fairy
Godmother." I immediately recognized that this title implied that there

would actually be a fairy godmother in the story. Accordingly, I quickly retracted the title and substituted "The Duck and the Old Lady." Therapists should not hesitate to change their minds in the course of storytelling if they suddenly realize that they can do better for the patient by doing so. It is unrealistic to require of ourselves that we create, on the spur of the moment, polished theatrical performances or cohesively written stories. In the split second between my stating the first title and then retracting it, I decided that my story would include an old lady who aspired to be a fairy godmother but who was unsuccessful. Hence, when I presented the second title I specifically omitted any reference to magic.

In the early part of my story the patient interrupted to point out that there were similarities between the story I was telling and a story I had told during a previous session. He was referring to a story in which a wise old owl was the conveyor of my therapeutic messages and that story as well dealt with the magic cure theme. His recognition of the similarities well demonstrates that the messages I communicate in my stories do sink in and are remembered.

This principle is again demonstrated by the sequence presented below which took place nine days later. On this day, instead of only the patient and his mother appearing for the session, his father and two younger siblings (his six-year-old brother and four-year-old sister) also appeared in the waiting room. The father was about to take the younger siblings out for a walk while the patient and his mother were in session with me. I invited the father to bring the children in because of my previous experience that their participation might be useful. The children were quite enthusiastic about the idea because they had heard from their brother such wonderful tales about the exciting things that go on in my office. Also, they had listened to some of the audiotapes that were made during their brother's sessions and had enjoyed what they had heard. George's father, however, was somewhat hesitant to come in because he feared the younger children would be disruptive. Accordingly, I told the younger children that they could come into the room as long as they behaved themselves and that if they did so, they might be allowed to participate in some of the games that George and I played, but I could not promise for certain that they would be invited to join us. The children were quite cooperative and did not interrupt George when he told this story on the television program.

Therapist: Good morning, boys and girls, ladies and gentlemen. Today is Friday, the 20th of April, 1973, and I am happy to welcome you all once again to "Dr. Gardner's Make-Up-a-Story Television Program." Our guest today is now going to tell us another one of his own original made-up stories. You're on the air.

Patient: The name of the story is: "Animals Who Can't Talk and Animals Who Can Talk."

Therapist: "Animals Who Can't Talk and Animals Who Can Talk." Okay. This sounds like a very good title for a story. Go ahead.

Patient: Once there were two animals and they couldn't talk and on the farm and on that farm there were cows who couldn't talk and all animals who couldn't talk. And there was another farm far, far away—there was another farm—and on that farm animals could talk and those animals said to the other animals, "Buh, buh, buh, buh," and the other animals didn't understand those animals.

Therapist: (interrupts) Excuse me, the animals who could talk or the animals who couldn't talk said, "Buh, buh, buh?"

Patient: The animals who could talk.

Therapist: Who could talk said, "Buh, buh, buh." Go ahead.

Patient: And the...what am I up to?

Therapist: You're up to—there were two farms. One farm had animals who couldn't talk and one farm had animals who could talk. And the animals who could talk said, "Buh, buh, buh," to the animals who couldn't talk. That's where you're at. Right?

Patient: (nods affirmatively)

Therapist: Now go ahead.

Patient: Then the animals who couldn't talk said (scratches ear)...didn't say anything, just went like this. (Patient's arms outstretched, shrugs shoulders, palms up, and has wistful expression on face.) That's all. And they—the animals who could talk—didn't know what that meant. And then finally the animals who could talk thought that they were saying it wrong. Instead of saying, "Buh, buh, buh," they said, "How come you can't talk?"

Therapist: Go ahead.

Patient: And then the animals who couldn't talk said (moves lips), just opened their mouths.

Patient's mother: (Gestures that therapist look at patient.)

Therapist: Do that again. I wasn't looking. Your mother said I missed something. What about the animals who couldn't talk? What did they do?

Patient: (Moves lips and mouth without sound coming forth.)

Therapist: Okay. Then what happened?

Patient: And then the animals who could talk said, "Ha! You still can't talk and I was trying to make you talk. I'm going to get a fairy godmother." And he just sat there and he didn't call for a fairy godmother. He didn't wish for a fairy godmother.

Therapist: Who didn't wish for a fairy godmother?

Patient: The animals.

Therapist: Which ones?

Patient: The ones who could talk, to make the ones who couldn't talk, talk.

Therapist: Oh, the ones who could talk wanted to get a fairy godmother in order to make the ones who couldn't talk be able to talk. Is that it?

Patient: (nods affirmatively)

Therapist: Okay, then what happened?

Patient: When he was just standing—sitting on the porch waiting for a fairy godmother...

Therapist: (interrupts) Who was standing waiting for a fairy godmother?

Patient: Uh (pauses).

Therapist: Who was waiting for the fairy godmother?

Patient: ...(mumbles)...

Therapist: Who?

Patient: The...(mumbles)...peeg...or the giraffe.

Therapist: A peeg?

Patient: A pig!

Therapist: A pig! Was this one of the pigs who could or couldn't talk?

Patient: Who could.

Therapist: Who could talk.

Patient: Or it could be a giraffe.

Therapist: A giraffe who could talk. So a pig or a giraffe was waiting for the fairy godmother. Okay.

Patient: And they just sat there doing nothing. They were looking up in the sky saying, "What happened to my fairy godmother? I probably didn't wish for one or say it out loud." And then he began to scream, "Fairy godmother" so loud that all the animals who could talk and couldn't talk ran away.

Therapist: Why did they run away?

Patient: Because he screamed so loud.

Therapist: Then what happened?

Patient: And then he said…

Therapist: (interrupts) Who's he?

Patient: And then the pig said, "Oh, wow, I really screamed loud that time. I scared all the animals who couldn't talk away. That's the name of the animals.

Therapist: What?

Patient: Couldn't Talk and Could Talk.

Therapist: Okay. His screams scared away all the animals who couldn't talk. Then what happened?

Patient: Then he said (in singsong manner), "Oh, I wish for a fairy godmother, a fairy godmother," and he sang and sang until he believed, until somebody, until he realized there's no such thing as a fairy godmother.

Therapist: Okay. You mean she never came?

Patient: No.

Therapist: Then what happened?

Patient: The end.

Therapist: Well, I have a question. What happened to the animals who couldn't talk? What happened to them?

Patient: They had to go to a teacher.

Therapist: Hh hmm.

Patient: They went like this (makes grimacing facial expressions) and the teacher couldn't understand what the animals were saying.

Therapist: So what happened then?

Patient: I'm all done.

Therapist: Well, did they learn to talk?

Patient: Yes. They said—they tried hard like this (makes facial contortions) and they made a couple of sounds: "Buh, buh, buh, yup, yup, yup," and then they started talking loud (voice gets louder): "Yup, yup, yup, yup, yup." And they talked so loud that they grew up to be a giant.

Therapist: Uh huh. I see. Okay. Is that the end of the story?

Patient: Yes.

Therapist: And what's the lesson of that story?

Patient: There are two lessons.

Therapist: What are the two lessons?

Patient: Never sit there but if you want a real fairy godmother don't believe in fairy godmothers. My third lesson is: *There's no such thing as fairy godmothers.*

The story demonstrates well how my messages from the sequence of nine days previously had been remembered by the patient and were retold in his story. One could argue that such repeating is not specifically therapeutic and that the child might be doing it merely to ingratiate himself with me. There is no question that this was probably going on. However, there is also no question that such repetition for the purpose of ingratiating the therapist is part of every patient's cure, regardless of age. It is hoped that the patient will reach the point at which new ways of thinking and doing things will be done for their own sake, rather than merely for the therapist's. In addition, I believe that George repeated my story because of his appreciation, at some level, that it had validity and that it offered him more promise for improvement than fairy godmothers.

Because the story had so many healthy elements, I decided not to alter it in my responding story. Rather, I decided to entrench the message by its repetition in the dramatic mode. The presence of George's younger siblings provided me with a source of willing recruits for participation in my planned theatrical performance.

Therapist: Okay. Now I'll tell you what. I think that was such a good story that instead of my making up a story, what I think we ought to do is let's make up a play. Okay? Do you want to make up a play in which we'll make up a play about your story? Do you want to do that?

Patient: What does that mean?

Therapist: Well, what we'll do is we'll act it out. We'll tell your story and we'll play the parts of different animals—you and me. Okay? Do you want to do that?

Patient: (nods affirmatively)

Therapist: (points to sister and brother sitting in another part of room) Do you want your brother and sister to be in the play?

Patient: (nods affirmatively)

Therapist: (speaking to brother and sister) Would you like to be in a play?

Voice heard from out of camera range: Yes.

Therapist: Okay, come on over here. We'll make a play now. I'll show you how we'll do it. (Sister Sue and brother Bob walk over to where patient and therapist are sitting. Therapist starts moving furniture around.) Let's make a play in which we have two farms. Come over here. (motions to Sue and Bob to come closer)

These are our two guests on our program today. (has Sue and Bob face camera) These two guests are going to be in the play. (moves microphone to side)

Patient: But how are you going to be by the microphone?

Therapist: The microphone will pick up our voices. Now here's what we're going to do. We're making believe that there are two farms. Okay?

Patient: (nods affirmatively)

Therapist: On one farm the animals can't talk and on the other farm the animals can talk. Now, let's make believe, first of all, the animals who can talk. Let's make some animal sounds. (points to patient) What kind of animal sound do you want to make? What kind of animal sound?

Patient: (just stares into space)

Therapist: (to patient while Sue and Bob just remain standing motionless) What animal sound do you want to make?

Patient: What kind of a sound...

Therapist: (interrupts) Any sound.

Patient:...does a giraffe make?

Therapist: I don't know. What kind of sound could a giraffe make?

Patient: (still pondering, while other children are still standing motionless)

Therapist: I don't really know. What's your guess? (after a pause) Well, pick an animal whose sound you know.

Patient: A pig.

Therapist: Well, how does a pig go?

Patient: Oink, oink, oink, oink.

Therapist: Okay, so you'll be the pig. (turns to Bob) Now what animal do you want to be?

Bob: Dog.

Therapist: You'll be the dog. What sound does the dog make?

Bob: Ruff, ruff!

Therapist: (turns to Sue) What animal do you want to be?

Sue: (in low voice) A dog.

Therapist: A dog. What sound does a dog make?

Sue: Ruff, Ruff!

Therapist: (to all three children) Okay, now, now all the animals make sounds. Let's make believe first we're the animals on the farm making the sounds. Okay, every animal make his own sound! Go ahead. Let's do it, (joins in with them) oink, oink, ruff, ruff.

Patient: Oink, Oink.

Sue: Ruff, ruff.

Bob: Ruff, ruff.

All: Oink, oink, ruff, ruff, oink, ruff, oink, ruff, etc.

Therapist: (to Sue) Okay, let's hear you.

Sue: Ruff, ruff, ruff, ruff.

Therapist: Okay, Now those are all the talking animals. Now—turn around (twists Bob around toward camera) so everybody can see you on television. All right? Now (places Sue in one spot) you stand over here. Okay. Now you (places Bob on his left side) stand over here so you'll be seen on television. Now, so those are the animals who can talk. Now, then, there are other animals who can't talk. They just go like (makes strained facial expression), "Mmmmmmmmmmm." Okay (points to Bob), you do that.

Bob: (tries to imitate therapist)

Patient: (to therapist) I hear noise out of you.

Therapist: Yeah, but I'm not saying. (points to Sue) Go ahead, you try words to do it.

Sue: (just stares at therapist)

Therapist: (grimaces and strains face again, trying to evoke some kind of sound) Go ahead (pointing to patient), you try to do it.

Patient: (makes contorted and strained facial expression)

Therapist: (joins patient and makes straining expression and sounds again) Now (placing right hand on Sue's shoulder and looking directly at her), you do that.

Patient: (interrupts) They should be...

Therapist: (interrupts while still looking at Sue) Go ahead.

Patient: ...like this (strains face and clenches hands).

Therapist: (again has strained facial expression as he joins in with patient) "Mmmmmmmmm," and they just can't talk. Then the animals...now the other animals come along and say, "Let's get a fairy godmother to help those animals talk." So let's call out for the fairy godmother. (shouts) "Fairy godmother."

Bob: (joins in with therapist) "...godmother."

Therapist: Go ahead. Call out for her.

All children: "Fairy godmother."

Therapist: (joins in) "Fairy godmother. Would you help those animals talk? (looks around at all the children) Go ahead, do it (points to patient). Yell out for the fairy godmother.

Patient: (shouts) "Fairy godmother. Will you help those animals talk?"

Therapist: (pointing to Sue) You say it.

Sue: (in rushed, garbled voice) "Fairy godmother. Will you make those animals talk?"

Therapist: (pointing to Bob) What about you?

Bob: (shouts) "Fairy godmother. Will you make those animals talk?"

Therapist: All right. Let's look up there. (They all look up at ceiling.) Do you see any fairy godmothers up there?

Patient: No.

Bob: (points toward window) Look up there—nothing!

Therapist: Let's yell louder. Maybe she'll come.

All shouting together: Fairy godmother!

Therapist: Yell louder. Maybe she'll—

All: (shouting even louder together) Fairy godmother!

Therapist: (showing increasing anguish) Fairy godmother, fairy godmother. (looks all around) Do you see any fairy godmother?

Bob: (turning around toward window and holding curtain open in one hand) No, she might be coming.

Patient: Just lights.

Therapist: (talking to Bob and then turning toward window and puts hand on curtain) Do you think she may be out the window here? Let's look out.

Bob: (as he separates curtain and looks out) She may be coming.

Therapist: (to Bob) Well, look out here. Do you see any fairy godmothers out there?

Bob: (looking out of window) No.

Patient and Sue: (looking out window from where they are standing)

Therapist: (to patient and Sue) Do you see any fairy godmothers?

Sue: (nods head negatively)

Patient: I only see the light but no fairy godmother.

Therapist: Let's try once more. Maybe she'll come.

All: (shouting loudly together) Fairy godmother! Fairy godmother. (all look around and up at ceiling)

Therapist: Will you come down and make the animals talk? (with dismayed expression on face) I don't see her. Do you see her?

Children: (seem completely absorbed and interested in what therapist is saying)

Therapist: Now what's going to happen? Now here are all the animals—let's make believe that we're all the animals who can't talk. Okay? (makes strained facial expression)

Children: (imitate facial expression)

Bob: (bends down for a second and pretends he's a dog)

Therapist: "We can't talk." Then what are those animals going to do? (directs attention toward patient) What's going to happen now? What are they going to do?

Patient: I think the other animals will tell where they know a good speech teacher.

Therapist: Right! So all the animals who can't talk go to a speech teacher. (looking at all three children) Who wants to make believe that they're the speech teacher? Who wants to be the speech teacher?

Patient: (raises hand)

Therapist: (pointing to patient) You be the speech teacher. Okay, we three are animals. (begins strained facial expression and makes garbling sounds again, and points to Bob) You do it.

Bob: (makes garbling sounds)

Therapist: (points to Sue) Okay, you do it.

Sue: (nods head up and down, smiling, tries to imitate garbling sounds)

Patient: (looking apprehensive) What should I do?

Therapist: Well, what does a speech teacher do?

Patient: Help people?

Therapist: All right. So what are you going to do?

Patient: Help.

Therapist: Okay, How are you going to help us speak?

Patient: By teaching you how to.

Therapist: Okay, make believe that you're the speech teacher teaching us how to.

Patient: Now say "Moo."

Therapist: (pointing to Bob) You try it first. You try to say "Moo."

Bob: Moo.

Therapist: (all excited) Hey, he said "Moo!" (pointing to Sue) Now you try it. (talking to patient) Teach her to say something.

Sue: Moo.

Patient: Say "Good."

Sue: Good.

Therapist: Okay, now tell me to say something.

Patient: Good, bad, and hat.

Therapist: What is that again?

Patient: Good, bad, and hat.

Therapist: Good, bad, and hat. Okay. (with strained facial expression) G...g...g It's very hard—you see, it's very hard to learn how to speak. It isn't easy. G...g...goo...goo...good. Hey, I said it. Hey, I can start to speak! (talking directly to patient) Now you say to the children, "It takes a lot of practice and you've got to work very hard."

Patient: It takes a lot of practice and you got to work very hard.

Therapist: (looking around at all three children) So, all of us, let's say we work very hard for a long time and we're all learning, and we can speak now. Okay?

Patient: (nods affirmatively)

Therapist: Okay. So everybody speak. Speak! Moo, moo.

Bob: Oink, Oink.

Therapist: Oink, moo, meow, oink.

Bob: Ruff, ruff.

Therapist: Ruff, ruff, ruff, meow.

Sue: (seems to be too entranced to join in making animal sounds)

Therapist: Hey, we're all speaking! Thank you very much, speech teacher (shakes patient's hand) for teaching us how to speak. (shakes hand again) Thank you very much. Let's shake this speech teacher's hand.

Bob: (shakes patient's hand)

Sue: (shakes patient's hand)

Therapist: Okay. And that's the end of the program. Let's say goodbye. The end.

Bob and *Sue:* (wave goodbye)

Patient: So short?

Therapist: So short?

Patient: Yes.

Therapist: Do you want to make it longer?

Patient: No.

Therapist: Do you want to add a part?

Patient: Nooooooo!

Therapist: Okay. Do you want to watch this?

All: Yes.

Therapist: Raise your hand if you want to watch this.

(Patient and Bob raise hands. Sue just looks amused and pensive.)

Therapist: Okay, we'll watch.

Again, the written transcript cannot fully convey the children's involvement in the play. They were all genuinely swept up in it and found it exciting and absorbing. The patient's comment at the end, "So short," was only final confirmation that he was having a good time and that the experience was a meaningful one for him. I added nothing new in the way of content; rather, I attempted to entrench the healthy message from his story in a powerful and absorbing manner. This experience marked a turning point in his therapy; following it there was very little talk of magic. This is not to say that there was absolutely no talk about magic; it is unrealistic to expect to remove such an attractive adaptation entirely. In fact, it is probable that none of us give up such hopes completely no matter how old we get. The important thing was that it was no longer a primary mode of adaptation for George.

3
MUTUAL STORYTELLING DERIVATIVE GAMES

When they're offered to the world in merry guise,
Unpleasant truths are swallowed with a will —
For he who'd make his fellow, fellow, fellow creatures wise
Should always gild the philosophic pill!
> — William S. Gilbert, *Yeoman of the Guard*

INTRODUCTION

During the first few years of utilization of the mutual storytelling technique, I found some children to be inhibited with regard to their freedom to create and verbalize stories. Accordingly, I began to think of other ways that could be useful in facilitating children's providing me with such material. Recognizing that children enjoy immensely playing board-type games, especially those in which there is a competitive element, a series of games was devised. These games involve traditional board-game materials such as dice, reward chips, and playing pawns. The introduction of the reward chips serves to enhance children's motivation to provide projective material. Whereas in the mutual storytelling technique no rewards are provided, in these games token chips are given, and the winner (the person who has accumulated the most reward chips) receives a prize.

Although reward chips are given, it would be an error for the reader to conclude that these games represent a kind of "behavior therapy." These games share with behavior therapy the use of reward chips, but the similarity ends there. In behavior therapy one uses rewards in order to change behavior at the manifest level. Behavior therapists differ with regard to their views about the presence or absence of unconscious processes and whether, if present, they play a role in symptom formation. But they are in agreement in not generally giving significant attention to unconscious processes in the therapeutic process. Many take the position that the symptom is basically the disease and its removal represents a cure.

My use of chips here serves an entirely different purpose. I am using them to reward the child for providing self-created free associations and stories, for psychotherapeutic use. My utilization of reward chips is based on the belief that unconscious processes do exist and that the understanding of them (especially by the therapist) plays an important role in the therapeutic process. In short, I am using reward chips for the elicitation of psychodynamically meaningful material, material derived often from unconscious processes. Behavior therapists, in contrast, use the reward chips to change behavior at the manifest level. We share in common the use of reward chips, but we use them for entirely different purposes.

It would be an error, also, if the reader were to conclude that I have absolutely no conviction for behavior therapy. This is not the case. One cannot deny the importance of positive and negative reinforcement in human development. One of the primary reasons why children are "good" is that they hope to gain the affection and love of their child rearers, and one of the main reasons why they inhibit themselves from being "bad" is their fear of loss of such affection. When two-year-old Johnny decides not to run into the street, it is not because he is aware of the fact that he may be endangering his life; rather, he restricts himself from doing so because of his anticipation that significant caretaking individuals will react with strongly negative feedback and even painful physical responses (a slap on the backside or a not so gentle wrenching of his arm) if he does so. The experimental rat presses the bar in order to obtain food pellets and will drop down to the random level of bar pressing frequency if the pellets are permanently withdrawn. So ubiquitous is this pleasure-pain principle that one could argue that behavior therapy is basically nature's form of treatment. In part, I agree that it is. However, the human brain is so complex and sophisticated that other mechanisms, beyond pain and pleasure, are operative, and so more sophisticated methods of psychotherapy are warranted when psychological disorders are present. This does not mean that we must select between the two. Rather, we can combine both approaches.

Furthermore, I generally prefer to utilize behavioral therapy techniques in the context of my psychotherapeutic program. I consider their isolated utilization to be somewhat artificial and sterile. For example, one could help an agoraphobic woman desensitize herself to her fear of open places by suggesting that she force herself to tolerate increasingly the fears that she experiences when she sets forth from her home. This would basically be the traditional behavior therapy approach. One might even try to quantify the times of exposure on a chart while pointing out to the patient her progressive improvement. My own approach would be to focus on what I consider to be the primary factors that are contributing to the agoraphobia, factors such as excessive dependency on the people with whom she lives and fears of asserting herself as an adult in a world of adults. This would not preclude, however, my encouraging desensitization and some kind of more informal assessment of her progress. Even the staunchest subscribers to the psychoanalytic theory would not dispute the value of desensitization. The crucial question is whether one believes that one can get a significant degree of symptomatic alleviation over a long period by merely focusing on the removal of the agoraphobic symptom. I believe that one is not likely to achieve long-term improvement by the behavior therapeutic technique alone. Even if one does, I would still consider the therapeutic work to have been only partially completed because the underlying factors that have contributed to the formation of the symptom have not been dealt with.

These games also make use of the competitive element. Basically I am using competition to enhance the child's motivation to acquire chips. There are some readers who probably would take issue with me on this point because of their belief that competition is basically a dehumanizing experience that we would do best to dispense with entirely. Obviously, I do not share this view. I think that one must differentiate between healthy and unhealthy competition, between competition that is humane and competition that is inhumane. In healthy competition, one strives to win but still has respect for one's opponent. In unhealthy competition, the primary purpose is to degrade and destroy for a variety of pathological purposes, such as hostility release, compensation for feelings of inadequacy, and self-aggrandizement. At any particular time there are thousands of people working in laboratories hoping someday to win a Nobel Prize. Although only an extremely small fraction of these individuals will attain their goal, most would agree that society is a better place for the existence of the prize. And one could say the same thing about a wide variety of other awards in the arts, sciences, and other fields of endeavor—awards that have served to enhance human motivation and striving toward excellence. If not for healthy competition, we might still be living in caves. If not for unhealthy competition, many people who reached premature death might have lived longer lives.

When using the games described in this chapter, the therapist should keep in mind these differentiations and do everything possible to keep the competition at a healthy level. Ideally, the patient and therapist will be so swept up in the game that both will forget whose chance it was and who is to get the reward chip. But even when this ideal is not reached, the therapist should strive to make the game so exciting that the child will frequently forget that it was his or her turn. When the child does appear to be more interested in acquiring chips than providing psychodynamically meaningful material, the therapist does well to discourage such preoccupations with comments such as: "Wait a minute. Don't throw the dice yet. I haven't finished giving my answer." "Hold on, I'd like to ask you a question about what you've just said." and "That's a very good beginning for your story. Now let's hear the middle and the end of your story. Every story has a beginning, a middle, and an end."

The general principle I follow when playing these games is that the child receives one chip for making a statement and two for telling a story. The statement option is introduced for children who are so restricted that they cannot relate a self-created story. As mentioned, the material so elicited should be used as a point of departure for various kinds of psychotherapeutic interchange. Often, the therapist may wish to respond with a story that is created to address itself to pathological manifestations in the child's story. For some children one might want to discuss the child's story at the symbolic level with comments such as: "Why did the cat run away from the rabbit?" and "Was there something else the cat could have done, something better than running away?" The rare child who is interested in an introspective inquiry might be asked: "Is there anything in your story about the three squirrels that is like what's happening in your house?"

THE BOARD OF OBJECTS GAME

In *The Board of Objects Game*, designed with N. I. Kritzberg, a board of sixty-four squares (a standard checker board serves well) or a larger board of one hundred squares is used. In each square is placed a small figurine of the type readily purchased in most stores selling children's games and equipment. (See p. 131.) The figurines include family members, zoo animals, farm animals, small vehicles (police car, fire engine, ambulance, etc.), members of various occupations (doctor, nurse, policeman, etc.), and a wide assortment of other common objects (baby bottle, knife, gun, lipstick, trophy, lump of brown clay, etc.). A

pair of dice is used, with one face of each die colored red. Last, there is a treasure chest filled with token reward chips.

The game begins with the child's throwing the dice. If a red side lands face up (and this should occur once every three throws of the dice) the child can select any object from the board. If the child can say anything at all about the object, he or she gets one reward chip. If the child can tell a story about the object, he or she gets two reward chips. The therapist plays similarly and the winner is the one who has accumulated the most chips when the allotted time is over. If a person is "lucky" and both red sides land face up, the player can select two objects and gets double rewards. The player may tell one story in which both objects are included or two separate stories. When commenting on, or telling a story about, an object it is preferable for the player to hold it and sometimes even move it about in accordance with what is going on in the story. The child will often do this spontaneously and the therapist should do so as well in appreciation of the enhanced efficacy of the dramatized communication. The therapist's various gestures, animal sounds, vocal imitations, accents, etc. can further involve the child and enhance receptivity to the therapeutic messages. After being used, the figurine can either be replaced on the board or placed on the side, depending upon the preference of the players.

Although the figurines are selected so as to elicit fantasies covering a wide range of issues usually encountered in most children's therapy, their exact nature, form, and variety is not crucial. The pressure of unconscious material to be released in a form specifically meaningful for the child is far greater than the power of the facilitating stimulus to distort the projected material. Accordingly, the therapist need not be too concerned about the selection of objects if he or she wishes to put together such a game. The usual variety of such figurines found in most toy stores will serve well.

Again, the therapist should try to create an atmosphere in which conversations may take place about the comments made or stories told, rather than one in which there is fierce competition for the accumulation of chips. The therapist plays in accordance with the same rules to create stories of his or her own that are either specifically related to the comments or stories just related by the child or else relevant in other ways to the child's life and problems.

The game is a very attractive one and it is a rare child who does not respond in the affirmative when shown it and asked: "Would you like to play this game with me?" Children below five or six, who have not yet reached the point where they can appreciate meaningfully the rules and organization of standard board games, will still usually want to "play." Some will enjoy throwing the dice until they get a red and will then choose an object. Such younger children may not be able to tell well-organized stories but may still provide meaningful, although fragmented, fantasies—especially because there is a reward chip that can be obtained for such revelations. The therapist must try to select from the disorganized fantasies those threads or patterns that are atypical, idiosyncratic, or pathological, and then use these as foci for his or her own responding comments. Often such younger children will be content to just play, fantasize, and collect chips without giving the therapist his or her turn. Generally, in such situations, I allow the child to tell a few "stories"—by which time I have gotten enough material to create one of my own. I then invoke my right to take my turn to tell stories and use the opportunity to relate my responding messages, either in story or nonstory allegory.

When the allotted time is up, the person with the most chips takes a prize from the box of *Valuable Prizes*. (See below.)

The aforementioned "rules" are those that I have found most useful. However, the therapist may wish to utilize his or her own variations and I, too, at times have modified the game (as in the aforementioned description of its use with younger children). I have found the game particularly useful with children at the kindergarten to second-grade level. At that age their reading ability is usually not great enough for them to play some of the more sophisticated games I describe in this chapter. Yet they do appreciate game structure and so generally become absorbed. At about the age of nine or ten, most children consider the game "babyish" and prefer the more advanced games described herein.

Clinical Example—The Case of Norman: The Cowboy Whose Gun Was Missing

Norman, a five-and-a-half-year-old boy, presented with a history of lag in his developmental milestones and coordination deficits. He had a tendency to withdraw and to "tune out," especially when an activity might expose his deficits. At such times he seemed to be in another world. A problem that was particularly apparent at the time the interchange below took place was inhibition of self-assertion. He could not fight back when teased by other children; accordingly he was being scapegoated.

The patient often spontaneously told stories about the various figurines on the *Board of Objects* without formally playing the game. The cowboy, which he chose to talk about in the interchange below, had a removable holster belt attached to which were two holsters with guns inside. In order to remove the belt, however, one had to pull the top half of the figurine away from the bottom half, to which it was attached by a small plug. If the holster belt were so removed and then the two halves of the body replaced, a waistline defect was still present where the holster belt had been. This is the interchange that occurred regarding the cowboy.

> *Therapist:* Hello, today is Monday, August 28th, 1972, and I'm here with Norman and he and I are going to play a game with these objects. Norman, can you pick one? The storytelling game. Okay. What is that?
> *Patient:* A cowboy.
> *Therapist:* Okay, that's a cowboy. What are you going to tell me about the cowboy?

Patient: Cowboys have guns.

Therapist: They have guns. Yeah.

Patient: And they shoot.

Therapist: Yeah. Go ahead.

Patient: Make believe he took his pants off.

Therapist: Okay.

Patient: He took his pants off.

Therapist: Yeah.

Patient: If he take his holsters with it only would that be as far as it would be?

Therapist: If you take his holster off what? I'm not clear what you're saying.

Patient: I think I'll try taking...

Therapist: Go ahead. Now what? You took off his holsters. Right?

Patient: Right.

Therapist: Now what did you ask me about that, about taking off his holster? I didn't understand your question. What was your question?

Patient: Is this as far as it goes when you keep the gun on but you take the holsters off?

Therapist: Yep. Right. You mean does the body go together with the feet after you take the holsters away?

Patient: Yeah.

Therapist: No, it doesn't. There's still a space there. What do you think about that?

Patient: Why is there still a space?

Therapist: Because that cowboy was made so he should have guns and when he doesn't have his guns his body and his feet don't go together. That's the way they made him. Do you know why they made him that way?

Patient: Why?

Therapist: What do you think? Why do you think they made him so that the gun should be there? Hh hmm?

Patient: Mmm.

Therapist: Why do you think they made him that way?

Patient: I don't know.

Therapist: Hh hmm?

Patient: I don't know!

Therapist: Does a cowboy need guns?

Patient: Yeah.

Therapist: What does he need them for?

Patient: Shooting.

Therapist: Now do you know why they made him with guns? Why do you think?

Patient: I don't know.

Therapist: What are the guns for?

Patient: Shooting.

Therapist: And why does he do that?

Patient: In case someone starts to bother him.

Therapist: Right, in case someone starts to bother him. Right. So what can he do in case...

Patient: (interrupting) Some Indians have bow and arrows.

Therapist: Right. Hh hmm. That's right.

Patient: Did you ever see a bow and arrow?

Therapist: Of an Indian? Sure. What would happen to that cowboy if he didn't have his guns?

Patient: I don't know.

Therapist: What would happen now? You say the guns are good because if someone starts to bother him then he could use them. Right?

Patient: Right.

Therapist: Now what would happen to him if he didn't have his guns?

Patient: If he had a bow and arrow (pauses)...

Therapist: Yeah and then what?

Patient: If someone comes along...(pauses)...

Therapist: Yeah.

Patient: ...and bothers an Eskimo.

Therapist: If someone comes along and bothers an Eskimo? Is that what you said?

Patient: He said, "If you don't go away, I'll kill you with this spear!"

Therapist: All right. Who says that? Who said that?

Patient: The Eskimo.

Therapist: Is the Eskimo the same as the Indian or is he somebody different?

Patient: He's somebody different.

Therapist: Okay. So what good is the spear then? How does the spear help the Eskimo?

Patient: He hunts with the spear.

Therapist: Right. What else does it do for him? How else does it help him?

Patient: I don't know.

Therapist: What did you say before about what the Eskimo does with his spear?

Patient: Hunts.

Therapist: Anything else?

Patient: Yes.

Therapist: What?

Patient: "If you don't go away I'll kill you with this spear."

Therapist: Right. And what is the person trying to do who the Eskimo says that to—the person to whom the Eskimo says, "If you don't go away I'll kill you with this spear"? What is that person trying to do to the Eskimo? Huh?

Patient: Trying to shoot him.

Therapist: All right. Now what about the cowboy and his gun? What is the good of the guns? What would happen to the cowboy if he didn't have his guns?

Patient: (accidentally drops the holster belt on the rug and can't find it) The guns disappear into the rug.

Therapist: Oh my, we can't find it.

Patient: I got a G.I. Joe at home.

Therapist: I want to ask you a question that you're not answering.

Patient: But he's a bigger G.I. Joe. These are smaller G.I. Joes.

Therapist: All right. I want to ask you one question now. What happens to the cowboy if he doesn't have his guns?

Patient: If he doesn't have—if he left his guns at his ranch...

Therapist: (interrupting) What would happen to him?

Patient: He would have to go back to his ranch.

Therapist: Why would he have to go back?

Patient: To get his guns.

Therapist: What does he need them for?

Patient: He says, "If you don't go away I'll shoot you."

Therapist: Right, if people bother him. Right? Is that right? Huh? Oh, here's the gun. Is that right that if people bother him he'll have the gun?

Patient: Hh hmm.

Therapist: Now why did they make this cowboy with guns then? Why did they make him with guns?

Patient: And then another boy comes along.

Therapist: Yeah and then...

Patient: "Then if you don't go away I'll jump on you." (hums to self; puts down the cowboy and picks up an airplane)

Therapist: What happened there?

Patient: New airplane and then he flew...(makes airplane sounds)...

Therapist: Then what happened?

Patient: And then the propeller breaks off.

Therapist: Then what happens?

Patient: And then the propeller broke my—and then his father...

Therapist: His father what?

Patient: Glues it back on.

Therapist: Hh hmm. And then what happens?

Patient: So it can never grow, so it cannot, so it can never, so it can't...

Therapist: Can't what?

Patient: So it can never—so the propeller can never come off again.

Therapist: Uh huh. Did he watch it himself to make sure that it didn't come off?

Patient: Yeah.

In this interchange I did not directly tell a story; rather, I tried to introduce my therapeutic communications in the context of the discussion about the cowboy and, subsequently, the Indians and Eskimo. I tried to communicate the importance of weapons in defending oneself. It was hoped that Norman would utilize this information in more effectively asserting himself. And this is what ultimately happened. Sequences such as these were contributory toward the patient's ultimately asserting himself more effectively with peers.

Some readers may have wondered why I did not make any comments about the use of guns as lethal weapons and their inappropriateness as a first line of defense (if not a last line of defense). At the time of this interchange (1972), I was not as appreciative as I am now of the insidious influence of gunplay in childhood. Had this interchange occurred at the time of this writing (1985), I would have emphasized that guns are just about the worst way of defending oneself and that they should only be used as a last resort and only then under extreme circumstances. I have come to appreciate that their utilization by children in "war games" contributes to the frivolous attitude that many individuals in our society have toward murder. It would be an error for the reader to conclude that I consider toy guns to play a central role in adult homicide. People who are homicidal generally are so because of severe psychiatric disturbance that has its roots in formidable family difficulties during childhood. Although the influence of childhood war games is small, it is nevertheless operative.

The interchange demonstrates well how many children of this age (including those without neurological impairment) will introduce new figures into the conversation without informing the listener of their appearance in his or her mind. This is what happened here with the sudden introduction of the Eskimo about whom I had heard nothing previously. However, the Eskimo and his spear certainly served as well as the Indian with his bow and arrow and the cowboy with his guns to not only manifest the patient's inhibition in expressing hostility but served as well as excellent objects for my own communications.

At the end of the interchange, the patient suddenly put down the cowboy and picked up a toy airplane. While flying it in the air he spoke about how the propeller had broken off and then how his father fixed it so it would never come off again. Classical psychoanalysts might consider this aspect of the child's story to represent a reaction formation or an "undoing" of castration anxiety. Breaking off of the propeller, according to this theory, would symbolize castration and the father's repairing it would represent the boy's fantasy that his father would undo the trauma.

I am dubious about this possible explanation. I think a more reasonable explanation is that it represents the boy's view that his father can correct and/or repair any injuries that may befall him. Another possible explanation is that the boy's father represents the therapist whose story had just served to help him feel more intact and helped him compensate for the feelings of impotence he felt prior to our interchange. Because of my uncertainty regarding the meaning of the story, I chose not to respond to it. Because I had already provided what I considered to be meaningful therapeutic communications, I had no trouble not doing so. Also, I have found that "overloading" can dilute and undermine previous messages that may have been effective.

THE THREE GRAB-BAG GAMES
The Bag of Toys Game

The games described in this section are attractive in that they appeal to the child's traditional enjoyment of the grab-bag game in which the child closes his or her eyes and pulls out an unknown object from a bag. In each, one reward chip is given for a simple response and/or two if the player can tell a story about the object that has been taken from the bag. The therapist enhances the child's curiosity and enthusiasm by occasional warnings not to peek and by exhibiting excitement when it is the therapist's own turn. The reward chips are contained in a treasure chest, which serves to further enhance their value. Again, the winner is the player who has accumulated the most chips at the end of the allotted time and he or she selects a prize from the same box of prizes described for previous games.

The Bag of Toys Game (See p. 141.) requires a bag clearly labeled BAG OF TOYS containing about forty to fifty figurines of the kind used in *The Board of Objects Game*. When putting his or her hand into the bag, the child is warned against peeking ("Keep your eyes closed. Remember, it's against the rules of the game to peek."), and spending time feeling the objects is also discouraged ("No fair feeling. Just pick out one of the objects."). After the object has been selected and used as a focus for comment and/or story, it is laid aside rather than returned to the bag. Again, the child will often add dramatic elements to the story and it behooves the therapist to do so as well. As is true for the other grab-bag games, the child's comments are used as a point of departure for psychotherapeutic interchanges.

Clinical Example—The Case of Bernard: Let Sleeping Dogs Lie, But Give Them a Bone

Bernard entered treatment at the age of seven-and-a-half because of significant classroom difficulties. He was disruptive in the classroom, fought frequently with his classmates, was not attentive to his studies, and concentrated poorly. Although very bright, he was not doing well academically. At home, he was frequently argumentative and often entered into power struggles with his parents. The parents often used him as a focus for their own marital conflict.

During his third session, the following interchange occurred while Bernard and I were playing *The Bag of Toys Game*.

Therapist: Okay, ladies and gentleman. This is Bernard and the date is April 19, 1974. Okay, you go first. No looking. Close your eyes. You can only open your eyes after you take the thing out of the bag.

Patient: (reaches into bag and pulls out a dog figurine)

Therapist: What's that?

Patient: A dog.

Therapist: A dog. Okay. Now if you can say anything at all about that dog you get one chip. But if you want to tell a story about that dog, a completely made-up story, you get two chips.

Patient: Once upon a time there was this dog. So this dog went away with his master. He was looking for hunting and they were hunting for ducks.

Therapist: Go ahead.

Patient: And when they came back he went to sleep.

Therapist: Hh hmm.

Patient: And after he woke up he got a bone and then he went back to sleep again.

Therapist: Excuse me. I'm a little confused. He went hunting with his master for ducks and then he went to sleep and when he got up there was a bone there for him?

Patient: Yeah.

Therapist: What about the — is that the whole story?

Patient: No.

Therapist: Okay. Go ahead.

Patient: And then he went back to sleep.

Therapist: Hh hmm.

Patient: Then he woke up and he went around with a boy.

Therapist: Hh hmm.

Patient: And he was walking him with the leash.

Therapist: The boy was walking this dog. Yeah. Go ahead.

Patient: And the boy hurt the dog.

Therapist: Go ahead.

Patient: He had to go to the, the — he had to go where? Where's the place that dogs have to go to when they're sick?

Therapist: Oh, a veterinarian?

Patient: Yeah.

Therapist: Well, how did the boy hurt the dog? What happened?

Patient: He was pulling on the leash too hard and his neck started to hurt.

Therapist: Go ahead. And they went to the vet.

Patient: And he fixed his neck up. And it took two days.

Therapist: Uh huh.

Patient: And then he went back and he had a bone, another bone.

Therapist: Uh huh.

Patient: And that's the end.

Therapist: Okay. Good.

Patient: I get two chips.

Therapist: Two chips. Right. Now it's my chance.

Patient: I'm winning.

Therapist: What? You're winning. All right. But I go now (reaches into Bag of Toys). Whoops. What do I have here? (picks out a boy figurine) I've got a...

Patient: (interrupts) It's a boy. Are you going to tell a story?

Therapist: Yeah. Right. I don't have to, but I want to. The same rules hold for me. It's a game. If I can say anything about the boy I get one chip, but if I can tell a story about the boy I get two.

Patient: If it's a tie then you mean we...

Therapist: (interrupts) Then we both get prizes. Right, if it's a tie. Okay.

The patient's story presents two themes, both of which were relevant to Bernard's difficulties. The dog's main activity appears to be sleeping. Although there is some mention of his going with his master and hunting for ducks, the emphasis is on his sleeping and on his acquiring a bone. The issue of his working for his reward is de-emphasized. This quality reflected well Bernard's attitude toward his schoolwork and complying with his parents' requests that he perform chores around the home. He much preferred to shirk responsibilities.

In addition, the story exhibits the magic-cure fantasy so frequently seen in children during the early phases of treatment. It is especially common among children who, like Bernard, do not wish to apply themselves. The dog is injured, goes to a vet, and is cured in two days. Little is said about any efforts on the dog's part to cooperate or inconvenience himself during the course of his treatment. The way in which the dog got sick is also of psychodynamic interest. We are told that the boy was pulling on the dog's leash too hard and this hurt the dog's neck. I believe that this image symbolized Bernard's relationship with his mother, who was somewhat rigid in her handling of him. Although she nagged, in part, in order to get him to do his homework and household chores, there was no question that her standards were high and she would have been "on his back" even if he were more receptive to her requests. She would insist, for instance, that he finish every bit of food on his plate and was rigid with regard to his bedtime. It was not surprising then that Bernard exhibited this fantasy. Depicting himself as a dog might also have been a reflection of his feelings of low self-worth.

It was with this understanding of Bernard's story that I told mine.

Therapist: Once upon a time there was a boy and he had a dog and this dog went out with him hunting, but instead of—they were going to go duck hunting—and when they got to the place where they were to hunt ducks, this dog suddenly decided to go to sleep. And the boy said, "Hey, come on. I brought you out here to hunt ducks, to help me hunt ducks. You're not doing anything."

And the dog just ignored him completely and went to sleep. And as the dog was sleeping he was dreaming that when he woke up there would be a big nice juicy bone there as a kind of surprise. And when he woke up, he looked around and he smelled around and there was no bone, and he was kind of disappointed. And the dog said to the boy, "Do you have a bone?"

And the boy said, "I would have given you a very nice juicy bone had you helped me with the hunting for ducks, but you didn't want to do that. Instead you just went to sleep. I'm not going to give you a reward." Do you know what a reward is? What's a reward?

Patient: It's something that you do very good on and you get something.

Therapist: Right. It's kind of a prize or present for doing something. He said, "I'm not going to give you a bone. You didn't help me hunt ducks. You just went to sleep."

Well, anyway, as they were walking home the leash that the boy had the dog on got caught in a bush. It stretched and it injured the dog's neck. The boy didn't want to injure the dog. It was one of these accidents that sometimes happen. Anyway, they had to go to a vet. The vet said to the boy and the dog, "Now look I'm going to give you some medicine. You have to take this three times a day." And also he said to the dog, "You have to do certain exercises with your neck in order to help the muscles get better and the tissues get better."

So they took the bottle of pills and when the boy gave the

dog the first pill, the dog didn't want to take it. And the boy said, "Listen, if you want to get better, you'd better take these pills."

The dog said, "Nah, I don't have to take those pills."

Patient: Dogs can talk?

Therapist: Well, you know, in my story a dog can talk. It's a make-believe story. And the boy said, "What about those exercises that the doctor said you should do, you know, stretch your neck and move it in different directions so that the muscles will get strong?"

He said, "I don't have to do that."

Well, a week later the dog had not taken any of the medicine and the dog had not done any of the exercises, and they went back to the vet and the vet said, "It doesn't look very good here. It doesn't look very good at all. Have you been taking your medicine?"

And the dog said, "Ah, I don't need that medicine."

And the vet said, "Have you been doing the exercises?"

And the dog said, "Well, I'm kind of busy."

He said, "Well, it's up to you. If you take the medicine and do the exercises your neck will get better. It's not going to get better on its own. It just doesn't happen like that, by sitting there and doing nothing. The only way that neck is going to get better is if you do the exercises and take the medicine." So what do you think happened?

Patient: He took the medicine.

Therapist: Well, he didn't like it. He didn't like it because he had to think about it three times a day, but he realized that the vet was right. And what do you think he did about the exercises?

Patient: He did them.

Therapist: Yeah. He found that the more he did the exercises, the faster his neck got better. And the lesson of that story is— well, actually there are two lessons to that story. One has to do with the duck hunting. What do you think the lesson of that part of the story is?

Patient: That if your neck gets hurt...

Therapist: (interrupts) No, the duck-hunting part. The story has two lessons. What do you think the lesson is about the duck hunting?

Patient: Hmm. I don't know.

Therapist: Well, what did we learn from that about— remember the boy and the dog and the hunting?

Patient: Oh, yeah, I remember.

Therapist: Okay. Go ahead.

Patient: The boy went duck hunting with his dog and the dog didn't want to go duck hunting, and he fell asleep. He wanted a bone, but in the morning when he woke up the dog found that there was no bone.

Therapist: So what did he learn from that?

Patient: He learned that if you do something the other person will get a bone.

Therapist: Put that in other words. I'm not sure I understand you.

Patient: If you help another person with hunting then you will get something.

Therapist: Right! You don't get something for nothing. If you're just going to sleep you're not going to get any of the rewards or prizes or things that come to those who work at it. That's the first lesson. So if you're going duck hunting, and if you're a dog, and you're helping a boy hunt ducks, he's going to be very unhappy with you if you don't work and he won't give you any presents, prizes, or rewards.

The second lesson is that if you are sick, if you have some problem like your neck is injured, you just can't sit around and wait for it to get better; you have to do the things the doctor says if you really want to get better. Usually things don't get better just by doing nothing. You have to do something about them. The end. Okay. I get two chips. Huh?

Patient: (nods affirmatively)

In my responding story, I communicated two messages to alter the unrealistic views of the world that Bernard held. I have found that such communications can be quite helpful in reducing such magical views of the world. I did not deal extensively with the issue of Bernard's mother's nagging him, as symbolized by the boy's pulling the dog's leash too hard. In my story the neck is injured by accident. I attempted here to convey to Bernard a feeling of his mother's psychological blindness with regard to this trait. More importantly, however, I was dealing with this directly with her and she was quite capable of reducing some of her pressures on him. Accordingly, I did not introduce anything into the story encouraging Bernard to handle this problem. In addition, it is unwise to try to introduce simultaneously too many themes into one's story. The child can just absorb so much at a time. When I have tried to introduce too many messages into my story, I have found the child to be overwhelmed and then he or she becomes bored and disinterested and tunes out from the multiple stimuli.

Clinical Example—The Case of Tom: The Bed That Dumped Its Occupants

Tom, seven years old, was referred because of significant disinterest in his schoolwork. Although he was very bright, he would spend hours in the classroom dawdling and preoccupying himself with nonacademic activities. Even when given individual attention by both his teacher and special tutors, he would not concentrate and would refuse to apply himself to his tasks.

An older brother, seventeen, had a neurologically based learning disability and was a significant disappointment to Tom's father. Over the years, Tom had observed frequent fighting between his father and older brother and this exposure was, without doubt, contributing to Tom's difficulties. In addition, his father was a somewhat aloof man who could not involve himself meaningfully with his children.

During his second month in treatment, the following interchange occurred while we were playing *The Bag of Toys Game*.

> *Patient:* (selects bed object) A bed.
> *Therapist:* A bed. What are you going to say about a bed?
> *Patient:* (mumbles)
> *Therapist:* What's that?
> *Patient:* This bed is plastic.
> *Therapist:* The bed is plastic. Okay, you get one chip for that.
> *Patient:* (mumbles)
> *Therapist:* Pardon me.
> *Patient:* I think we're going to have a tie today.
> *Therapist:* We're going to have a tie? Well, maybe.
> *Patient:* Yeah.
> *Therapist:* Hmmm. Who can tell?
> *Patient:* Once there was a bed and it was a very hard bed and
> it was very mean.
> *Therapist:* It was very mean?
> *Patient:* Yeah, it was a very mean bed.
> *Therapist:* How was it mean?
> *Patient:* If someone laid on it, it would dump—it would tilt

itself—and it would dump everybody off and the lady liked it until one day she died. And that's the end. It's short. It's like yours, a little short one.

Therapist: Uh huh. I see. Let me understand something. This bed was mean and it dumped everybody off it who would want to lie on it. Is that it?

Patient: Yeah.

Therapist: And the lady who owned the bed died?

Patient: No, the bed died.

Therapist: The bed died.

Patient: Make believe.

Therapist: Yeah. How did the bed die?

Patient: By doing that when everybody, when…when… when he tilted himself always he was getting weaker and weaker 'till he died.

Therapist: I see. Okay. You get two chips for that story. Now it's my chance.

I considered the bed to represent the patient's father. In his comment about the bed he stated that it was plastic. And this was reminiscent of his father's personality—especially his lack of feeling. But more important, the bed's practice of dumping everyone who tried to use it is a good representation of his father's rejecting attitudes. Those who would try to get close to his father, as symbolized by getting into the bed, would be rejected. Finally the bed dies. This, I believe, represents Tom's hostility toward his father being released in symbolic fashion. The lady, who owned the bed, represents his mother. Although not stated, the story suggests that even she was dumped from the bed and this too is a good representation of the parental relationship.

With this understanding of Tom's story, I related mine.

Therapist: Now it's my chance. All right. Let's see what I have. (reaches into the Bag of Toys and pulls out a table) A table!

Patient: That's a table?

Therapist: Yeah, what do you think it is?

Patient: Yeah, oh yeah. (patient throws bed onto nearby chair)

Therapist: What are you doing? Do you want to keep your things over there?

Patient: Yes.

Therapist: Okay, now we'll keep things over there. This

table. The table didn't like people to sit next to it. I get one chip. Now for my story.

Once upon a time there was a table and this table, when people would put food on it, it would wobble. It would go (imitates by sound wobbly table)…let's say this was food here…somebody put a plate on it or something (puts reward chip on table to simulate a plate of food). It would go (imitates wobbly sound while shaking table) and it would knock it off. They'd put it back on and (imitates wobbly sound again and puts back chip) it would knock it off. It just didn't like to have food on it. Once in a while it did. Once in a while you'd put food, you'd put a plate on it and it would let the plate stay. But other times it just didn't want the plates and it would go "ooooooohhhhh" and the plates would go off.

So the people in the family decided that the best thing that they could do was to see what the table's mood was. If they saw the table was going to shake they'd put a little something on it. If the table would shake they'd just take it off and then they'd say, "Okay, we'll just use another table. That's all." But if they put something on it and the table let it stay, then they'd all sit around and they would then use it. Now sometimes they would get angry at the table…

Patient: (interrupts) They should—you know what they should do? Cut it if it shakes all the plates out. Cut it in half.

Therapist: Cut it in half?

Patient: Yeah.

Therapist: Why do that?

Patient: Just do it.

Therapist: Why? Are you saying that—why should they cut it in half if it—you mean when it shook the plate?

Patient: Yeah.

Therapist: Why cut it in half? What would that do?

Patient: They should.

Therapist: But why? What would that accomplish? What would that do if they cut it in half?

Patient: Nothing. It would just, you know, then it would be no good and then they'd be sad about it.

Therapist: It would be no good?

Patient: Yeah, then it wouldn't have—it wouldn't be—then he wouldn't have a lot of fun or anything.

Therapist: Who's that, the table?

Patient: Yeah.

Therapist: Oh, in other words…

Patient: (interrupts) They would shake it and shake it and everything.

Therapist: You mean they would punish him that way? Is that what you are saying?

Patient: Yeah.

Therapist: I see. Would he still shake things off the table if they cut him in half?

Patient: No.

Therapist: Why not?

Patient: He wouldn't have two legs to do it.

Therapist: I see. Well, now one of the kids in the family thought that would be a good idea to cut the table up in half and to hurt it that way. But one of the teenagers, an older kid, said, "No, that's foolish because that table is still good. Sometimes it stays still and sometimes it lets us put plates on it. We might as well use it when we can and when we can't we'll just use another table and this way we can get some use of the table because it's a very fine table. It's a very good table." So they said it was a good table and there's no reason ruining it or cutting it up. So what do you think finally happened? Hmm?

Patient: Uh, they didn't…(pauses)…

Therapist: They didn't what?

Patient: They didn't ruin it.

Therapist: They didn't ruin it. What did they do?

Patient: They just left it alone and they wouldn't use it anymore.

Therapist: At all?

Patient: Yeah.

Therapist: Or did they use it when it wasn't rocking around?

Patient: No, they didn't use it at all.

Therapist: No, that's not how my story ends. In my story, they use it when it's not rocking around and when it is rocking around they don't use it. That's how my story ends. So I get two chips for that.

Patient: That was a long one.

Therapist: Okay, let's put this table over there. Okay, you go now.

In situations in which a child's mother and/or father have significant inhibitions in involving themselves with a child, one should not encourage the child to attempt to establish a deep involvement with such parents. In fact, it would be cruel to do so because it would only increase the child's frustration and resentment and this could only intensify his or her difficulties. Accordingly, in such situations, I generally try to help the child appreciate that the parent has deficiencies with regard to providing affection, but I try to help the child recognize that such a parent can still provide affection at times. It behooves such children to develop realistic views of their parents and to involve themselves when such involvement is rewarding and to remove themselves and seek gratifications elsewhere when the parent is not inclined to provide it.

In my story, I make this recommendation symbolically. The table in my story (like the bed in Tom's story) represents the father. Just as the bed dumps those who would try to sleep in it, my table wobbles and shakes off any food that would be set on it. However, my table is not uniformly rejecting. There are times when it will allow the food to remain. Those who use the table learn to test it first to determine whether the food will be allowed to stay. In this way, I encouraged Tom to approach his father and involve himself with him when the latter was receptive and to remove himself when his father was not.

During the telling of my story, Tom suggested that the people cut the table in half as a punitive action, as well as a way of preventing it from shaking off the food. Again, he was not only expressing his hostility in an extreme way but also trying to find a method of stopping the rejection. Neither of these represented reasonable adaptations. He could not kill his father, nor could he prevent his father from rejecting him. Accordingly, I rejected these alternatives for incorporation into my story in order to maintain what I considered to be the healthier adaptations.

The transcript does not fully communicate the various movements of the table and plates that were utilized to enhance Tom's interest. Although he stated in the end that it was a long story, he did appear to be involved significantly throughout most of it.

The Bag of Things Game

The Bag of Things Game requires a bag clearly labeled BAG OF THINGS, in which are forty to fifty objects that are far less recognizable than those in the BAG OF TOYS. Whereas in *The Bag of Toys Game* the objects are readily identified (soldier, car, boy, fire truck, etc.), in *The Bag of Things Game* objects have been specifically selected because they are not clearly recognizable. Accordingly, the bag contains various kinds of creatures, monsters, wiggly things, a lump of clay, a few blocks, a plastic ring, an odd-looking seashell, some strange-looking robots, and assorted figurines that vaguely resemble people or animals. Because they are not clearly recognizable, they tend to be less contaminating of the child's fantasies than toys in *The Bag of Toys Game*. Often the child tends to anthropomorphize the objects, but their amorphous quality allows their utilization for a wide variety of fantasies. In the course of play, used objects are laid aside and dramatizations are encouraged.

Although *The Bag of Things Game* was designed to circumvent the problem of contamination of projected fantasies, my experience with the game did not prove the instrument to be significantly superior to *The Bag of Toys Game* or *The Board of Objects Game*. In all of these games (and the other projective games described in this chapter), the external facilitating stimuli do not appear to differ with regard to their capacity to elicit meaningful material. I believe that the reason for this is simply (as mentioned before) that the pressure of unconscious processes to express relevant psychodynamic material is far greater than the capacity of the external eliciting stimulus to contaminate such fantasies. Although the objects in this game are more amorphous and less recognizable than those in the other games described thus far, they do not appear to affect significantly the nature of the fantasies that they evoke. However, it would be an error for the reader to conclude that this game should therefore be dispensed with. It is another variation that can serve to facilitate the child's telling self-created stories when other games are losing their novelty.

Clinical Example—The Case of Betty: Get Off My Back

Betty came to treatment at the age of eight because of shyness, generalized tension, and poor peer relationships. She was quite tight, restricted, and inhibited in expressing emotions. She feared asserting herself and was easily scapegoated. Her parents were highly intellectualized professional people who were similarly fearful of expressing feelings. During her second month of treatment, the following interchange took place while playing *The Bag of Things Game*.

> *Patient:* (picking from the bag) I hope I get something good.
> *Therapist:* I hope so too.
> *Patient:* (holding up an amorphous creature with a similar

smaller creature sitting on its head) What's this?

Therapist: What does it look like to you?

Patient: I don't know what it is.

Therapist: Well, make it into anything you want. People see it differently. Call it whatever you want, what it looks like to you.

Patient: It looks like some kind of monster or something like that.

Therapist: Okay, do you want to call it a monster?

Patient: Okay.

Therapist: Now, if you can say something about that monster you get one chip.

Patient: The monster had a little monster sitting on the top of his head and he was green.

Therapist: Very good. You get one reward chip. Now you can get two more if you can tell a completely made-up story about that monster, one completely made up from your imagination.

Patient: Once upon a time there was this monster. And he had this little monster sitting on the top of his head. And he (the big monster) wanted the little monster to get off because he was heavy and he was bothering him.

Therapist: You mean the little monster was bothering the big monster?

Patient: Yeah.

Therapist: What was the little monster doing?

Patient: He was poking him and he was very heavy.

Therapist: So then what happened?

Patient: So the big monster was walking along one day and the little monster fell off his head, landed on the sidewalk, and he died. The end.

Therapist: Is that the whole story?

Patient: Yes.

Therapist: Okay.

The story is a clear statement of the patient's feeling of impotence regarding effective self-assertion. Just as she cannot effectively defend herself against those who tease her (many of whom were smaller than herself), the monster (who symbolizes Betty) is unable to assert himself and use his own powers to rid himself of the little fellow who is bothering him and is a heavy weight on his head. The problem is solved by the little monster's conveniently falling off and dying. No effort is required of the big monster, no self-assertion, no struggle, no anxiety.

The game continued.

> *Therapist:* Okay. Now it's my turn. I wonder what I'm going to get. I hope it's something good. Let me see. (Pulls out a red creature with large lobster-like claws. On its head is a little yellow creature with similar, but much smaller, claws.) Wow, look what I've got. What do you think that is?
>
> *Patient:* It looks like some kind of a lobster or something like that.
>
> *Therapist:* Okay. We'll call it a lobster. Once upon a time there was this lobster. And on his head sat this obnoxious little lobster. And the little lobster was always poking the big lobster. And he would take his little claws...do you see his little claws here?
>
> *Patient:* Yes.
>
> *Therapist:* Well, he'd take his little claws and he'd sometimes pinch the big lobster on the ears. And he'd poke him with his claws too. So what do you think the big lobster did?
>
> *Patient:* I don't know.
>
> *Therapist:* Well, try to guess.
>
> *Patient:* The little lobster fell off?
>
> *Therapist:* Well, that's how it happened in your story but it didn't happen in mine. First, the big lobster kept hoping that the little lobster would fall off and hit his head and even die, but as much as he wished that that would happen, it didn't. He wished it very hard. He would go, "Oooh, oooh, I wish so hard that he falls off." But the little lobster just kept sitting there and poking the big lobster, and biting him with his claws.
>
> And sometimes the big lobster used to cry because it hurt him so when he was poked and bitten. And he'd cry, "Oooh, ooh, you're hurting me." But because he didn't do anything the little lobster just kept on bothering him and biting him.
>
> *Patient:* Did he bleed?
>
> *Therapist:* Yes, a little bit. In fact, it was the day that he began to bleed when the lobster's teenage brother was passing by and he saw what was happening. And he said to the lobster, "Why are you letting him do all those terrible things to you? You have very big claws and you could easily get him off your head. Look how tightly closed you keep your claws." (Therapist now talking to patient and pointing to tightly closed claws.) Do you see how

tightly shut he keeps his claws?

Patient: Yes.

Therapist: Why do you think his claws are shut so tight?

Patient: Because he's scared?

Therapist: Right! Because he's scared. So what do you think happened then?

Patient: He opened them up?

Therapist: Right! He was very scared to do it and his knees were knocking and his claws were chattering like this (therapist chatters his teeth) and he was scared all over. And the teenager said, "Go ahead, snap at him. You'll see how fast he'll jump off your head." So the big lobster snapped, but it was a very soft and low snap, and so nothing happened. "That's no snap," said the teenager. "Do it harder," the teenager said. Well, the big lobster was even more scared, but he did it.

What do you think happened then?

Patient: The little lobster still stayed?

Therapist: No! The little lobster began crying, "Ooooh, oooh, you've hurt me. Look what you've done to me. I'm bleeding. Mommy, mommy, I'm bleeding." And he jumped off the big lobster's back and went crying to his mother.

And the teenager said, "You see. That wasn't so bad. I knew you could do it."

And how do you think the lobster felt then?

Patient: He felt very good.

Therapist: Right! He felt wonderful. And after that, whenever the little lobster wanted to get on his head to poke him, he would just snap his claws and the little fellow would run away. But at other times, when the little lobster wanted to be friendly and play, they had a good time together. And do you know what the lesson of that story is? What we can learn from that story?

Patient: If someone bothers you, don't let him do it?

Therapist: Right! If someone bothers you, don't let him do it. It may be scary at first, but if you still fight—even though you're scared—you'll get people to stop bothering you. The end.

The message of my story is obvious. The patient's solution to the problem of dealing with those who bothered her was totally maladaptive. Mine served, I believe, to encourage greater self-assertion, and this is what ultimately happened in the patient's treatment. Stories such as this played, I believe, a role in bringing about such changes.

When rereading this transcript for publication, I realized that I made a therapeutic error in my responding story. The big lobster hopes that the little lobster will get off his head and then wishes very hard that he do so. After that he cries when the little lobster maltreats him. Then, at the advice of the teenager, he asserts himself by using physical force. It would have been better had I had the big lobster ask the little lobster to stop maltreating him and then to make various threats before resorting to physical action. The reader does well to note my utilization of the teenager in this story. I often have found teenagers useful as the supreme authorities in my stories. As all the world knows, teenagers are omniscient and omnipotent and are viewed as such, not only by themselves but by younger children. They serve well, therefore, as high authorities in children's stories, and therapists who are not utilizing their services are depriving themselves of valuable sources of wisdom.

Clinical Example—The Case of Ronald: The Robot Baby Who Receives Unconditional Positive Regard

Ronald, age seven, exhibited many social perceptual difficulties as a manifestation of his neurologically based learning disability. He was of at least average intelligence and did not have significant visual-perceptual or auditory-perceptual problems. However, he did behave differently from other children, mainly because of his impulsivity, angry outbursts, and insensitivity to the nuances of appropriate social interaction.

While playing *The Bag of Things Game*, he drew an object that closely resembled a robot. There was a slot in the back enabling one to use the figurine as a bank. This is the interchange that took place.

Therapist: Just stick your hand in and take whatever one you want. One thing, please.
Patient: (taking figurine out of bag) Ooh, what's that?
Therapist: I don't know. What does it look like to you?
Patient: Bank.
Therapist: A bank? I guess it can be used as a bank.
Patient: But how would you get the money out of it?
Therapist: I think it's more than a bank—well, what does it look like?
Patient: A bank because of that (points to a slot in the back).
Therapist: Right. You can put money in it. But what is the

bank? I mean, there are things like piggy banks. What is that? What kind of a bank is that? This is a treasure chest bank here we're keeping the reward chips in. What kind of a bank would you call that? What does that look like?

Patient: Maybe a robot bank.

Therapist: Now if you want to say something about the robot you get one chip and if you can tell a story about it you get two.

Patient: Once upon a time there was a robot and it had one little baby and everybody loved that little baby. Everybody came to visit him. And they loved that little baby so much. The end.

Therapist: I have a question about that. What was there about that baby that they loved so much?

Patient: Uh, his eyes. They liked to play with that baby.

Therapist: Hh hmm. What else made them like the baby?

Patient: Everything.

Therapist: Is that it?

Patient: (whispers) Yeah.

Therapist: Okay. You get two.

The story is typical of those told by many children with minimal brain dysfunction. Having few assets that they consider worthy of gaining them the affection of others, they hope to be loved for innate qualities. In this case, the baby is liked because of his eyes. In addition, we are told that people like to play with the baby, but again, no specific ingratiating qualities on the baby's part are described. Last, when I specifically asked the patient, "What else made them like the baby?" he replied, "Everything." Again, this is an avoidance answer and does not provide specifics.

With this understanding of Ronald's story, I related mine after choosing a somewhat nebulous little wiggly creature from the bag.

Therapist: Now it's my chance. (holds up figurine) What does this look like?

Patient: I don't know.

Therapist: Okay, let's just call him a baby. Okay?

Patient: Okay.

Therapist: Once upon a time there was this baby and everybody looked at this baby and everybody said, "Ooh, what a cute little baby. Isn't that a nice little cute baby? Ooh, how cute." (pretends he's kissing baby while making kissing sounds) They used to coo with him and they would hold him and hug him. "Ooh, what a cute little baby."

This little baby, as he grew up, he found that people weren't cuddling him so much and weren't saying, "Ooh, what a cute little baby." And he thought that just by sitting there and doing nothing that people would continue to love him. Well, that's how it is with babies. Babies can sit and do nothing and everybody will love them, or most people will love them. But as you get older, if you want to get people to like you, you have to be doing things. You have to be nice to them or make things that they may like or do things for people and you just can't sit there and smile and expect everybody to love you.

But he didn't know this, so when he became five, six, seven years old and he would just sit there and do nothing he found out that people weren't going over and saying, "Ooh, how lovable you are. Ooh, we like you so much." And he got kind of lonely because they weren't loving him like they used to when he was a baby. But then when he started doing things—when he started being nice to people, being friendly, and he started learning a lot of things that made him interesting to talk to—then people started liking him more and he wasn't so lonely.

And do you know what the lesson of that story is?

Patient: No.

Therapist: Try to figure it out. What do you think the lesson is?

Patient: (silent)

Therapist: Well, do people like you for sitting there and doing nothing?

Patient: No.

Therapist: Do they like little babies when they sit there and do nothing?

Patient: Yeah.

Therapist: Yeah, but when you get older what happens?

Patient: They don't like you anymore.

Therapist: Right. And what do you have to do when you are older in order for people to like you?

Patient: Be nice to them, make things that will make a person happy.

Therapist: Right. Right. And that's how you will get friends when you're older. The end. Okay. I get two chips for that. Right?

Patient: Right.

Therapist: Okay. Your chance.

The purpose of my story is obvious. I attempted to help the patient appreciate that one is loved for assets and qualities that attract people, and that if he is to be liked by others he must apply himself. Children with neurologically based learning disabilities must be strong adherents to the work ethic if they are to overcome their deficits. And it is the purpose of therapy to help bring about such commitment. Elsewhere (Gardner, 1973c) I discuss in detail this important aspect of self-esteem development.

The Bag of Words Game

The Bag of Words Game requires a bag labeled BAG OF WORDS. In it are approximately four hundred words, each of which is printed with thick ink (a "Magic Marker" or "Flair" pen will serve well) on a 2"x3" card. Different colored cards and inks can be used to make the game more attractive. Words have been chosen that are most likely to elicit comments and stories relevant to issues commonly focused on in therapy, e.g., breast, anger, mother, father, boy, girl, foolish, doctor, love, and hate. A full list of the words I have found most useful follows; however, readers are likely to think of a number of words on their own and may find some of my words less useful than I have found them. In accordance with the aforementioned principle of the pressure of unconscious material being more powerful than the contaminating effect of the eliciting stimulus, the specific choice of words is not vital. Occasional cards provide the child with extra reward chips ("You get two extra reward chips"), and these increase the child's excitement while playing the game. Used cards are laid aside and dramatizations are encouraged. Again, the child's responses are used as points of departure for therapeutic interchanges.

accident	automobile	bathroom	blame
adult	ax	bathtub	blood
afraid	baby	beat	boast
airplane	babysitter	beautiful	boat
allowance	backside	beaver	body
alone	bad	behavior	book
ambulance	bad habit	belly button	bottle
anger	bad luck	best	bowel movement
animal	bad thoughts	bicycle	boy
annoy	ball	big	boyfriend
ant	balloon	bird	Boy Scout
ape	bang	birthday	brag
apple	bare	birthday party	brat
ashamed	bath	black	brave

bread	daughter	game	joke
breast	dentist	garbage	joy
bug	die	garbageman	judge
build	dinosaur	gift	kangaroo
bully	dirty	girl	kill
calf	dirty trick	girl friend	kind
cake	dirty words	Girl Scout	king
camera	discover	God	kiss
camp	disgusting	good	knife
camp director	doctor	grab	lady
candy	dog	grade	lamb
car	doll	grandfather	large
care	dollar	grandmother	late
cat	draw	grown-up	lollipop
catch	dream	gun	lonely
cheat	dumb	hamster	lose
chewing gum	early	happy	love
chicken	egg	harm	lucky
child	enemy	hate	mad
children	escape	healthy	magic
Christmas	eyeglasses	hear	make
cigarettes	fail	heaven	make-believe
circus	fall	hell	man
clay	famous	hen	manners
clean	fat	hide	matches
climb	father	hit	mean
clothing	fear	hole	medal
clown	feeling	holiday	medicine
club	fight	homework	mess
cockroach	finger	honest	message
compliment	fire	hope	milk
conduct	fire engine	horrible	mirror
cookie	fireman	horse	mistake
cop	fish	hospital	model
counselor	fix	house	mom
cow	flour	hug	money
cowboy	food	hungry	monkey
cry	fool	hurt	monster
cripple	foolish	ice cream	mother
crook	forget	ill	mouse
cruel	fox	Indian	mouth
crybaby	freak	insult	mucus
cuddle	friend	invisible	mud
curse	frog	jail	nag
dad	fun	jerk	naked
danger	funny	job	nasty

The Psychotherapeutic Use of The Talking, Feeling, & Doing Game

naughty	like	slob	threaten
new	lion	sloppy	thumb
nice	lipstick	sly	tickle
nightmare	little	small	tiger
nipple	pray	smart	toilet
note	present	smell	tooth
nurse	president	snail	touch
old	pretty	snake	toy
operation	prince	sneak	train
ostrich	princess	soap	treat
owl	principal	soldier	tree
paint	prize	son	trick
parent	proud	song	tricycle
parrot	psychiatrist	sore loser	trip
party	psychologist	sorry	truck
pass	punish	spanking	try
pay	pupil	spear	turtle
peacock	queen	spend	ugly
penis	quiet	spider	upset
pet	rat	spit	vagina
phony	refrigerator	spoil	vomit
pick on	respect	sport	water
picture	robber	steal	weak
pig	rotten	stick	weep
piggy bank	sad	stingy	whip
pill	scaredy-cat	stink	whisper
plan	scary	stone	win
play	school	story	wish
playground	scold	strong	wipe
please	scoutmaster	student	wolf
poison	scream	stupid	worm
poke	secret	suck	worry
police car	secret plan	surprise	worst
policeman	see	sword	young
polite	selfish	talk	zoo
pony	share	teacher	
poor	sheep	teacher's pet	
praise	shoot	tease	
reward	shout	teenager	
rich	shy	telephone	
right	sick	television	
laugh	silly	temper	
lazy	sissy	tantrum	
leave	sister	thank	
letter	skunk	therapist	
lie	sleep	thief	

Clinical Example—The Case of Marc: The Man Who Picked the Big Coconuts Off the Palm Tree

Marc came to treatment at the age of seven because of tics, excessive tension, and agitated behavior in the classroom. His mother, a very buxom woman, was quite seductive with him. Near the end of his first month in treatment, the following interchange took place while playing *The Bag of Words Game*.

Patient: I've got the word *tree*. Once there was a tree and it was a talking palm tree.

Therapist: A talking palm tree. Go ahead.

Patient: It was so full of coconuts that he couldn't even move or talk. He was too heavy. So one day it decided that it would quit and just try and make all the coconuts come off, but they wouldn't come off. So he looked around until he found somebody with a gun shooting birds, and he asked him if he would...

Therapist: (interrupts) Who is he now?

Patient: He was just looking—the palm tree was looking around and he just found someone.

Therapist: Oh, the palm tree wanted to get his own coconuts off?

Patient: Yeah.

Therapist: Okay. It was a *he* palm tree?

Patient: Yeah.

Therapist: And then he finally found someone with a gun.

Patient: Yeah.

Therapist: Okay.

Patient: Who was shooting birds with a shotgun. But it wasn't easy because he just had to look around because he couldn't move. So he called him and he asked him if he would shoot them off. And he (the man) said, "I won't shoot them off, but I'll pick them off. I love coconuts." The end.

Therapist: So what happened?

Patient: And the lesson was if you're a palm tree and you have coconuts on you, you shouldn't just try and take them off, but if you're a palm tree there's nothing you can do.

Therapist: Wait a minute. The lesson is if you're a palm tree, what?

Patient: There's nothing to do except stay where you are just like other trees.

Therapist: And don't do what?

Patient: Don't try to take your coconuts off.

Therapist: Why not?

Patient: Because they're supposed to come off theirselves.

Therapist: I see. So what was the trouble? Did this palm tree get into any kind of trouble by having this man shoot the coconuts off?

Patient: The man said that "I wouldn't, um, I won't shoot them off but I'll pick them off because I love coconuts."

Therapist: So he picked them off.

Patient: Yeah.

Therapist: The man picked off the coconuts. I'm not clear what the lesson is.

Patient: The lesson is that if you are a palm tree you shouldn't want to make your coconuts come off because they'll come off themselves and all that you should do is stay where you are just like other trees.

Therapist: Hh hmm.

Patient: They don't move.

Therapist: Okay. Now it's my chance.

Although Marc represented the tree as male, I considered it to represent his mother. The coconuts, being round and filled with milk, serve well as a breast symbol. They are high up on the tree and inaccessible. The central theme of the story is whether or not the coconuts will he made available to those on the ground. We are told that the tree was so full of coconuts "that he couldn't even move or talk." This, I believe, represented Marc's view of his mother as being buxom and that her breasts were the most prominent part of her anatomy. Marc's mother was well-endowed in this area and was a very seductive woman, as well.

The man with the gun, I believe, represents Marc's father. He has a powerful phallus which somehow enables him to gain access to the coconuts, that is, the mother's breasts. There is some ambivalence on Marc's part regarding whether or not the coconuts should come off the tree. The tree asks the man to take the coconuts off (with the help of his powerful weapon), but the man refuses to shoot them off. Rather, he decides to pick them off stating, "I love coconuts." Although Marc's presentation is somewhat confusing, the main element that comes through is that the tree is advised not to encourage premature removal of the coconuts; rather, it should wait until they come off naturally.

In essence, I considered this story to reflect Marc's wish that his father not have such ready access to his mother's coconuts, that is, her breasts. He would prefer that she withhold them from access to him as long as possible. However, he sees his father as having the power to get them at his will, but he gets his father to take them by hand, rather than with a gun. Possibly, this represents Marc's fear that his father might destroy the coconuts and then they would be completely unavailable to him. If his father has to get the coconuts he might as well preserve them. However, Marc would much prefer the tree to be less receptive to the father's ready access to them. The story reveals, as well, his appreciation that his mother wishes to provide the father access, and this is symbolized by the tree's wishing that the coconuts would come off. It was with this understanding of Marc's story that I related mine.

Therapist: Okay. Now it's my chance. (picks card from bag) I've got the word *boy*.

Once upon a time there was a palm tree and this palm tree had many coconuts on it, and there was a boy who lived next door to the property where this palm tree was. He used to look up at that palm tree and he would say, "Boy, those would be great coconuts to have. That would be terrific if I could have those coconuts. I'd like to get them off that tree. I'd like to split a couple open and eat the coconut and drink the milk that's in the inside and..."

Patient: (gestures to speak)

Therapist: Do you want to say something about that?

Patient: I just wanted to say that I hate coconut trees.

Therapist: You hate coconut trees. Anyway...

Patient: (interrupts) Coconut juice!

Therapist: Anyway, in my story this boy liked coconut juice and he liked those coconuts, and he used to eye those coconuts every day. And one day he thought, "Gee, it would be great to get those coconuts." But he knew they belonged to the man next door.

So one day—he knew that if he went on the property there or tried to climb the tree to pull down those coconuts the man would get very angry. So one day he thought he would get a gun, and probably shoot down some of those coconuts. Anyway, as he was taking aim to shoot down a coconut, just at that moment, the owner of the house—the owner of the coconut tree—came out and he saw the boy and he said, "What are you doing, sonny?"

He said, "Oh...I...uh." He was really trying to think of some kind of a lie but he really couldn't because it was obvious what he was really doing and he sort of had to confess that he was going to try to shoot down the coconuts.

Patient: (interrupts) I know what he could say.

Therapist: What could he have said?

Patient: He could have said that he was trying to shoot down birds.

Therapist: Well, the man could see that he was aiming directly at the coconuts and he wouldn't have gotten away with that story. So he had to kind of confess that he was trying to shoot down the coconuts.

And the man said to him, "I'm very sorry. Those coconuts are mine. I'm not letting you shoot them down. But there are two things that we can do. One, I'll give you one of the coconuts because there are lots of coconuts on my tree. However, my suggestion to you is that you plant your own coconut tree or save up some money and buy some coconuts from a store or buy some coconuts from someone else because I'm not selling any." What do you think the boy did?

Patient: He did what the man told him to.

Therapist: What did he decide to do?

Patient: He decided to save up his money and buy more coconuts or buy it from somebody else.

Therapist: Right. He got a job as a newspaper delivery boy and saved up some money and bought some coconuts. In addition, every once in a while the man let him have some of his coconuts and let him know that those were really his and he couldn't have them, but that he could have a little bit. But the main thing was that the boy learned that he couldn't get them from the man so he had to get them elsewhere.

And the lesson of that story is: If you like coconuts and the coconuts you like are owned by another person, ask him. Perhaps he'll give you some or a little bit. But if he won't give you all, which is usually the case, because nobody is going to give you all the coconuts he owns, then try to get them elsewhere, like earning some money and buying some, or planting your own coconut tree. That's the lesson of that story. Anything you want to say about that story?

Patient: (nods negatively)

Therapist: Did you like that story?

Patient: (nods affirmatively)

Therapist: Good. What was it about the story that you liked?

Patient: Well, the coconuts.

Therapist: What was the main thing about it that you liked?

Patient: When he was trying to shoot down the coconuts.

Therapist: Hh hmm. Okay. When he was trying to get down the coconuts. Okay.

In my story I tried to communicate to Marc the fact that his mother's breasts were his father's possession. However, he could have some physical gratifications with her, but only to a limited extent. The father, however, does not react punitively. Rather, he is willing to allow Marc some of these physical gratifications, but encourages him to seek them elsewhere through his own efforts, both in the present and in the future. This is typical of the kind of stories I utilize in helping youngsters resolve oedipal problems.

In Chapter One I discussed my views on the Oedipus complex. I stated that, when I do see oedipal problems in boys, they are generally the result of maternal seductivity with or without paternal castration threats (overt or covert). In Marc's case, his mother was extremely seductive. She wore low-cut blouses and tight-fitting clothing, invariably used perfume, and spent significant time at beauty parlors. In addition, she undressed in front of Marc up to the time he began treatment. In my responding story, I introduced the element of sharing. As mentioned, this is a central factor in the resolution of oedipal problems. My telling Marc that the man (equals father) will occasionally allow him to have some coconuts, but he must get most of those he wants elsewhere through his own efforts, is a way of giving Marc some oedipal gratifications, but to a limited degree. It was not that I was going to actually encourage Marc to caress (pick) his mother's breasts; rather, I was only suggesting with symbolism that he could get some kind of physical and possessive gratifications in his relationship with her. I do not recommend, however, that Marc wait until he is an adult; rather, I suggest that he obtain at that time substitute gratifications elsewhere. And these are important elements in my helping boys deal with oedipal problems.

SCRABBLE FOR JUNIORS

Whereas in the standard game of adult *Scrabble* (manufactured by Selchow & Richter Co., Bay Shore, New York) the players form their words with letter tiles on a blank playing board, in the child's version, *Scrabble for Juniors* (also manufactured by Selchow & Richter Co.) simple words are already printed on the board and the child attempts to cover the board letters with his or her own letter chips. (See p. 168.) In the modification of the *Scrabble for Juniors* game devised by N.I. Kritzberg and myself, all the letter tiles are first placed face down along the side of the playing board. The patient and the therapist then select seven letter tiles each and place them face up in front. The game proceeds with each player in turn placing two letters over those on the board. The patient is advised to try to so place the letters that he or she will be working toward the completion of a word. The player who places the last letter necessary to finish a word (this need not be the final letter of the word; it can be anywhere in the word) receives a reward chip. If the player can say anything at all about the word, he or she gets a second reward chip. And if the child can tell an original story about the word, he or she gets two extra reward chips. (Accordingly, the maximum number of chips obtainable for completing a word is four.)

Generally, I try to let the patient be the first to complete a word in order to learn those issues that are uppermost in the child's mind at that time. This information enables me to relate more meaningful communications when my turn comes to comment on or tell a story about a word that I have completed. Because the players' letter tiles are placed face up, I can see what letters I can place on the board that would make it most likely for the patient to complete his or her word first. In addition, I may fail to complete a word that I am capable of and "by mistake" use the letter elsewhere. Although I, like most therapists, am a firm believer in being totally honest with my patients, there are times in child therapy when a little duplicity is justified because it serves the purposes of the child's treatment.

Sometimes children will focus on a particular word on the board and try to complete it because they are especially eager to tell a story about it. In such situations, the therapist can be fairly certain that the word has triggered significant associations. More often, however, the child's choice of a word is dependent upon the letters he or she happens to choose. In addition, most children tend to favor words that are closest to their side of the playing board. In spite of the drawbacks implicit in these determinants of the words chosen, my experience has been that the completed word will generally be used in the service of expressing those issues most pertinent to the child at that time.

The Psychotherapeutic Use of The Talking, Feeling, & Doing Game

Again, the winner is the player who has accumulated the most chips at the end of the allotted time. A slow pace is encouraged so that the words, comments, and stories can serve as points of departure for discussion. Dramatizations are also encouraged during the course of play. The game is useful from the late first-grade to about the fourth-to-fifth-grade level. Older children find the words too "easy."

My attempts to use the standard adult *Scrabble* game with older children have not worked out well. They tend to get much too involved in the point values of the various letters and so swept up in the strongly competitive elements in the adult version that comments and story-telling tend to take a secondary role. Accordingly, I do not have adult *Scrabble* available in the office as one of the games the child can choose to play. Also, the child is no match for the adult because of the latter's larger repertory of words. If the therapist then plays with full conviction and honesty, the child will be demeaned. If the therapist feigns ignorance to equalize the game, the strongly competitive factors intrinsic to the game will still serve to contaminate it for therapeutic purposes.

Clinical Example—The Case of Cary: The Frog and the Seal

Cary entered treatment at the age of ten because of a number of difficulties—mainly interpersonal. He refused to fight back when teased or picked upon and so was easily scapegoated, even by younger children. The only way he was able to attract friends was to beg them to come to his house where his parents had always made sure there was a plethora of toys and attractive games. He was very tearful of new situations and would often be unable to fall asleep for two or three nights prior to an anticipated event.

During his third session we played *Scrabble for Juniors*.

Therapist: Now Cary has finished the word *lily* for which he gets a chip. Now, wait a minute, hold it; don't go on yet. If you can say anything at all about the word *lily*, you get a second chip—anything at all.

Patient: What do you mean?

Therapist: Just say anything at all about a lily, any sentence which includes the word *lily*.

Patient: A lily grows on a pond.

Therapist: A lily grows on a pond. Okay, so you get a second chip. Now, if you can make up a story about the word *lily*, any story at all, but it must be completely made up from your own imagination, then you get two more.

Patient: Once a frog sat on a lily in the swamp and then the frog jumped off onto another lily.

Therapist: All right, that's a good beginning of a story, but that's not a whole story. A story has a beginning, a middle, and an end.

Patient: Hhmmm. I can't think of one.

Therapist: Well, try. See, if I can tell a story about a lily I can get two as well, although you end up with four, I can end up with two. So, you know, the person who has the most chips wins, so if I can tell a story about a lily I can get two and then we'd be even.

Patient: What I said was a beginning. Right?

Therapist: Okay, well, say it again. The frog jumped...

Patient: A frog jumped on a lily in the swamp and then it jumped off to another lily.

Therapist: Okay.

Patient: And then—and then the lily started floating down the pond.

Therapist: Okay.

Patient: Then there was this waterfall and the lily fell right into the waterfall.

Therapist: The lily fell into the waterfall?

Patient: Hh hmm.

Therapist: And the frog was on it?

Patient: (nods affirmatively)

Therapist: Then what happens?

Patient: The frog died.

Therapist: Okay, you get two for that. Now.

Patient: (interrupts) I still have one more letter to go.

Therapist: Okay, yeah, but now it's my chance to tell a story. You put it down later. I can get two for telling a story about a lily.

I considered the frog to symbolize Cary. His being on a lily pad is a reflection of Cary's feeling that his situation is an unstable one and that he could easily "sink." Worse, he could meet his doom and be helpless to prevent his demise. Floating down the river and being killed by being thrown over the waterfall is a poignant statement of his feelings of impotence with regard to the destructive forces of the world.

It was with this understanding of Cary's story that I related mine.

Therapist: Once there was a frog and he jumped on a lily pad and he noticed that the water was kind of moving, that it wasn't just a stagnant pond. The water was kind of moving and he saw that the water was moving kind of rapidly. It became more and more rapid and then he heard some noise and it sounded like a waterfall, and he realized that the lily was moving toward a waterfall. So he leaped off onto another pad and then leaped to another one, and leaped from pad to pad until finally he got to shore. He went along the shore and there he saw that there really was a waterfall and he was glad that he had looked around and was careful and had avoided the catastrophe of going over the waterfall.

And the lesson of that story is: Look around you and listen. It may help you avoid trouble.

In my story I tried to impress upon Cary the fact that he has the capability to protect himself against the dangers of the world, that if he uses his senses and utilizes foresight he can prevent many of the calamities that may befall him. Cary was clearly not trying very hard to deal with his difficulties, and my hope was that my story might contribute to his taking a more active role in solving his problems.

The game continued.

Therapist: You got the word *seal.* You get one chip for the word *seal* and another one if you can tell something about the word *seal.*

Patient: I once saw a seal.

Therapist: Okay. Two more for a story.

Patient: There were two seals swimming in the Atlantic Ocean and they were swimming really far out and they would have fun. They were playing around and one time the seal—there was this big fish and the seal saw it and started to swim away and the big fish saw it and went and tried to eat it.

Therapist: Tried to eat one of the seals? Yeah, go ahead.

Patient: And then they went over a rock and then the fish hit a rock and the seal got away.

Therapist: Wait a minute, now. There were two seals. Right?

Patient: Right.

Therapist: And were any of them hurt by the big fish or what?

Patient: No, the big fish was hurt.

Therapist: Oh, the big fish hit a rock and that's why the seals got away?

Patient: Right.

Therapist: And they weren't hurt at all?

Patient: Right.

Therapist: I see. Okay. Now it's time for me. Did you take your two chips?

Patient: No.

Therapist: Take two chips for that.

In this story the seals, who represent Cary, are confronted with a big fish who tries to eat them. The latter represents, I believe, Cary's tormenting peers and all others who may be hostile to him. The problem of their attacking him is readily solved without any effort on Cary's part. The pursuing fish conveniently hits a rock and the seals get away. The story reflects Cary's wish that his problems will be neatly solved by external events favorable to him, with no effort on his part necessary to bring about the desired changes in his situation.

With this understanding of Cary's story, I responded.

Therapist: Once upon a time there were two seals. They were out in the ocean there swimming and all of a sudden this big fish came along and the fish started to attack them. Now that was kind of foolish of that fish because these were two seals against one fish, and they were very good friends and they started to fight this big fish. And the first seal was really happy that he had such a good friend because this good friend helped him fight the big fish. In addition, all of a sudden they saw a rock near the shore, and they took this rock and they threw it right at the big fish — they threw it right at the big fish. And this hit the big fish right on the head and that big fish then swam away and they got rid of that guy, and they were glad that they had fought him.

One of the fish would have hoped that the big fish might swim into a rock or something like that and in this way they would be able to avoid a fight, but the second one said, "Listen, that's not going to happen. Those big fish don't swim into rocks. He has eyes and he has fins and that's not going to happen to him. If we want to get rid of him we've got to hide and throw some rocks at him." And that's exactly what happened.

And the lesson of that story is: If you are a seal and if a big fish is trying to bite you, there are two things you can do, among other things. You can have a friend and the two of you can fight

The Psychotherapeutic Use of The Talking, Feeling, & Doing Game

the big fish or you can do some things, like throw rocks at that fish. But don't just sit back and hope that the big fish will swim into a rock and hurt himself and then go away. Things like that just don't happen. The end.

Okay, I get two chips for that.

In my story I attempted to impress upon Cary the fact that his somewhat magical solution to his problem of being scapegoated was unrealistic. The seal who hopes that the fish will hit a rock and thereby cease his pursuit is dissuaded from this passive and dangerous way of handling the situation. Rather, the seals fight and are successful in driving away their tormentor. In addition, they make use of the strength they have in numbers. In this way, I hoped to provide Cary with the motivation to make friends, in part, so they might serve as his allies against those who bullied him.

Clinical Example—The Case of Timothy: The Seal and the Cat

Timothy entered treatment at the age of nine-and-a-half because of severe behavior problems in school. He was disruptive in the classroom and irritated both his teacher and other children with his antics. A mild neurologically based learning disability was present; however, this was only a small contribution to his academic difficulties. In addition, his parents had been separated but did not get divorced and had been living apart for two years. His father, although consistent in providing for his family's financial needs, was erratic with regard to his visits. When he did come to the home, his relationship with Timothy was poor in that he had little interest in those things that involved Timothy.

After about a year and a half of therapy, Timothy exhibited significant improvement in his classroom behavior and, in addition, was able to better handle the angry feelings he felt toward his father. Specifically, there was far less displacement of such anger toward classmates and a healthier adjustment to the reality of his relationship with him. It was during this period that the following interchange took place, while playing the *Scrabble for Juniors* game.

Therapist: Okay, you finished the word *seal* for which you get one reward chip. If you can say anything at all about the word *seal* you get a second chip.

Patient: Once upon a time there was a seal...

Therapist: (interrupts) No, no, no. That's a story. First, just say anything at all about the word *seal*—just a statement about the word *seal*.

Patient: The seal is an animal that lives in the cold.

Therapist: Okay, you get one for that. Now, you can tell a story about the word *seal*.

Patient: Once upon a time there was an Eskimo hunter who was going to catch a seal and there was a couple of the seals. This one seal said, "I'm too smart for that guy." And like he, um, uh—so he put some bait, you know, kind of like fishing, you know, fish and he got the bait and he caught the seal, and the seal was, you know, he killed the seal or put him in a zoo, more or less, put him in the zoo. And in the zoo he didn't have as much fun. He was in the zoo, you know, bored.

Therapist: Hh hmm.

Patient: He couldn't catch his own fish and stuff so he was bored. That's where I quit. That's my story.

Therapist: That's the whole story. Lesson?

Patient: That don't think you're so smart on catching in traps.

Therapist: Don't think you're so smart...?

Patient: Don't think—don't be so sure in traps.

Therapist: Can you be a little bit more specific?

Patient: Like, um, don't...that's what I really mean...don't, uh...

Therapist: Don't what?

Patient: Just because you see a little piece of bait lying out you don't just get it.

Therapist: Hh hmm.

Patient: Because it might be led to a trap.

Therapist: Hh hmm. Okay, you take two chips.

Patient: I got two chips already.

Therapist: You got one for completing the word *seal* and saying seals live in the cold. Take two more for the story. Okay.

I considered the seal to represent the patient and the Eskimo trapper those around him whom he considers to be malevolent. There is a healthy element in the story, in that the seal's wise-guy attitude is being criticized. However, the seal does get caught and this, I believe, is a statement of the patient's feeling that he is somewhat helpless to protect himself from those who would be malevolent to him. Being put in the zoo symbolizes, I believe, the patient's feeling that he is entrapped by overwhelming forces.

With this understanding of the patient's story, I related mine.

> *Therapist:* Now wait a minute. It's my chance to tell a story now. Okay, you want to wait.
>
> *Patient:* (proceeding with the game) Yeah.
>
> *Therapist:* Just hold up. Now I tell a story about the word *seal* and I can get two chips for it. Once upon a time...actually you get one for getting the word, one for saying something about it, and two for the story. Okay?
>
> *Patient:* (nods affirmatively).
>
> *Therapist:* Now I go. I get two if I can tell a story.
>
> Once upon a time there was a seal and this seal lived up north where it was cold and there were Eskimos who were constantly trying to capture seals. So this seal's mother and father said to him, "Now listen, you know the Eskimos are out to catch us and we have to be very careful. We have to watch out for their traps and watch out for their bait."
>
> Well, this seal was kind of a wise guy and he said, "Ahh, I don't have to watch out for their bait. I don't have to watch out for their traps. I don't have to watch out. Nothing is going to happen to me."
>
> So whereas the other seals listened very carefully to their teachers and their mothers and fathers regarding the kinds of traps the Eskimos used and the kinds of bait that they used, this seal didn't. And sure enough, one day he got caught in a trap, but fortunately only his fin got caught. He was able to pull himself out of it and he got away. And he had his fin, his little paw—I don't know what they call them—the seals have little flappers. His flapper was...(to patient's mother) what do they call it?
>
> *Patient's mother:* Flipper.
>
> *Therapist:* Flipper. His flipper had a little piece of flesh nipped off, but otherwise he was all right. And he came back to his parents and he was bleeding, leaving a kind of trail of blood, but they managed to fix him up.
>
> And for the rest of his life he remembered that little experience and every time he looked at his flipper and saw the scars there it reminded him to be careful. And, of course, after that he learned very much about the kinds of traps that Eskimos have and how to avoid them.

And what do you think the lesson of that story is?

Patient: It's your story, not mine.

Therapist: Okay, the lesson of that story is that often it pays to learn about the things that can be useful to you in life and that can often save you a lot of trouble. The end.

Patient: You can see the scar on his flipper. Nothing was...nothing was...he didn't have anything cut off.

Therapist: No, no. Just a...

Patient: (interrupts)...scar.

Therapist: A scar and a little piece of tissue was taken out, but the scar filled that up. Okay, I get two chips.

In my story, I confirmed the healthy element in Timothy's story by reiterating the inappropriateness of the wise-guy attitude. However, in my story the seal, although scarred, learns that one can avoid certain dangers by considering their possibility in advance. The scar serves as an ever-present reminder of his trauma and helps him remember to avoid difficulties throughout the rest of his life. My main message here, of course, was that one need not be helpless with regard to dangers that may be present; one has the power to avoid them if one wishes to attend to them. I was referring here not only to the patient's classroom difficulties, but to his problems with his father as well.

Subsequently, the following interchange took place.

Therapist: Okay, you completed the word *cat*. Wait, you get one chip for the word *cat*.

Patient: A cat is an animal. It's a smaller animal related to the lion.

Therapist: Okay, now you get...

Patient: (interrupts) Then there's tigers; zee, um, chet...cheetahs and jaguars are all cats.

Therapist: All right, now if you can tell a story about the word *cat* you get two more.

Patient: Once upon a time there was a cat and the cat really liked these people, you know. They didn't think—they didn't like him, you know. They...

Therapist: (interrupts) Wait. The cat liked the people, these people?

Patient: Yeah.

Therapist: Go ahead.

Patient: And it kept on…(mumbles)…

Therapist: What?

Patient: And the cat didn't like the people…the cat liked the people, you know. The people didn't like the cat and the cat's an old bugger.

Therapist: Wait. The cat liked the people, but the people didn't like the cat.

Patient: Yeah.

Therapist: Okay.

Patient: And, um, they'd tell the cat, "Get lost, you old cat." The cat came back the very next day. The cat would not stay away. Hey, that rhymes!

Therapist: Okay, go ahead.

Patient: And they did it again. They kept on doing it and doing it because the cat like was abandoned and he wanted someone to own him, you know, love him.

Therapist: Hh hmm.

Patient: And the cat…they'd kick it out and it kept on doing it and this cat came back (sings) the very next day. The cat would not stay away.

Therapist: Okay.

Patient: And, um, so the cat…so the cat foretold them, "Don't think that…" the cat…well, they looked around the place where there were rats, you know, rats and mice.

Therapist: Yeah, I'm not clear. What's that about rats and mice?

Patient: Well, the people lived around a place where there were rats and mice and stuff.

Therapist: Yeah.

Patient: And the cat killed them all, you know.

Therapist: Yeah.

Patient: The cat was hanging around and when the cat was hanging around there weren't any mice, so they decided, "Hey, that cat's really helpful. He gets rid of the rodents and stuff." So they got the cat and the moral of the story is like you don't just kick around someone because you don't like them, like they might be very useful and they like you. That's the moral of the story.

Therapist: Hh hmm. Okay. Okay. You get two for that. That was a very good story.

I considered the cat to represent the patient himself and the owner, his father. At first, Timothy is abandoned; however, when he proves that he has a worthwhile skill he is then reaccepted into the household. The story reveals the patient's lingering feelings of rejection; however, it also reveals his appreciation that one way one can counteract rejection is to exhibit useful and ingratiating qualities. The fantasy, therefore, is a reflection of a healthy adaptation. However, it does reveal the fact that Timothy has not completely given up his hope to regain his father's affection. With this understanding of the patient's story, I related mine.

Therapist: Okay, now it's time for me to tell my story. Once upon a time there was a cat and he lived with this man and this man decided that he didn't like this cat too much. The cat was all right in some ways, but he decided that he didn't want him. So he told the cat to leave. And the cat went out and he was very unhappy. He said, "Aw, come on, let me come back and live with you."

The man said, "Ah, you're no use."

And the cat said, "I'll show you. I'll show you that I can be useful. You don't like me anymore and you won't let me live with you anymore. Okay, we'll see."

Anyway, the cat went to a nearby house and there were some people there who were really having a lot of trouble with mice and rats and things like that. And he said to them, "You know, I can be very helpful to you in killing off these mice and rats."

And they said, "You can? Would you come to live with us?"

And he said, "You people look like you'll appreciate me." So he went to live with these other people and he was very useful, and they gave him a good home, they gave him good food, and they gave him a good place to sleep.

And then the other man that he had left realized that he had made a mistake in sending this cat off, but it was too late. The cat had already lived with these other people, but he saw his first owner once in a while. He would see the old owner once in a while and the old owner realized that he had made a big mistake in sending this cat off, but it was too late. The cat had another home. And the cat realized a very important lesson, which was what?

Patient: It's your story!

Therapist: Okay, the lesson is that if someone doesn't like you or, you know, may like you very little, it doesn't mean that no one else in the whole world will like you. There are always other people in the world who can appreciate the good things in you. The end. Anything you want to say about that story?

Patient: (nods negatively)

Therapist: Okay.

Whereas in Timothy's story, his father's appreciation of him and reconciliation with his father are accomplished, in my story there is no reconciliation. To foster such reconciliation would have been unrealistic because of the long period that the patient had been separated from his father and the fact that there was absolutely no reason to believe that the father was going to return to the home. However, I did emphasize the ingratiating qualities that the patient possessed so as to reinforce this element from his story.

More significantly, however, in my story the cat finds love and affection in another home but still maintains some relationship with the previous owner. My attempt here was to help Timothy appreciate that others can show him affection in compensation for the deprivations he suffers in his relationship with his father. This need not mean, however, that he has to break completely his relationship with his father; rather, he can maintain gratifying relationships with a number of individuals.

THE FEEL AND TELL GAME

In the three grab-bag games, the bags are open at the top and the child merely retrieves an item from the bag. In *The Feel and Tell Game*, objects are placed in a double canvas bag bound at the top. On the outside of the bag are written the words FEEL AND TELL. (See p. 180.) The child is merely asked to feel an object through the double canvas bag and state what he or she believes the object to be. Because the bags are bound at the top, the child cannot stick his or her hand inside the bag in order to identify the object. A chip is given for merely stating what the child guesses the object to be. It is not necessary for the child to identify accurately the object; it is only necessary for the child to make a guess regarding what the object might be. Because the objects have been selected for their amorphous shape or unusual configuration, it is not likely that the child will identify most of them correctly.

The child obtains one chip for making a guess (any guess will do), a second for making a statement about the object, and a third for

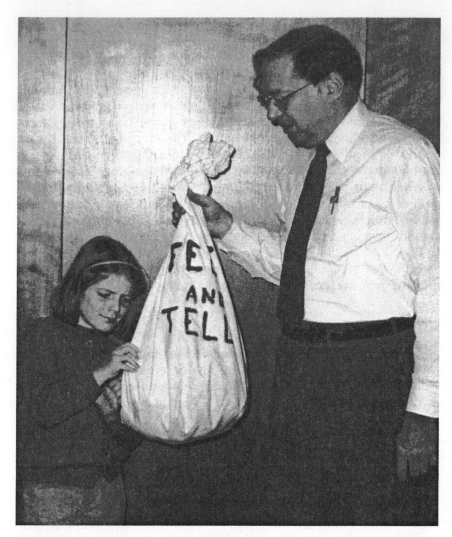

telling a story about the object. The game, in a sense, can be considered a "tactile projective game." The more successful the examiner is in utilizing objects that are amorphous, the greater the likelihood the child's projections will be the primary determinant of what he or she considers the object to be. Accordingly, the examiner does well to select objects that are not easily identifiable while being felt through a double canvas bag. Often, junk items that should have been thrown out long ago serve well for this purpose. In the illustration, the reader is shown those objects that I utilize in my *Feel and Tell Game*. (See p. 181.) I am sure that most people have similar collections of junk objects that can now be put to good use.

Clinical Example—The Case of Mary:
The Kangaroo in the Mother's Pouch

Mary was referred for treatment at the age of nine because of fear
of going to school. She was significantly dependent on her overprotec-
tive mother and presented with a typical picture of separation anxiety
disorder. As is often the case in such families, her father was passive
in his relationship with her mother and viewed the mother's overprotectiveness to be a manifestation of superior maternal capacity. Each
morning, when Mary's mother would prepare her to go to school, she
would complain of a variety of somatic difficulties: headache, stom-
achache, nausea, fever, pain in the joints, and so forth. Typically her
mother would indulge these complaints and often kept her home from
school, even though there was rarely evidence for bona fide illness.
During her second session, the following interchange took place:

> *Therapist:* Okay, Mary, here's how this game is played. I'll
> hold up this bag. What does it say on this bag?
> *Patient:* (looking at the bag) Feel and Tell.
> *Therapist:* That's right. Now the way this game is played is
> that you have to try to figure out what's in the bag by just feeling

it. Actually, it's a double bag and there's a string on the top so that you can't put your hand inside. And you can't look inside either. You have to try to guess what's in the bag, or the two bags, by feeling through them. Okay, let's see you do it.

Patient: (feeling the bag) I don't know what this is. What is it?

Therapist: As I told you, you're supposed to try to guess what you think is in there. There's no right answer. Just saying what you think is in there will get you a chip. Then you'll get another chip if you can say something about that thing. And then you'll get two more chips if you can tell a story about that thing. Okay, let's see you make a guess.

Patient: (feeling different objects in the bag) I don't know what these things are. This one feels like a kangaroo. Yes, I think it's a kangaroo.

Therapist: That's a very good answer. You get a chip for that. (Therapist gives the patient a chip.) Now you can get another chip if you can say something, anything at all, about the kangaroo. Let's see you do it.

Patient: The kangaroo was in his mother's pouch.

Therapist: That's a very good answer. The kangaroo was in his mother's pouch. You get a chip for that. (Therapist gives the patient another chip.) Now let's see you tell a story about a kangaroo. It must be a completely made-up story. It can't be about anything that really happened to you or to anyone you know. It can't be from television or books. It has to be completely made up. Okay, let's see how good you are at making up a story about a kangaroo. If you can, you get two more chips.

Patient: Well, once there was this baby kangaroo. And he was in his mommy's pouch. He liked it there. The end.

Therapist: What you've said so far is a very good beginning for a story. But every story has a beginning, a middle, and an end. Now tell us the middle of your story. Go ahead.

Patient: I can't think of anything else. That's all I can think of.

Therapist: You know, if you want to get two chips, you have to tell a whole story.

Patient: That's all I can think of.

Therapist: Okay, you get one chip for that story, because it's only a part of a story. I hope that you'll be able to tell longer stories next time and then you'll get more chips.

Patient: Okay.

The fact that the patient envisioned a kangaroo is in itself of significance. The object she was feeling (a small, somewhat round teddy bear) in no way had the configuration of a kangaroo. The fact that she felt it to be a kangaroo is a statement of the power of the projective process, and this is an important principle for the therapist to appreciate when utilizing this game. The greater the disparity between the objects and the child's fantasy regarding its identity, the greater the likelihood that powerful forces are distorting the item for the purposes of satisfying unconscious needs. A kangaroo, of course, lends itself well to symbolizing a maternal figure. I consider it to be equal (if not superior) to the cow in this regard. The baby in the pouch (of course) symbolizes the patient and the kangaroo her mother. Although the story is a short one, it is, in essence, a complete story. The little baby kangaroo wants to stay in the pouch and remain indefinitely in a dependent state. That is essentially the whole story and when the patient initially said that it was the end of the story, I was basically in agreement with her. However, in the hope that I might get more material and elaborations, I encouraged her to add more to the story—but I was unsuccessful. With this understanding of the patient's story, I told mine:

Therapist: Okay, now I'll tell my story. Once upon a time there was a kangaroo. And this kangaroo liked to stay in his mother's pouch. It was nice and warm in there and the nipples of her breasts were always next to him. Whenever he wanted to suck on the warm milk, he could do so. And his mother didn't mind his staying there, even though other kangaroos his age were already outside and not spending so much time in their mothers' pouches.

Well, one day, while this kangaroo was resting comfortably in his mother's pouch, he suddenly heard some noises outside. They got louder and louder and he began wondering what they were. He stuck out his ear, above the edge of his mother's pouch, and he could hear other children kangaroos laughing, singing, and dancing, and having a lot of fun. Then he pulled himself up above the edge of the pouch and looked down to see what was happening down there. Then he saw all the kangaroo kids having a good time. The children kangaroos were jumping up and down and they were having a grand time, laughing, singing, and dancing, and things like that.

Well, he wanted to join in the fun but he was scared to leave his mother's pouch. He was frightened that something terrible would happen to him out there. His mother was always telling him to play near her or to stay inside because there were rough kangaroos outside who might hit him. Also, she had warned him a lot about getting hit by cars, getting drowned, getting taken away by strangers, and even such things as getting stabbed and shot. And so, when he was thinking about leaving the pouch, he began to think about all these things his mother said could happen, all these terrible things that he didn't want to happen to him.

Well, as he was thinking about these things, the other kangaroos outside started calling up to him and asked him to come out of his pouch and play with them. The kangaroo told them that he was very busy and that he would come out some other time. But they could see by the look on his face that he was frightened. And so they started calling him "scaredy cat" and other names like that. They started yelling up, "Hah, hah, hah, the baby's afraid to go out and play" and other things like that. This made the kangaroo feel very embarrassed. He also felt very sad. He really wanted to go out and play and he really wanted the other kids to stop calling him names like that. (Therapist now turning toward patient) So what do you think he did?

Patient: He just stayed in the pouch and didn't listen to the other children.

Therapist: Well, a part of him wanted to do that because he was scared to go out, and he wanted to remain in a safe place in his mother's pouch. However, another part of him wanted to go out and play with the other kids and join in the fun. Also, he didn't want the kids to be teasing him that way and calling him all those terrible names. So, he decided that he was going to try to go out of the pouch, even though he was very scared. And so, little by little, he pulled himself out of the pouch and little by little, more and more of him came out. As he was doing that, the little kangaroos outside were all cheering him for trying. And this gave him more confidence that he could do it. But the more he was outside the pouch, the more scared he became. A few times he went back in, and then the other kangaroo children started laughing at him and calling him names. But, when he pulled himself out, they cheered him and that made him feel better. (Therapist again turning to patient) So what do you think finally happened?

Patient: Well, I think that he was still too scared to get out.

Therapist: Do you think that's a good thing?

Patient: I don't know.

Therapist: Well, would you like to hear my opinion about that?

Patient: Yes.

Therapist: Well, in my opinion, it would have been better for the kangaroo to go out, even though he was scared at first. And that's exactly what happened. He finally got out. It took some time, but he finally did it. He was scared at first, but, after a while, he got used to being outside and he found that it was a lot of fun to play with the other kangaroos. And each time he did it, it was easier and easier, and that's how he got over being scared to play with the others and being scared of being out of his mother's pouch.

My story obviously needs no explanation. It encourages desensitization to a fearful situation and is part of the treatment of any child with fears.

THE ALPHABET SOUP GAME

The *Campbell's Alphabet Soup Game** is packaged in a container that closely resembles a very large can of Campbell's tomato soup. (See p. 186.) The container is quite attractive and therefore readily appeals to the child who is looking over the toy shelves for a game to play. The equipment consists of a plastic bowl filled with plastic letters and two spoons. The modification that I have found most useful therapeutically is for the patient and therapist to each scoop a spoonful of letters from the bowl and form a word with them. The patient (whom I generally allow to go first) gets a reward chip for having been able to form a word. If the child can say anything at all about the word, he or she gets a second reward chip. And if the child can tell a story about the word, he or she gets two extra reward chips. I then similarly respond to my word. The responses, of course, are used as points of departure for psychotherapeutic interchanges.

The game can then proceed in a number of ways. One variation is for the players to attempt to form other words from the same batch of letters in order to obtain more reward chips. When the player is no longer able to, he or she can take a second scoop by "paying" two chips to the bank. These can be added to the original group of letters (the preferable alternative because there are then more letters with which to form words), or serve as a replacement for them. Sometimes trading letters with one another adds to the enjoyment of the game. Or the two players can decide to trade their whole batch of letters with

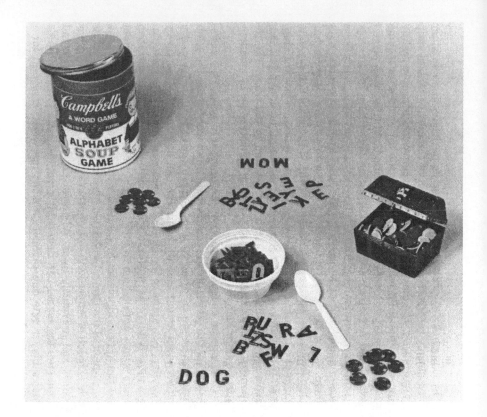

one another, to see if they can form other words not previously used. Whatever the variations utilized (and I am sure the reader can devise his own) the basic principle holds that a player gets one reward chip for the word, a second for a comment, and two more for a story. Again, the winner is the player who has received the most reward chips at the end of the allotted time. He or she, of course, receives one of the *Valuable Prizes* from the previously described box of prizes.

> *This game is no longer being manufactured. The interested reader, however, should be able to put together a reasonable facsimile. All that is necessary are two spoons, a soup bowl, 1" plastic letters available in most toy stores, and a treasure chest of reward chips.

Clinical Example—The Case of Larry: The Boy Who Felt His Mother's Breasts

Larry entered treatment at the age of seven and a half because of compulsive touching of walls and furniture. He was a very tense boy and intermittently exhibited tics of the neck and shoulders. On occasion, his tics took the form of yawning and throat-clearing sounds. However, the verbal tics were not that prominent that one could justifiably consider him to have a Gille de la Tourette's syndrome.

Excessive masturbation was also described by the parents. At the end of the initial interview, while I was standing and talking with the parents and Larry, he began to caress his mother's breasts. She continued to talk to me as if nothing were happening. When I brought this to the family's attention the father stated that he had not noticed that anything was happening and the mother said that Larry caressed her breasts on occasion, that it was an innocuous practice not associated with sexual excitation by either of them, and that she did nothing in response.

In my subsequent evaluation, I found the father to be a man who compulsively spoke about sexual matters—especially in a humorous way. The mother was coquettish and undressed frequently in front of Larry. On one occasion, early in treatment, Larry wrote the following note to his mother: 'F-ck sh-ter old god damn mommy. Happiness is watching mommy pull her god damn f-ckin pants down."

I considered Larry's tensions to be related to pent-up sexual excitation which could not be released directly. As expected, many of his stories revealed sexual and oedipal themes. My responding communications attempted to help him resolve his oedipal conflicts. During the second month of treatment the following interchange took place, while playing the *Alphabet Soup Game*.

> *Therapist:* What word do you have?
> *Patient: Jug.*
> *Therapist:* Okay. Now you get one chip for completing the word *jug*. Now if you can say something about *jug* you can get another chip, and if you can tell a story about *jug* you can get two more chips.
> *Patient:* Don't you get—um, oh yeah.
> *Therapist:* Go ahead.
> *Patient:* Okay. I'm going to tell a story and...
> *Therapist:* (interrupts)...and say something. Go ahead.
> *Patient:* Okay. A jug could hold flowers.
> *Therapist:* Okay, that gets another chip. A jug could hold flowers. All right. Now a story can get you two more chips.
> *Patient:* Okay. Once there was a girl and she was picking flowers. She was cutting off flowers on one of her trees and...(pauses)
> *Therapist:* Yeah. Go ahead. And...
> *Patient:* And she was putting it in her mother's jug. So...(pauses)
> *Therapist:* Go ahead.

Patient: And so when she was putting it in she brought the jug over so she could put in all the flowers that she got and it broke because she dropped it.

Therapist: What broke?

Patient: The jug.

Therapist: Okay. She dropped the jug, yeah, as she was putting the flowers in?

Patient: Yeah.

Therapist: Yeah. Go ahead. You don't have to wait for me. Go ahead. You tell your story.

Patient: And…(pauses)…she—so she—so she stopped to think and her friend and her friend's mother were going out to the flower shop and she—and that was the same flower shop where her mother bought the jug so the girl asked her friend's mother if she could go. And she said, "Why?" And she told her the story and then she went to buy her a new one. And so when they got back her mother was just coming back and then she put the same kind of flowers—she just—since she broke that one she cleaned it out and then the flowers that she picked out of the dirt she put in so that…

Therapist: (interrupts) Oh, did they bring her another jug—this friend and the mother?

Patient: Yeah, but she went.

Therapist: She went with them. And she got another jug.

Patient: Yeah.

Therapist: Go ahead. And then what happened?

Patient: That's the end.

Therapist: And she put the flowers in?

Patient: Yeah.

Therapist: Okay. And the lesson of that story? What do we learn from that story?

Patient: That you should tell your mother if you do something or something bad happens. Or you shouldn't take a jug or a vase and, um, and bring it in the front but in the back you could just take another vase or make your own. You don't have to take your mother's vase or jug.

Therapist: You don't have to take your mother's vase or jug, or, or…

Patient: Jug.

Therapist: …or jug. You can get another one. Is that it? I'm not clear what that last part is.

    Patient: You can make one of your own or you can buy one, or if you have your own you should use your own.

    Therapist: Hh hmm.

    Patient: You shouldn't use your mother's.

    Therapist: Hh hmm. You should use your own.

    Patient: Yeah.

    Therapist: Okay. Very good.

I understood the jug to represent Larry's mother's vagina. The flowers, which were taken from a tree, in this case I felt were phallic symbols. Although flowers are traditionally a female symbol, in this situation I considered them more likely to represent male genitalia in that they were inserted into a jug. In addition, their being taken off a tree suggests that Larry is acquiring his father's genitalia for his own purposes.

Although Larry represented himself as a girl in this story, I did not consider him to have a sexual orientation problem. Children will often represent themselves as a person of the opposite sex to disguise the figure and prevent realization that they are talking about themselves. As the girl consummates the sexual act, that is, as she inserts the flowers into the jug, it drops and breaks. I felt that this represented Larry's basic feeling that his mother's genitalia were "too hot to handle." By dropping the jug he avoids getting "burned," that is, suffering various anticipated repercussions for this "transgression." In addition, the jug's dropping represents his ambivalence about consummating the sexual act. Dropping the jug prevents the flowers from remaining in it.

He then acquires a jug on his own. I considered this to be a healthy step in the alleviation of his oedipal problems. By getting his own jug he gives up the quest for his mother's. I believe that this story revealed, in symbolic form, an appreciation of messages that I had communicated in previous sessions in which I advised Larry to consider alternative sources of gratification, both in the present and in the future. This, of course, is an intrinsic part of helping a child resolve oedipal difficulties.

With this understanding of the patient's story, I attempted to form a word from my own letters that would enable me to respond appropriately. This is the interchange that followed.

    Therapist: Now it's my chance. Okay?

    Patient: (nods affirmatively)

Therapist: Now I've got the word *box*, (spells) b-o-x. Now I get a chip for the word *box*. All right?

Patient: (nods affirmatively)

Therapist: And, let's see now, if I can tell something about the word *box* I can get a second chip. I'll say that a box—there are some boxes that are very pretty, very fine boxes. So I get a chip for that. Okay?

Patient: (nods affirmatively)

Therapist: Now if I can tell a story about the word *box* I get a third one. Right?

Patient: (trying to form new word with his letters)

Therapist: Listen, do you want to hear my story or do you want to try to make your word now? What do you want to do?

Patient: Hear your story.

Therapist: Okay, then leave this and then you'll try to make another word from your letters after I finish. Okay?

Patient: (nods affirmatively)

Therapist: Okay. Once there was a girl and she wanted to take some flowers off a tree and her mother had a very beautiful box—and this box had been given to the mother by the father—and the father told the girl that she could look at the box once in a while and she could use it once in a while, but that she couldn't have it for herself. It wasn't hers, that it was the mother's. It was a very fine, beautiful box.

Now one day the girl wanted to put the flowers in that box—the flowers that she had picked—and she was kind of scared about that. She was afraid that if she put the flowers in that box, that her father would really get very very angry at her and he might beat her, hit her, or punish her very severely. And so as she was putting the flowers in the box—and her hands were shaking—in fact, it was so much so that she almost dropped it, her hands were shaking so.

Her father came in and he said, "What are you doing?"

And she said, "I'm oh, I'm just using this box for some flowers." She had to tell him what she was doing. It was clear what she was doing.

And the father said, "You know what I told you about that box. That's not your box. That box belongs to your mother. You can use it a little while, but if you want to really keep those flowers, you'd better get your own. And you can use that box for a while to keep those flowers in, but I want you to go to a store with your own allowance and buy your own box and then you can transfer the flowers to that box from the one I gave your mother."

The girl wasn't too happy about it because she thought the box was quite beautiful and she said, "Gee, I wish I had a box like that someday."

And the father said, "Well, someday you may. There's no reason why you shouldn't and when you're older you may get one like that. At any rate, now you can't have it. You can only use it a little bit once in a while."

And so she put her flowers in the box and then she went to the store. She took some of her allowance and some money she had saved and bought herself a box, and then put the flowers in that.

And do you know what the lesson of that story is?

Patient: (nods affirmatively)

Therapist: What is the lesson?

Patient: If somebody has something and you want it, you can't have it.

Therapist: Or they may let you use it a little bit, but you can go out and get your own. Do you know what the other thing is called when you get your own?

Patient: No.

Therapist: It's called a substitute. Do you know what the word *substitute* means? What does *substitute* mean?

Patient: Well, is it the kind of person who like when the teacher is absent a substitute comes in?

Therapist: Right! You get a substitute teacher. Right. Okay. So I get two chips for that one. Right?

Patient: Right.

Therapist: Okay.

Patient: I get 50¢ allowance.

Therapist: Who gets 50¢?

Patient: Me, and my brother.

Therapist: Yeah. What do you spend it on?

Patient: ...(mumbles)...

Therapist: What?

Patient: I save it.

Therapist: Uh huh. Are you saving up for something?

Patient: Yes.

Therapist: What?

Patient: At Woolworth's they have a motor that I want to get.

Therapist: Hhmmm. Good. Okay. Let's turn this off.

In my story the box is very much the mother's. However, the girl (again representing Larry) was permitted to use it once in a while, that is, share mother's affection with father. I emphasized the fact in my story that the box is the mother's and that it was given to her by the father. In my story I introduced the element of Larry's fear of paternal retaliation if he were to take his mother's box and use it for himself. Although this issue did not come up specifically in Larry's story about the jug, I knew it to be one of his problems and a significant element in his tension. Because his story contained what I considered to be part of a healthy resolution of the oedipal conflict (namely, acquiring a substitute gratification), I decided to focus on what I considered a still-to-be-resolved element in Larry's oedipal difficulties.

In my story the father does not react punitively to Larry's "transgression." He does allow him to use the box once in a while. He encourages Larry, however, to purchase his own box with money saved from his own allowance. Here, I introduced the notion that Larry will have to apply himself if he wishes to get the same kinds of gratification from a woman that his father enjoys.

In helping a boy resolve oedipal difficulties, I try to help him appreciate that his mother's affection must be shared with the father. He can get some physical contact with his mother but cannot enjoy the intense degree of intimacy that his father does. The younger the child, the less likely he is to appreciate that such intimacy involves sexual intercourse. However, the young child is generally not particularly interested in that kind of experience; rather, he is more interested in generalized physical contact, sole possession, and occasional physical pleasure.

We continued to play the game and it was now Larry's chance to form a word.

Therapist: Okay. Now what word did you make?

Patient: Gun.

Therapist: Okay. You get a chip for the word *gun*. Now you can get a second one if you can tell a story with the word *gun*.

Patient: Okay.

Therapist: Or you can say something about the word *gun*. Do you want to say something about...

Patient: (interrupts) You need a license to have a gun.

Therapist: Okay. You need a license to have a gun. That gets a chip. Now a story.

Patient: Um. Once there was a man who had a gun and he found a spaceship—part of a—when he was in the ocean on a boat by himself 'cause he was fifteen years old. So...

Therapist: (interrupts) Did you say he was on a spaceship or he found a spaceship?

Patient: He found part of a spaceship in the ocean when he was on a boat because he's old enough to have his own boat.

Therapist: He found a spaceship in the ocean?

Patient: Part of it.

Therapist: It was floating in the ocean or it was underneath the ocean?

Patient: Floating.

Therapist: Okay.

Patient: Do you know, when a rocket blasts off if it has three stages the stages fall off them?

Therapist: Oh, so he found one of the stages.

Patient: You don't have a capsule, just a stage.

Therapist: Okay. So he found one of the stages floating in the ocean. Go ahead. Then what?

Patient: And he wanted it so he had a rope. So he took the rope and he tied it onto the boat and he tied it on to that part and he got on and he took the motor off of his motorboat and put it on the rocket ship, the stage of the rocket ship.

Therapist: Oh, he took the motor off his boat and he put it on the rocket ship.

Patient: Yeah.

Therapist: Okay.

Patient: So that would move and pull the boat. So when he was moving along he found he went deep, deep, deep into the ocean, all the way in. Out there, there were sharks and whales and it was very rough. It was so rough that he fell off the rocket ship. So there was a shark in the water coming toward him; so there was only one thing that he could do. There was an island and the only problem was that it was full of snakes. So the rocket ship went down. So quickly he took the motor off and put it back on his boat. He started it up and he went past it, but he just got a little bite in his foot, and he went back home and he didn't want to go back in the ocean again. That's the end.

Therapist: Okay. And the lesson of that story?

Patient: If you have your own boat or if you're in the ocean and see something that you want, like something big, you can't have it unless it's like a toy gun or something. You can't take something big.

Therapist: Oh, you can have a toy gun, but you can't have a big rocket stage. Is that it?

Patient: Yeah.

Therapist: Because? Hhmm? Because?

Patient: Because it's too big and anyway there's nothing more you could do with it and there's no room for it.

Therapist: Uh huh. Okay. Very good. You get two chips for that. Okay. Let's turn the tape recorder off while I try to get a word, and then I'll tell a story about my word.

Patient: Turn it off.

In this story, we again see strong oedipal themes. The patient wishes to hook his boat up to a rocket ship stage that is floating in the ocean and to be pulled around by it. He would take the motor off his own boat and attach it to the rocket ship stage. I believe that the rocket ship capsule probably represents Larry's father and that the stage that fell off it, Larry's mother. In essence, he has his father discard his mother and she is then available to him as she floats in the ocean. Larry's motor, as a symbol of his genitalia, is hooked up to his mother. However, it is she who pulls him around, and this, I believe, symbolizes his dependency rather than his sexual ties to her. However, the father once again appears—this time as a school of sharks and whales. He immediately "fell off the rocket ship" and tries to find safety on a nearby island. However, "the only problem was that it [the island] was full of snakes." Again, the punitive retaliating paternal figure appears to be ubiquitous. Accordingly, he flees from the scene suffering only a "little bite" in his foot. The story ends with his not returning to the ocean again.

This story is a dramatic statement of Larry's oedipal fears. The retaliating father is ever-present. However, his "bark seems worse that his bite" in that Larry suffers only a "little bite" in his foot. I believe that this represented an appreciation of my message given in the previous story that father will not be as punitive as Larry anticipates. In addition, in the "lesson" Larry sets his sights on smaller prey, namely, a toy gun—in other words, something closer to Larry's size and his ability to handle. One could argue that the rocket ship stage represents Larry's father's penis and that the story reveals Larry's desire to acquire his father's penis and his fear that such acquisition will be met by powerful and dangerous retaliation. This interpretation does not preclude my original. Rather, it is probable that both are operating simultaneously here. And, they are not inconsistent with one another in that they both serve the purpose of Larry's desire for a more intimate involvement with his mother. In short, if the rocket ship represents Larry's mother, the story reveals his attempt to "hook on" to her. If the rocket ship represents Larry's father's penis, the story reveals Larry's desire to acquire this large penis for the purposes of becoming more attractive to his mother so that he can "latch on" to her.

It was with this understanding of Larry's story that I responded as follows.

> *Therapist:* Now I've got the word *pet*. Okay?
> *Patient:* (nods affirmatively)
> *Therapist:* Now I get a chip for the word *pet*. I can get a second chip if I can tell a story about pets. Okay? Or a second chip if I can say something about pets. People like their pets and sometimes they don't want to share their pets, or they don't want to share their pets all the time. And now if I can tell a story about the word *pet*, I'll get two more chips.
>
> Once upon a time there was a man and he had a boat and he was riding his boat in the ocean—it was a motorboat—and he saw a stage of a rocket that was floating in the ocean. And he said, "Boy, it would be great to have that great rocket and then I could really zoom around the ocean here, zoom around the water, zoom around the island, and everything else."
>
> Well, he didn't know that the sharks who lived in that water and the snakes who lived on the islands had kind of adopted that stage—that rocket stage—as a pet. They liked it and they would swim around it. They would play in it and they would go inside it. The sharks would swim through it; the snakes would swim through it. And when this man put his motor on that stage, they got very upset and they said to him, "Listen, that's ours, that rocket stage. You can't have it. We'll let you play in it a little while, but you're going to have to get your own."
>
> Well, he said, "No, I want it all my own."
>
> And they said, "Listen, you can't have it all your own. It's

ours. You can play with it a little bit." And he realized that the sharks meant business and the sharks and snakes were really kind of powerful.

But he said, "Well, what can I do?"

And they said, "Well, look at this ocean—we're near Cape Canaveral here and they fire off these rockets every once in a while and there are other stages here which fall into the ocean. Now we suggest you go over there and find out when they're going to shoot off the next rocket and then you just take your boat out into the ocean along the path of the rocket, and I'm sure you'll be able to get a stage."

So what do you think happened?

Patient: He got one.

Therapist: He got one! How did he get it?

Patient: He found out when the next rocket was going off and then one that fell.

Therapist: Right! That's exactly what happened.

Patient: Are you finished?

Therapist: Did you think I was finished?

Patient: Yeah.

Therapist: Yeah, I was finished, but I was just trying to talk about the lesson of it. That's what I was trying to do. What do you think the lesson of that story is?

Patient: Same as mine.

Therapist: What's the lesson?

Patient: In my story it was that if you want something, you can't have it if it's too big or something, like if it's very big and you just want it, like the rocket stages there's no use for it. You take it out of the water or something and there's no place to keep it.

Therapist: Hh hmm.

Patient: Or back in the water if you have a dock.

Therapist: Hh hmm. Well, in my story what does the man do when he finds out that the sharks and the snakes won't let him have that rocket, except that they'll let him play with it for a little while?

Patient: He has to get his own.

Therapist: Right, so that if you want a rocket stage and it's already adopted as a pet by sharks and snakes, then go and get another one. There are usually others around. The end.

Okay. Now I get two chips for that story. Look, I'll tell you.

Would you like to watch some of this now?

    Patient: Yeah.

    Therapist: Okay, let's watch some of it now.

    Patient: (counting the reward chips) It's even.

    Therapist: It's even. Right. So we both get prizes.

In my story, the sharks and snakes do permit Larry to spend some time with their rocket ship stage. However, they are firm in not permitting him full ownership of it. However, they suggest that he acquire his own and inform him that there are many other rocket ship stages that fall into the waters because they are quite close to Cape Canaveral.

The post-story discussion revealed that Larry did appreciate my message. On the clinical level Larry did subsequently enjoy an alleviation of his tics and touching compulsion. I believe that interchanges such as those presented here played a significant role in the alleviation of his difficulties.

As mentioned earlier in this book, I consider less than one percent of all the patients I have seen to be suffering with what could justifiably be referred to as oedipal problems. All of the rest have problems which are better explained by other mechanisms. However, when I do see oedipal problems, very specific family problems are operative. As discussed in Chapter One, I consider oedipal difficulties to rest on a foundation of parental deprivation of affection. The child's preoccupation with possession of the opposite-sexed parent is related to the desire to compensate for the frustrations felt over not being given the affection, love, attention, guidance, and protection that it wants. Furthermore, there is usually some seductivity by the opposite-sexed parent but no sexual fulfillment. The child is titillated but not given sexual gratification. Accordingly, we are not dealing with sexually abused children; rather, we are dealing here with children who have parents who are sexually seductive, but not to the point of providing gratification. When the seductive parent is a mother, there may be castration threats (overt or covert) by the father. These are not necessarily present and are not, as Freud believed, an intrinsic part of the paradigm.

Larry's mother was very seductive with him. She allowed him to play with her breasts (through clothing) but denied that there was any sexual excitation for either her or him. Larry's father was observer to this practice and considered it innocuous. I believe the excitation so produced contributed to his tics and generalized tension. His father's compulsive talk about sexual matters also contributed to Larry's excitation, but I could not find therein specific evidence for castration threats. I did not consider Larry's problems to be the result of normal sexual cravings; rather, I considered them to be the result of specific family factors that engendered the development of the oedipal paradigm.

THE PICK-A-FACE GAME

Creative Playthings manufactured wooden plaques depicting various facial expressions. (See p. 199.) Although not designed specifically to be utilized as a therapeutic game, they lend themselves well to this purpose. Unfortunately, Creative Playthings is no longer in business. The same game can be devised by mounting pictures of various facial expressions on small wooden plaques.

I have used these faces primarily as a mutual storytelling derivative game, which I call *The Pick-a-Face Game*. For this purpose, I use the plaques, a pair of dice (one side of which is covered), and a treasure chest of reward chips. The tiles are placed on the table face up. Each player in turn throws the dice and if a die lands with a covered facet up, that player is permitted to select any face. One point reward chip is then given. If the player can make a statement about the face, he or she receives another chip. And, if the player can tell a story about the face, he or she receives two more reward chips. Again, the material so elicited is used as a point of departure for a wide variety of therapeutic interchanges. Although these specific facial expressions might be restricting of free fantasy, my experience has been that they are not. A child will generally ascribe to them a wide variety of emotions that are likely to be present in most self-created stories. After a face is used, it is turned over. The person who has the most chips at the end of the allotted time receives one of the prizes.

Clinical Example—The Case of Gloria: Make Believe There's No Trouble, and You Won't Be Bothered By Things

Gloria was eight years old when her parents brought her for treatment. The main problem was poor performance at school in spite of high intelligence. She spent most of the day in class involved in her own fantasy world. She was oblivious to her poor report cards, notes of complaint sent home by her teacher, and threats of parental punishment for her lack of commitment to her education. Gloria's father had his first heart attack at the age of 38 and his second at 44. Two years prior to the beginning of treatment, he had undergone a bypass opera-

tion. Both parents had made every attempt to cover up the import of the father's illness and had used a wide variety of ploys to protect her from the knowledge of his condition. In the first few months of treatment, I impressed upon them the importance of giving her accurate information. Although they complied with my request in this area, they did so without full conviction. The result was that Gloria continued to utilize the denial mechanisms she had learned from her parents. I believed that if they had had greater conviction for my recommendation, Gloria would not have been so denying.

In her fifth month of treatment, while playing *The Pick-a-Face Game*, the following interchange took place:

Therapist: Okay, the dice say you can pick a face. Which face are you going to pick?

Patient: I'm going to pick this one here. It's a smiling face.

Therapist: Okay. You get one chip for picking that face. (Therapist gives patient a chip.) Now you can get another chip if you can say something about that face.

Patient: He's smiling.

Therapist: What's he smiling about?

Patient: He's smiling because he's happy.

Therapist: What's he happy about?

Patient: He's just happy. He's not happy about anything. He's just happy.

Therapist: You can't just be happy about nothing unless you're dumb or something like that. You have to be happy about something.

Patient: Okay, he's happy because his mother bought him some ice cream.

Therapist: Okay, you get a chip for that. (Therapist gives patient a reward chip.) Now you can get two more chips if you can tell a story about that boy and his smiling, happy face.

Patient: Okay, let me think...Once upon a time there was a boy. And he was a happy boy. He was a very happy boy. He was the happiest boy in the whole world. He got good grades in school. He got all As. He got As in conduct. The teacher said that he was a "pleasure to have in the class." And he was happy at home. Everything was good at home and he was happy there. And he had lots of friends who liked him very much. One day the family went on a picnic and they had a good time. They went home and the children watched television and then they went to sleep. The end.

Therapist: That was a fairly good story, but I've heard better ones. It didn't seem to have very many exciting things happen in it. Can you jazz it up a bit? Can you add things to make it more exciting?

Patient: I can't think of anything else.

Therapist: You know, in every family, both good things and bad things happen. What about this family? Did only good things happen to them? Or were there some bad things that happened also?

Patient: Only good things.

Therapist: Only good things? Nothing bad at all? Never at all?

Patient: Never at all.

Therapist: You know, in any family, things can happen like people getting sick or things like that. Didn't that ever happen in their family?

Patient: Well, once one of the children got the flu and had to stay home from school for a few days. But the parents were always okay.

Therapist: Anything else you want to say about that story?

Patient: No, I'm finished.

I considered the story to represent Gloria's significant utilization of denial mechanisms. The child in her story is doing well in school; Gloria was doing abominably. The family of the child in Gloria's story are all happy; all is going well with them, and neither of the parents is sick. This, of course, is opposite to what was the situation in reality for Gloria. With this understanding of Gloria's story, I proceeded as follows:

Therapist: Okay, it's my turn. The dice show that I can pick a face now. I'm going to pick this one. (Therapist selects a face with a smile.) Once upon there was a boy named Jack, and he was always smiling. I didn't say that he was always happy; I only said that he was always smiling. In fact, he was the kind of a person who would smile even when he was sad, even when he was unhappy, even when he was very unhappy, even when he was very, very unhappy. In fact, Jack thought that the best thing to do about bad news was to make believe that it didn't exist, to make believe that it just wasn't there. Of course, that doesn't help anything because when you make believe that a problem isn't there—when it really is—then you don't do anything about the problem. Did you ever read any stories of mine that tell about people who do that kind of thing, people who don't talk about problems when they really have them?

Patient: No.

Therapist: Try to think hard. Don't you remember the stories I gave you?

Patient: No.

Therapist: Think again. When you first came here, I gave you a book and I told you to read the stories either by yourself or with your parents. Do you remember that book?

Patient:...Oh, yes.

Therapist: You remember the name of that book or what it was about?

Patient: There was some stories in it, but I don't remember.

Therapist: Do you remember one about an ostrich?

Patient: Oh, yeah, it was about an ostrich who put his head in the sand.

Therapist: No, it was just the opposite. Do you remember what it said about the ostrich and whether or not it put its head in the sand?

Patient: I don't remember. I thought he did when there was trouble.

Therapist: No, he does just the opposite. He wouldn't do such a stupid thing. When there's danger, the ostrich either looks at it and thinks what to do or runs away, but never makes believe that there's no danger. Only people think that way. And they think that ostriches do it that way also, but they don't. They're wrong. Do you remember that now?

Patient: Yes.

Therapist: Do you do that?

Patient: No.

Therapist: What about in school?

Patient: I don't think so.

Therapist: Well, I think you do. I think you make believe that there's no trouble in school, when there really is. What do you think about that?

Patient: Well, maybe I do it a little bit.

Therapist: Well, give me an example of a time when you do it, a time when you say you do it a little bit.

Patient: I don't remember now.

Therapist: Okay, I'll continue with my story about the boy Jack, who was always smiling. One day Jack learned that his mother was sick and that she would have to go to the hospital. She was very sick and they thought she might die but they didn't know for sure. When Jack first heard the news, he was sad for a short time. Then, he pushed the whole thing out of his mind and began smiling. He just smiled and made believe that there was no trouble. His teenage brother, Fred, however, came up to him one day and asked him what he was smiling about. Jack said that he was very happy. His brother Fred said, "I don't know what you're so happy about. Mom's very sick."

Jack answered, "I don't want to talk about it. I don't want to think about it."

The big teenage brother Fred then said, "Well, I think you'd better think about it, because it's really going to be terrible around here if something bad happens to her, like if she dies."

Jack then began to scream and shout and said, "I told you, I don't want to talk about it."

Again, Fred told him that it was important to talk about it. Jack then ran off into his room and began to cry. As he lay in bed, he thought of himself out in the cold snow, starving and freezing, and that made him even more upset. Finally, his older brother Fred came into the room and heard him mumbling, "I'll freeze to death. I'll starve to death. No one will take care of me."

Fred then said, "I see now why you didn't want to talk about things. You think that if something happens to Mom that you'll freeze to death or starve to death, and there'll be no one to take care of you. But you've forgotten one important thing."

And Jack said, "What's that?"

And Fred said, "We still have a father. If something happens to Mom, we still have Dad."

As soon as Jack heard that, he felt better. He realized then that he had forgotten that his father would still be around and could be a substitute if anything happened to his mother. Do you know what a substitute is?

Patient: Yes, like a teacher, a substitute teacher.

Therapist: That's right, when your teacher is sick, you get a substitute teacher who takes over for her. And a father can be a substitute for a mother if the mother gets sick. Well, anyway, when the boy heard that, he realized that he had been stupid for not talking more about it and making believe that there was no trouble. And his teenage brother too helped him realize that it is important to talk about problems and that if you do, you can often do something about them and that if you don't, then they often get worse. Do you know what the lesson of my story is?

Patient: Talk about things.

Therapist: Right!

I cannot say that this was one of the most successful interchanges I've ever had with a child who exhibits denial mechanisms. However, a little progress was made. It takes many bricks to build a house and every brick contributes.

THE MAKE-A-PICTURE STORY CARDS

The Make-a-Picture Story Cards (MAPS) (Schneidman, 1947) is a valuable instrument. In fact, I consider it to be one of the most useful diagnostic and therapeutic instruments in the child therapist's armamentarium. First, I will discuss its standard use as a diagnostic instrument and then the modifications that I utilize for therapeutic purposes.

Diagnostic Utilization

The instrument consists of 22 cards (See p. 205.) on each of which is depicted a scene, e.g. a doctor's examining room, the attic of a house, an empty street, a stage, an empty raft floating on the ocean, a forest, and so forth. In addition, there is a blank card. No figures, either animal or human, are present in any of the scenes. In addition, there is a collection of figurines, both human and animal. Some of the human figures appear to be typical family members, but others are readily identified as a pirate, clergyman, soldier, doctor, nurse, Santa Claus, superhero, and maid. A few animals are also included, such as a snake and a dog. The patient is asked simply to look through the pictures and select one. Next, the patient is asked to review the figurines, select one or more, place them on the selected scene, and then create a story. I consider the stories to be valuable sources of information about underlying psychodynamics.

As a diagnostic instrument, I consider *The Make-a-Picture Story Cards* (MAPS) to be superior to *The Thematic Apperception Test* (TAT) (H. Murray, 1936) and the *Children's Apperception Test* (CAT) (L. Bellak and S.S. Bellak, 1949), which it resembles. In the TAT and CAT, the scenes, although designed to be somewhat vague, still in-

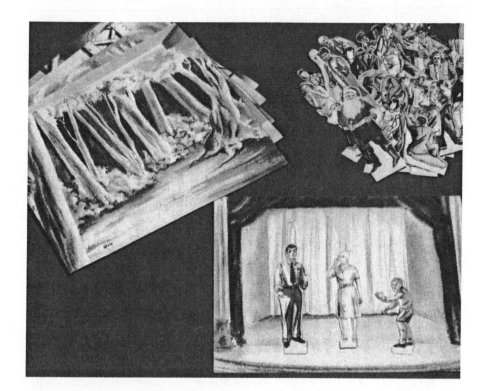

clude figures that are definitely recognizable. In the TAT, one can state easily whether the depicted people are male or female, young, middle-aged, or elderly. In the CAT, there is even greater specificity with regard to the activities of the various figurines (invariably animals). Accordingly, although there is a universe of possible responses to the TAT and CAT cards, there is still a certain amount of contamination of the child's fantasies by the eliciting stimuli. The MAPS pictures, however, are created by the child. Thus, there is less contamination than one has with the CAT or TAT instruments, and so there is a larger universe of responses that may be elicited. For this reason I consider the MAPS instrument to be superior to the TAT and CAT.

However, there is one major drawback to the utilization of the MAPS cards. Specifically, the facial expressions on all of the figures appear to this examiner to be somewhat grotesque, macabre, and hostile. At best, they are poorly drawn; at worst, they are morbid. My experience has been that one gets more hostile and morbid fantasies than would be obtained from more neutral and/or benevolent figurines. Accordingly, in order to offset the contaminating effect of this drawback of the instrument, I generally present the child with both the figurines provided by the manufacturer and my own set of small play dolls that I traditionally use in my work with children. When the instrument is used in this way, I have found that I get a better balance of fantasies.

Therapeutic Utilization

The MAPS cards lend themselves well to therapeutic utilization. All one needs to do is add the treasure chest of reward chips to the aforementioned equipment and one has what I consider to be an extremely valuable therapeutic game. (See below.) The game begins with the child's being told that he or she will receive one chip for creating a picture by placing one or more figurines on the selected card. An additional chip is given for a statement about the picture and two more for a self-created story. Again, the therapist plays similarly and the material so elicited is used as a point of departure for a wide variety of psychotherapeutic interchanges. The winner is the person who has accumulated the most chips at the end of the allotted time.

Of the various mutual storytelling derivative games described in this chapter, I consider this one to be the most valuable. One of the problems with the other games is that the unconscious well appears to run dry quickly after four or five stories, and the material then elicit-

ed tends to be more stereotyped and less idiosyncratic. Somehow, the MAPS cards and figurines appear to give the unconscious "new" ideas. However, with the MAPS these are less likely to be contaminations than with the other instruments; they are more likely to be catalysts for the expression of important psychodynamic themes.

Clinical Example—The Case of Ruth: The Army of Babysitters

Ruth entered treatment at the age of six, when she was in kindergarten, because of "hyperactivity and poor attention span." Because of these symptoms the school considered her to be suffering with a neurologically based learning disability. Although the school authorities were aware that both of her parents were suffering with serious physical illnesses, they still considered Ruth to be neurologically impaired, and the question was raised about her repeating kindergarten and possibly entering a class for learning-disabled children. In addition, Ruth exhibited manifestations of depression, withdrawal, apathy, disinterest in play, and generalized sad affect.

My own evaluation revealed absolutely no evidence for the presence of neurologically based deficits. There were, however, definite family problems that provided a much more likely explanation for Ruth's difficulties. When Ruth was three, her father developed signs and symptoms of a brain tumor. This was diagnosed and removed; however, his prognosis was considered guarded. When I saw her at six, her father exhibited mild neurologically based sensorial deficits — deficits that were probably not apparent to the unsophisticated observer. However, because he was bald and did not wear a hairpiece, his operative scars were readily apparent. He was back at work and, I suspected, was not functioning at the same level of performance that he was at prior to his illness.

About one year prior to her initial visit, when Ruth was five, her mother exhibited various sensory and ocular changes that were ultimately diagnosed as multiple sclerosis. During the subsequent year she suffered with a number of significantly severe exacerbations, some associated with sight loss (bordering on bilateral blindness) and intermittent weakness in both lower extremities (that required the assistance of crutches or a cane).

In her projective play, Ruth routinely cluttered every scene with as many humans and animals as were available. When administered the MAPS cards, Ruth covered every card with as many figurines as she could find. I considered such utilization of the play dolls to be a manifestation of her separation anxiety and the desire to compensate for the potential loss of one or even both of her parents. By cluttering the scene with as many human and animal figures as possible, she reassured herself that there would be substitutes for these potential losses. In line with this, I considered her symptoms of hyperactivity and attentional deficit to be concomitants of the fear that she felt in relation to her parents' illnesses. Furthermore, I considered her depression the predictable result of the spectre that hung over her household. Her depression served as a confirmation of my view that when someone is depressed, there is either something in the patient's reality that justifies a depressed reaction or he or she views the situation in such a way that depression is a predictable effect.

During her third month of treatment the following interchange took place while using *The Make-a-Picture Story Cards* as a point of departure for mutual storytelling.

> *Therapist:* Good afternoon, boys and girls, ladies and gentlemen. Today is Monday, the 28th of December, 1931 — I mean 1981 — and my guest and I are playing games. Now what we have here are these cards and our guest selects one card and then we have all these dolls here. We have these regular kinds of colored dolls like this, and we have these black and white flat dolls like this — and you pick whichever ones you want — and you put them on whatever scene you want and then you tell a story about it. Okay?
>
> *Patient:* Okay. All right. (Patient creates a picture.)
>
> *Therapist:* Let's see the card you have here. Now what is this card of? What does that show?
>
> *Patient:* The baby of the house.
>
> *Therapist:* The baby of the house.
>
> *Patient:* It's a picture with the mother, and the father, and the baby.
>
> *Therapist:* Okay, the mother, father, and the baby. Go ahead.
>
> *Patient:* Okay. I'll set this up.
>
> *Therapist:* Set it up.
>
> *Patient:* One day the mother and the father with their little baby went into the mother's and father's bedroom. The baby was bouncing and bouncing and bouncing and bouncing on the bed. "It's time for bed, Junior," said mother. Junior fell asleep right away.
>
> *Therapist:* It's time for bed and then Junior fell asleep right

away. Okay, then what happened?

Patient: Then the mother and father climbed into bed. Junior was their only child.

Therapist: Junior was their only child and they climbed into bed with Junior.

Patient: And that night they had a real big dream.

Therapist: They had a dream. Yeah.

Patient: About them having a family to...

Therapist: A dream that what?

Patient: About a family babysitting Junior.

Therapist: Oh, a family was babysitting Junior.

Patient: And they were out shopping for the night.

Therapist: The family was outside for the night? The babysitting family?

Patient: No, the regular family. The mother and the father had gone out for the night and this other family was babysitting little Junior.

Therapist: Oh, in other words when the mother and father were out, this whole family was babysitting Junior. Is that right?

Patient: Hmm. (Patient adds family of five to the scene.)

Therapist: Okay, this *whole* family was babysitting Junior. Then what happened? Where are they out? Now they're in bed there with Junior?

Patient: Yeah, but they're dreaming.

Therapist: Oh, they're dreaming that they went out. They really weren't out. They were just dreaming that they were out and they were dreaming that this whole family was babysitting.

Patient: Yeah.

Therapist: Okay, then what happened?

Patient: Then when they woke up in the morning the baby started to...

Therapist: When they woke up in the morning, they what?

Patient: When they woke up in the morning the mother said to Junior, "We'll have a family babysit you today."

Therapist: The mother told Junior they're going to have the whole family babysit. Okay.

Patient: Junior soon got down behind mother. He didn't want mother to go to work. "I'm sorry, Junior, but I can't take care of you, but..." (mumbles)...

Therapist: (interrupts) Wait a minute. Junior didn't want

Mommy to leave for work and Mommy said what?

Patient: "I'm not going to work, Junior. I..." (mumbles)...

Therapist: I'm not going to what?

Patient: "I'm not going to work yet."

Therapist: "I'm not going to work yet?"

Patient: "Because you're going to have a new baby sister. Besides, you're already very little. I know that. You'll have to do with your new friend in the house."

Therapist: Wait a minute. You'll have to what with your new friend in the house?

Patient: "You'll have to do good with your new little kid in the house."

Therapist: "You'll have to do good with the new little kid in the house?" You mean the brother or the sister?

Patient: Yeah.

Therapist: Uh huh.

Patient: One day, mother and father came home with twins!

Therapist: Wow! They came home with twins. Oh, twins. Instead of coming home with one, they came home with two. Then what happened?

Patient: Mother said, "Meet..." I mean Mother said to Junior, "Meet Peter and your sister Ann."

Therapist: "Meet Peter and your sister Ann?"

Patient: Yeah.

Therapist: Oh, okay. So there was a Peter and Ann. Then what happened?

Patient: Peter's nickname is *clean*.

Therapist: Peter's nickname is what?

Patient: Is *clean*.

Therapist: Is *clean*?

Patient: Yes.

Therapist: Clean is his nickname and Ann's nickname is what?

Patient: Is *dirty*.

Therapist: Peter's nickname is *clean* and Ann's nickname is *dirty*. Okay. Then what happens?

Patient: That night the mother and father slept in the bed with Peter on the floor and the two twins at the foot of the bed.

Therapist: Okay. Okay, Peter on the floor and the two twins on the bed.

Patient: And they woke up in the morning and they had no

more troubles with babysitting, because the whole family was babysitting! (Patient now takes out the remaining dolls [about 15] and fills up all the remaining spaces.)

Therapist: They had no more troubles because the whole family...you mean, this wasn't a dream. They really were there?

Patient: Hh hmm.

Therapist: Is that the end of the story?

Patient: Yes.

Therapist: Okay. Now it's my chance to tell a story. Okay?

Patient: Oh, brother!

Therapist: Brother. You don't want me to tell a story?

Patient: Well, you can, but you can't use some of these characters.

Therapist: Okay. Which characters can I use and which characters can I not use?

Patient: Well, one thing. I just don't think you should use just those four. (Patient sets aside four adult dolls, two males and two females.) You can use any of the others.

Therapist: I can't use these four?

Patient: Yeah.

Therapist: I can't use these four over here, but I can use any of the others?

Patient: Yes.

Therapist: Okay, I can use any of the others. Why can't I use these four over here?

Patient: Because I'm going to need them for my next one and I think I might want them. I know what they might do.

Therapist: Okay. I will not use them. I will use these others. Okay?

Patient: Okay.

My slip at the beginning of this interchange, in which I gave the date as 1931, rather than 1981, like the overwhelming majority of slips, is not without psychological significance. The year of my birth is 1931. I suspect that I too was anxious about Ruth's parents dying ("Send out not for whom the bell tolls, it tolls for thee.") and probably unconsciously wished to regress back to a point where I could start all over again as a way of forestalling the inevitable. Had Ruth been old enough to understand the significance of this slip I would have certainly discussed it with her. It probably would have provided her some psychological benefit. Knowing that others have similar concerns can in itself be therapeutic. I suspect, as well, that other therapeutic benefits might have been derived from such a discussion.

This story is typical of those Ruth told in the early phases of her treatment. Rather than simply have a single babysitter, she has a whole family babysitting. She starts off as an only child and when mother is expected to come home with one new baby, she comes home with two. By the end the babysitting family expanded to include just about every doll in sight, resulting in a total coverage of the card that she had chosen. Her final request that I not use the four adult dolls in my story was, I believe, a reflection of her separation anxiety. She wanted to save them for herself, a symbolic reassurance that she would not be separated from them. I then told my story.

> *Therapist:* Once upon a time there was a family and in this family was a mommy and a daddy. There was a baby and there was a girl. Okay? They lived together. Now this girl's father got sick one day, and he had to go to the hospital. But he came back! While he was away she was scared that he might not come back, but he came back and then her fears were over. But while he was there the mother said to the girl, "Are you scared that Daddy may not come back?"
>
> And she said, "Yes, I am scared."
>
> The mother said, "Well, it would be sad if he didn't come back. However, there are many other people in the world. There's this man over here. (Therapist picks up male doll.) There's an uncle. (Therapist displays another doll.) There's a grandpa. (Therapist picks up a third.) There's a grandma (and a fourth). There are lots of other people. In fact, while Daddy was in the hospital, Grandpa came to the house to stay. Now when Daddy came back the grandpa went home and lived with Grandma."
>
> One day Mommy had to go to the hospital and the little girl got very sad, and she was worried that her mother might not come back. But the daddy said, "Do you remember what your mother said when I was in the hospital?"
>
> And the little girl said, "Yes."
>
> And what had the mommy said to the little girl when the daddy was in the hospital?
>
> *Patient:* I want to…(mumbles)…
>
> *Therapist:* What?

Patient: Let me think.

Therapist: Okay, you think.

Patient: That it would be sad if he didn't come back.

Therapist: That he would be dead?

Patient: It would be sad if he didn't come back.

Therapist: It would be sad...

Patient: (interrupting) Because there are lots of other people in the world.

Therapist: Right! If he didn't it would be very sad, but there are lots of other people in the world. Right. And then what happened was that the mommy had to go to the hospital. And what did the daddy say to the girl?

Patient: Probably the same thing.

Therapist: Which was?

Patient: It would be sad, but there are lots of other people in the world.

Therapist: Right. And he said, "There's Grandma." And Grandma came to the house and Grandma stayed at the house to help take care of the little girl and the baby while Mommy was in the hospital. Did the mommy come back from the hospital? (All this is done with appropriate doll transfers.)

Patient: I don't know.

Therapist: Yes, she did. She came back and the little girl hugged her and kissed her, and her daddy hugged her and kissed her, and the baby hugged her and kissed her, and everybody was glad she was back. And the grandma said, "Okay, I don't have to stay here any more now, because your mommy is back." And Grandma went home and stayed with Grandpa.

And then what happened was when the weekend came they had dinner guests. There was an uncle who came and there were friends. (Again appropriate dolls are introduced and removed.) There was a cousin—a teenage cousin. Here is a teenage cousin. And there was a boy. He was 12. He came. And there was another girl. And there was another uncle. And there was an aunt. And there were lots of friends and relatives that came. And so this made the girl feel very good, because she knew there were a lot of people in the world and that if ever anything were to happen to anybody in her family, like her mother or her father—if they were to get sick—she knew that there would be other people who could help take care of her.

And although she thought it would be very sad if something were to happen to one of her parents, she knew that there were a lot of other people. And do you know what the lesson of that story is?

Patient: No.

Therapist: What do we learn from that story?

Patient: Let me try and remember now. I don't know.

Therapist: We learn that if something happens to your mother or your father...

Patient: Don't worry—that there are lots of others in the world.

Therapist: Right. Although it's very sad, there are lots of other people in the world. Okay? Now would you like to watch this television program?

Patient: Of course...

Therapist: Okay, let's watch it.

Whereas in the patient's story the scene is cluttered with a multiplicity of figures simultaneously, in mine a more realistic approach to the parental substitute problem is provided. Specific individuals are defined and they are placed on the scene one or two at a time. At no time is the scene cluttered with a host of figures. I provided reassurance about the presence of substitutes, but introduced a healthier utilization of such surrogates, namely, one or two at a time rather than a horde. This is certainly more consistent with what would be her situation if her parents were indeed to die.

Ruth's therapy was conducted at what I considered to he a low level of efficiency. Had her parents not been sick, she probably would not have needed treatment. The most therapeutic experience that Ruth could have would be the total and complete cure of both of her parents. Because no one could honestly reassure Ruth that her parents would completely recover, it is not likely that her therapy could be completely successful.

At the time of this writing, she has completed three years of treatment. Fortunately, her mother is enjoying a prolonged period of remission from her multiple sclerosis and her father's condition still remains stable. There is no question that these are important factors in her improvement, although I would like to think that her therapeutic experiences have played some part. However, she still exhibits significant insecurity about her situation. In the middle of her second year of treatment she saw the movie *Annie* and became preoccupied with children who live in orphanages. This was primarily reflected in her therapeutic play. Clearly, she identified with the children whose parents had died and envisioned herself being placed elsewhere if this calamity were to befall her. Even though I had early in treatment advised the parents to discuss with Ruth who she would be living with if they were to both die, she still persisted in believing that she would somehow be cast out into an orphanage. Reassurances such as those provided in the aforementioned story played some role in reducing this fear.

CONCLUDING COMMENTS

I consider the mutual storytelling derivative games to be valuable therapeutic instruments. Although they are basically quite similar to one another with regard to the "rules," they are generally not considered so by most children (especially younger ones). The situation here is similar to that which is found in children's games in general. Many board games are basically identical with regard to the fundamental rules of play; the differences are the figures and equipment that are utilized when playing the seemingly different games. Accordingly, children are used to this sort of thing and generally do not object to these similarities in the derivative games. They are generally less valuable than pure mutual storytelling because the fantasy created with "Dr. Gardner's Make-Up-a-Story Television Program" is essentially completely free of external contaminations. These games should then be viewed as instruments of second choice. It is preferable for the therapist to be presented with a free self-created fantasy that is told into the atmosphere. Although the external facilitating stimuli here do provide some contamination, my experience has been that the pressure of the unconscious to project fantasies relevant to issues meaningful to the child at that particular time are far more powerful than the capacity of the external facilitating stimulus to provide significant contamination.

The mutual storytelling derivative games are generally useful for children from about the age of four (the earliest age at which I treat) to about eleven. At that age, children begin to appreciate that their stories are revealing of underlying psychodynamic processes over which they are likely to feel anxiety and/or guilt. Accordingly, most will then refuse to play the game with rationalizations such as: "This is a baby game" and "I'm not in the mood to play those kinds of games." This is one of the reasons why I devised *The Talking, Feeling, & Doing Game*, which I will be discussing in detail in the next chapter. Another reason for the game's development was that there were some children who were still not providing me with psychologically meaningful material, even though I presented them with one or more of the games described in this chapter. *The Talking, Feeling, & Doing* Game proved useful not only in eliciting material from these more resistant children but by extending, as well, the upper age limit for obtaining useful projective material that could readily be utilized in therapy. I found that I could engage most children up to the age of 14 or even 15 with *The Talking, Feeling, & Doing* Game, five or six years after the mutual storytelling technique and its derivative games were no longer therapeutically useful.

4

THE TALKING, FEELING, &
DOING GAME

When the One Great Scorer comes to
Write against your name—
He marks—not that you won or lost—
But how you played the game.
      — Grantland Rice

  The mutual storytelling technique (Chapters One and Two) proved useful in facilitating children's telling self-created stories and providing other fantasy material that was of value in therapy. There were, however, children who were not free enough to tell stories using the relatively unstructured format of "Dr. Gardner's Make-Up-a-Story Television Program." It was for these children that the derivative games (Chapter Three) were devised. However, there were still some children who were so inhibited, constrained, or resistive that even these more attractive modalities did not prove successful in getting them to reveal themselves. It was for these children that *The Talking, Feeling, & Doing Game* (Gardner, 1973a) was devised. This game proved useful in engaging the vast majority of such children. In addition, for children who were free enough to reveal their fantasies, it proved useful as another therapeutic modality.

THE BASIC FORMAT OF THE TALKING, FEELING, & DOING GAME

  The game is similar in appearance to the typical board games with which most children are familiar. (See p. 218.) It includes a playing board, dice, playing pawns, a spinner, a path along which the pawns are moved, reward chips, and cards that are drawn from the center of the game board. This familiarity, as well as the fact that it is a game, reduces initial anxieties and attracts the child to the therapeutic instrument.

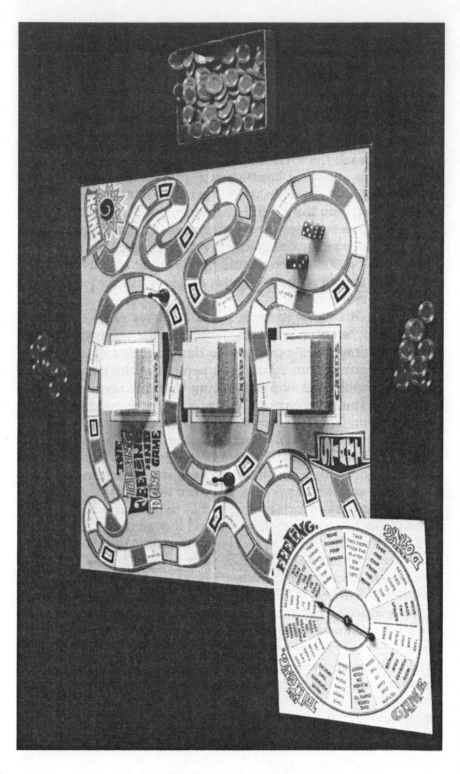

The Psychotherapeutic Use of The Talking, Feeling, & Doing Game

To begin the game both the therapist and the child place their colored pawns at the START position. Alternatively, they throw the dice and move their pawns along a curved path of squares which ultimately end at the FINISH position. For younger children, one die can be used. A pawn can land on one of a number of squares: white, red, yellow, SPIN, GO FORWARD (a specific number of squares), and GO BACKWARD (again, a specific number of squares). If the pawn lands on a white square, the player takes a Talking Card; on a yellow square, a Feeling Card; and on a red square, a Doing Card. If the pawn lands on SPIN, the player spins the spinner and follows the directions. Generally, these provide gain and loss of chips, or forward and backward movement of the playing pawn. Similarly, landing on GO FORWARD or GO BACKWARD squares results in movement of the pawn. The spinner and movement squares are of little, if any, psychological significance. They are included to insure the child's fun and relieve some of the pressure associated with a high frequency of drawing only the aforementioned three types of cards.

Of course, the core of the game is the directions and questions on each of the cards. As their titles imply, the Talking Cards instruct the player to make comments that are primarily in the intellectual and cognitive area. The Feeling Cards focus primarily on affective issues. The Doing Cards usually involve playacting and/or some kind of physical activity. The child is given a reward chip for responding to each of the cards. Although a token reinforcement is provided, the game is by no means a form of behavior therapy. Positive reinforcement is not being given for behavioral change at the manifest level. Rather, the child is being reinforced for providing psychodynamically meaningful material for psychotherapeutic utilization. The child's and the therapist's responses are used as points of departure for psychotherapeutic interchanges.

There is no actual time limit for the game. Both the therapist and the patient play similarly, and each responds to the cards. The first player to reach the FINISH position receives five extra reward chips. The second player continues to play until he or she also reaches the FINISH position. If the game is interrupted prior to one player's reaching the FINISH position, the player who is closest to that position receives three extra reward chips. The therapist should discourage active competition on the child's part for the acquisition of chips. The game should be played at a slow pace, and each response should serve as a point of departure for psychotherapeutic interchange.

There are 104 cards in each stack. I always randomize them and have never "stacked the deck" with specific cards that I hope the child will draw. The cards are so designed that any card will be relevant to any player. About five percent of the cards in each stack are so simple and nonthreatening that just about any child will respond. These are basically placed there for the extremely fragile child who would be threatened by the cards that will touch on basic problems of living. These simpler cards insure that the child will get chips and thereby remain motivated to participate in the game. The most liberal criteria are used when deciding whether or not a child should be given a chip for responding. Again, the therapist wants to do everything possible to draw the child in and maintain his or her interest. Some typical low-anxiety cards: "How old is your father?"; "What's your lucky number? Why?"; "What is your telephone number?"; "What is your address?"; "What's your favorite flavor ice cream?"; "What present would you like to get for your next birthday?"; "What's your favorite smell?"; "Make believe you're blowing out the candles on your birthday cake."; and "Make a funny sound with your mouth. If you spit, you don't get a chip."

The remaining questions and directions are far richer psychologically and are at the "heart" of the game. These are not as anxiety provoking as a request to make up a story that will reveal free fantasies; however, they provide highly meaningful therapeutic material. Some typical cards: "All the girls in the class were invited to a birthday party except one. How did she feel? Why wasn't she invited?"; "Everybody in the class was laughing at a girl. What had happened?"; "A boy has something on his mind that he's afraid to tell his father. What is it that he's scared to talk about?"; "What's the worst thing a boy can say to his mother?"; "Suppose two people were talking about you, and they didn't know you were listening. What do you think you would hear them saying?"; "What things come into your mind when you can't fall asleep?"; "If the walls of your house could talk, what would they say about your family?"; "Tell about something you did that made you proud."; and "What's the worst thing that ever happened to you in your whole life?"

The child's responses are usually revealing of the psychological issues that are most relevant to him or her at that point. The questions and instructions cover the wide range of human experiences. The material elicited is likely to be relevant to the etiology of the child's disturbance. The questions are designed to direct the child's attention to the basic life conflicts which are being resolved in inappropriate and maladaptive ways by the symptomology. They direct the child's attention to the issues that I referred to previously, that is, the basic life conflicts that are at the foundation of psychopathological processes. As mentioned, each response serves as a point of departure for therapeutic interchanges. The therapist does not merely provide the child with a chip and then race on with the game to see who can reach FINISH first. Rather, the therapist tries to get as much "mileage" as possible from each response, using his or her discretion in deciding how much discussion is warranted for each patient. Highly defensive and resistant children will not be able to tolerate the kind of in-depth discussion in which the healthier child can readily participate.

The therapist answers the same questions as the child. The greater the therapist's knowledge of the child's problems, the more judicious will be his or her responses. Obviously, it is not the therapist's role to provide answers relevant to his or her own life problems. Rather the responses should be designed to provide therapeutic messages pertinent to the child's difficulties. I always respond honestly. Often I will provide a response that will relate to an experience of mine in childhood that is relevant to the patient's problems. Children generally enjoy hearing about the events of their parents' lives that occurred at that time in the parents' childhood that corresponds to the age of the child at the time of the conversation. Such discussions draw children closer to their parents. The same principle holds in therapy. Such revelations, then, can contribute to a deepening of the therapist-patient relationship. As mentioned, a good relationship is crucial if therapy is to be successful. Without it, there will be little receptivity to the therapist's messages and practically no identification with him or her.

Many therapists, especially those with a classical psychoanalytic orientation, may take issue with the freedom with which I reveal myself. They would argue that I am contaminating terribly the therapeutic field and making the patient's free associations practically useless. I am in full agreement that such revelations contaminate the patient's free associations. I am not in agreement, however, that the classical approach is without its drawbacks. It does indeed provide the so-called "blank screen" for the purest projections. However, the acquisition of such information is done in a setting which, I believe, is antitherapeutic. It creates a distance between the therapist and the patient that compromises the development of a good therapist-patient relationship. The patient's thoughts and feelings about the therapist become distorted and divorced from reality. The situation increases the likelihood that the patient will develop delusions about the therapist and will idealize him or her. It will widen the gap between them as the patient comes to view the therapist as perfect. We can love most those whom we know nothing about—but such love is more delusional than real, based as it is on a paucity of information. What is gained in the way of pure free associations is more than counterbalanced, I believe, by the losses of a compromised therapist-patient relationship and the antitherapeutic experience of the patient comparing him- or herself negatively with the therapist. *The Talking, Feeling, & Doing Game* provides the therapist with the opportunity to reveal defects in a noncontrived and nonartificial setting. He or she thereby becomes more human to the patient, and this is generally salutary for the therapist-patient relationship. In addition, my revelations are not those that would compromise my own privacy and that of my family. Even with these restrictions, there is enough that has gone on in my life to provide me with a wealth of potential information for revelation.

I uniformly answer all questions. Some highly defensive children, however, may find it difficult to do so. Sometimes, I will inform such children that failure to answer the question will result in their not getting a reward chip, and this will lessen the likelihood that they will win the game. Some children are motivated by this "threat" and try to respond to the card. On occasion, a child will refrain from answering most cards but still involve him- or herself in the game. Many of these children listen attentively to my responses and, I believe, gain thereby from the game. Although I am working here in a partial vacuum because I am not getting as much information from the child as is desirable, my knowledge of the child's history and background provides me with enough information to give responses to the cards that are meaningful to the child and pertinent to his or her problems.

The question is sometimes raised about winning and losing when playing therapeutic games with children. *The Talking, Feeling, & Doing Game* obviates this problem. It may not be immediately apparent to the therapist that the main determinant as to who wins the game is luck. If each player answers each card, the determinant as to who wins the game is the dice. If a player obtains many high throws, then he or she will reach FINISH earlier and thereby acquire fewer chips. If a player obtains a larger number of low throws, more chips will be acquired when going from START to FINISH. Because low and high throws average out for each player, the number of wins and losses also average out over the course of treatment.

Although *The Talking, Feeling, & Doing Game* was originally devised to engage resistant children in therapy, it has proved useful for less defended children as well. In fact, it has proved to be the favorite therapeutic activity of the children in my practice. Many other therapists have informed me that this has been their experience as well. This therapeutic boon is not without its drawbacks, however. One danger of the game is that it will lure the child (and, unfortunately, the therapist) away from utilizing techniques that are more likely to elicit "deeper" psychodynamic material. Dealing with this material is also important in therapy. Accordingly, the therapist should not injudiciously "respect" the child's wishes to devote the entire therapeutic experience to this technique. The game is generally useful for children over the age of five or six, the age at which they begin to appreciate the give-and-take structure of board games. At that age, of course, the therapist may have to read the cards to the child (or read along with the child), but this is not an impediment. Whereas the mutual storytelling technique and its derivative games are generally not useful above the age of 11, one can get a few more years mileage from *The Talking, Feeling, & Doing Game*. My experience has been that it can be useful up to the age of 14 or 15.

Although primarily designed to be used in the one-to-one therapeutic situation, the game can be used in child group therapy as well (preferably for small groups of three to five children). When so utilized, the therapist can use a child's response as a point of departure for group discussion. The game is particularly useful in child group therapy because it provides intrinsic structure in a situation that traditionally tends to become unstructured (the children tend to become playful, rambunctious, distracted, etc.). In addition, it facilitates discussion of problems in a setting in which such conversations are usually difficult to accomplish because of the reticence of most children to engage in them.

Generally, the material elicited when utilizing the mutual storytelling technique is closer to pure dream and free fantasy than that revealed in *The Talking, Feeling, & Doing Game*. The "Make-Up-a-Story Television Program" is so structured that there are no specific stimuli around which the stories are told. Traditional play materials such as dolls and puppets, although valuable and frequently effective catalysts for story elicitation, do contaminate the story and tend to "draw" the child's projections into specific directions. The cards in

The Talking, Feeling, & Doing Game are similarly contaminating. However, I believe that the "push" of the unconscious material to be released in a form specific for the child's needs at that particular time is far stronger than the "pull" of the evoking stimulus and its power to significantly alter the projected material. Accordingly, the "channeling" of the projections is not very significant.

First, I will describe some common responses I provide for each of the three categories of cards. Then I will present some clinical vignettes in which I demonstrate my utilization of the game in the treatment of children.

EXAMPLES OF CARD RESPONSES
Talking Cards

Human behavior lends itself well to being divided into thoughts, feelings, and actions. It was from this observation that I decided to name this game *The Talking, Feeling, & Doing Game*. Furthermore, the sequence here is also important. Thoughts generally precede feelings, and feelings precede actions. Certainly, the sequence is applicable for fight-flight reactions. One sees a danger. A possible emotional reaction is fear. In response to the fear, one flees. Another possible emotional reaction is anger. Then, one fights and the anger enhances one's efficiency in protecting oneself from the attacker. For emotions such as sexual arousal and hunger, feelings may precede thoughts. One feels hungry, then one experiences thoughts related to food acquisition. Then one takes action and attempts to obtain food. Because therapy is more likely to deal with fight-flight emotions then those related to eating and sexual arousal (not that these aren't involved in treatment at all), I decided to place *talking* before *feeling* in the name of the game.

The Talking Cards encourage the child to speak about his or her opinions on a wide variety of subjects. The questions are designed to elicit information related to the fundamental problems of life with which all children are confronted. The solutions to these problems can either be adaptive or maladaptive. We refer to a maladaptive solution as symptomatic. The game is designed to elicit discussion of these issues in the hope that the child will learn how to deal better with these problems of life and thereby not have to resort as frequently to the pathological adaptations.

It is vital for the therapist to appreciate that *there are no standard answers for the therapist to provide*. Rather, each response must be tailored to the particular child with whom the therapist is playing the game. Accordingly, it would be an error for the therapist to use the responses I provide here in the models I have created for the therapist's answers. Rather, they should be viewed as selected examples of the *kinds* of responses that I might provide and as guidelines for the therapist's own responses. Just as the therapist's responding story in the mutual storytelling game is tailored to the patient's story, the therapist's answers in this game are also designed to fit the patient's needs.

Question: What sport are you worst at?

Response: I never really was very good at sports. So there are a lot of sports I am pretty bad at. Of the sports that were commonly played in my neighborhood when I was kid, I would say that the one that I was worst at was basketball. I guess that I didn't try hard enough. It's not that I was born a klutz; I just think that I didn't work at it enough. I used to feel pretty bad when kids would choose up sides and I was the last one to be chosen. Had I worked harder at it, it probably wouldn't have happened to me.

The card "What sport are you worst at?" essentially forces the therapist to reveal an area of weakness. Even if the therapist were an Olympic decathlon champion, he or she would still be provided with the opportunity to talk about a sport in which there is weakness. Besides providing the aforementioned benefits of such revelation, I use the response to put in a plug for the work ethic. The response also provides the child with the knowledge that I too had my rejections and that I too was not chosen for involvement in various activities when I was a child. This is a universal phenomenon, and it is helpful for the child to know that the therapist too suffered such rejections. It contributes to a sense of communion with the therapist and this cannot but be therapeutic.

Question: What things come into your mind when you can't fall asleep?

Response: If I had let someone take advantage of me during the day and didn't do anything about it, it would tend to linger on my mind. I would keep thinking about what I should have done and how I didn't do it. This might interfere with my falling asleep. I would keep thinking of the thing over and over again—especially how I might have said something or done something, but I didn't say or do anything at the time. I'm sorry then that I didn't speak up or do something. But later, it was too late. And there may be nothing that I can then do about it. So I have trouble falling asleep because I keep thinking about what I should have done. Sometimes however, there is something I can do about it and then I do it at the time. Then I get it off my chest. Then I feel better. Then I can fall asleep more easily. I did the thing that I was supposed to do.

For example, something happened when I was a young kid that caused me to lose a lot of sleep for a few nights. I was in junior high school at the time. I was walking out of a classroom. Some kids in the class made some kind of a smoke bomb and threw it into one of the desks. The teacher wasn't there, and as they left the room, the smoke started to pour out of the desk. I was scared that the desk would catch on fire. I wanted to run over and pull everything out of the desk because I was so scared that the whole school might burn down, but I was afraid that the other kids would call me "chicken." So I walked out of the classroom with the others. About five minutes later I heard a fire alarm bell and I wasn't surprised. It was a big school with almost 1,000 kids. And we all quickly left the building. As we got outside, I could see the smoke coming out of the classroom. The fire engines came and put out the fire. Fortunately, it was caught in time and no one was hurt. Also, the fire didn't spread too far. The kids who lit the smoke bomb were kicked out of school.

I was really sorry that I hadn't had the guts to pull the stuff out of that desk and stomp on it. I think there were other kids in the classroom that wanted to do the same thing, but none of us had the guts. For the next three nights, I kept thinking about how much trouble I would have saved everybody—especially those boys—if only I had done what I knew was the right thing. I know some kids probably would have laughed at me, but I would have known I was doing the right thing. It was a big mistake. And I still remember it after all these years, even though I only lost some sleep for a few nights.

Although my response at the beginning is designed to be general, the example I give makes particular reference to self-assertion. In particular, I focus on the importance of doing what one considers to be "right" even though it may be the unpopular thing. I try thereby to encourage self-assertion. Such comments are especially helpful to children with self-assertion problems. The pent-up resentments that such children cause themselves can distract them from learning in school. It also contributes to their becoming targets for bullies and scapegoaters. And this too can interfere with learning as the child comes to dread school attendance.

Question: What's the best story you ever heard or read? Why?

Response: Of all the books that I ever read when I was young, the one that I remember to have been the best was the one describing the life of Thomas A. Edison. As you probably know, Thomas A. Edison was one of the greatest inventors who ever lived. Although he wasn't the only man to work on these things, his inventions were important—giving us the electric light bulb, the phonograph, and the moving picture camera. He was a poor boy who lived in Ohio. He was a very hard worker and was an extremely curious person. He was immensely interested in how things work.

He had a laboratory near his home and it is said that he would sometimes work most of the night on his inventions. He loved learning about how things work, and he loved trying to figure out better ways of doing things. To this day, people all over the world use his inventions. To this day, he is remembered as having given mankind some of its greatest inventions. He must have really felt great about himself because of all the good he did for mankind. It is mainly his curiosity and hard work that did these things both for himself and for others. It was Thomas A. Edison who said: "Genius is 1 percent inspiration and 99 percent perspiration." Do you know what that means?

Edison epitomizes the gratification and fame that can come to someone who is strongly committed to the work ethic. I emphasize here the great benefit that can come to others from the efforts of a strongly motivated person. My aim here is to engender some desire on the child's part to view Edison as an admirable figure worthy of emulation and inspiration. Obviously, one such message is not going to achieve this goal. However, the seed is planted and with reiteration over time it is quite possible that Edison will become incorporated into the child's psychic structure and join with other introjects to serve as a model for identification and emulation. Younger children, obviously, will not understand the quotation about genius and perspiration. However, even they can be engaged in a discussion of it if the words they do not understand are explained.

> *Question:* Suppose two people you knew were talking about you and they didn't know you were listening. What do you think you would hear them saying?
>
> *Response:* I might hear the people saying that I'm the kind of a person who is direct and honest. Although people might disagree at times with what I've said, they would agree that I am direct about what my opinions are and don't pussyfoot about them. They know that when they ask me a question, they'll get an honest and direct answer with no hedging, beating around the bush, or saying things that aren't true. I am not saying that they would say that I never lied in my whole life and that I never will, only that they are pretty confident that I'll be honest with them. You see, I believe that there is truth and wisdom to the old saying that "honesty is the best policy." If you tell a lie, you have to go around worrying that people will find out that you've lied. Also, lots of people feel bad about themselves when they lie; they feel guilty about it. And when people find out that you've lied, then they don't trust you even when you've told the truth. So these are the main reasons why I find it better to tell the truth, rather than to lie. What's your opinion on this subject?

Identification with the therapist and modeling oneself after him or her is an important part of the therapeutic process. This is very similar to the educational model in which the child learns, in part, because of identification with the teacher and the desire to gain the same gratifications that the teacher enjoys from learning. The therapist not only serves as a model for learning, but should be serving as a model for other desirable attributes as well, for example, healthy self-assertion, sensitivity to the feelings of others, feelings of benevolence toward those who are in pain, handling oneself with dignity, and honesty. This card enables the therapist to provide examples of such traits. However, the therapist should select traits that are particularly relevant to the child's problems. Furthermore, the therapist must avoid presenting these with a flaunting or holier-than-thou attitude.

> *Question:* Make believe that you're looking into a crystal ball that can show anything that is happening anywhere in the whole world. What do you see?

Response: I'm looking into a crystal ball. There's a cloud there, and I can't see anything now. Wait a minute...wait a minute...it's starting to clear. I think I can see something now. Oh, yes, it's a big auditorium. In the front rows are lots of children, school children. In the back rows are all the parents. There's something happening on the stage. There are teachers sitting up there and, oh yeah, there's the principal. He's standing in the front and he's giving something to a child. It looks like he's giving her an award. She certainly looks proud. Now the principal is shaking her hand and everybody's clapping. Now he's making another announcement. And here comes another child up on to the stage and everybody's clapping. He's then giving her an award and the principal's making a little speech about her. There's a big smile on her face. Obviously, she's also won a prize or award. Now she's walking off the stage and everyone's clapping.

My message here is clear. I am trying to help the child gain an appreciation for the rewards of successful schoolwork. I focus on the internal reward, the sense of pride and gratification. I also describe the external rewards: the applause of the audience, the speech of the principal, and the prizes. The dramatic element here serves to enhance the child's interest and increase the chance that my messages will be heard.

Question: Tell about something you did that you are ashamed about.

Response: I had an experience many years ago, when I was a medical intern, that was very embarrassing. It was so embarrassing that I still remember it clearly to this day. It happened when I was an intern. An intern is a young doctor just out of medical school. Well, one Friday morning the resident, the doctor who was my boss, told me that I should prepare a speech about one of the patients that I was treating. He told me that I was to give it the first thing the following Monday morning. He told me to look over the patient's present and past charts as well as to study all the old X-rays. The patient had been sick for many years, and there was a lot of material to cover. He told me that it was important that I do a good job because this was the biggest conference of the month and that all the doctors in the hospital would be there. The hospital had over 200 doctors and it was a very important conference.

Anyway, Monday morning I got to the hospital and started

to work with my patients. I noticed that none of the other doctors were there and wondered where everyone was. Suddenly, the telephone rang and I answered. It was the resident. He was very upset and he asked me why I wasn't at the conference. I was so surprised and shocked that I almost fainted. I realized that I had totally forgotten about the conference. I had prepared nothing! I was sick to my stomach. I immediately grabbed the patient's chart, the two X-rays that I could find, and rushed to the conference room.

What I should have done was to publicly announce that I was unprepared and to express my apologies. However, I tried to get away with it. I tried to go through the chart and give a speech about the patient, when I had very little information. I didn't lie or anything like that. I just tried to take a little information from one place and a little from the next but it didn't hang together. Finally, one of the older doctors who organized the conference interrupted me and suggested that we discontinue the conference. I was humiliated. But I was also relieved. I certainly learned an important lesson that day. And I have never again forgotten to prepare a speech. That event took place many years ago, and although it was painful and embarrassing, I learned an important lesson.

The question "Tell about something you did that you are ashamed about" again requires the therapist to reveal an area of imperfection. In the vignette that I selected, I also provide a message about preparing things in advance, thinking ahead, and thereby protecting oneself from humiliation. This message is likely to be of some relevance to most children in treatment.

Question: If you became mayor of your city, what would you do to change things?

Response: If I became mayor of my city, I would do everything in my power to bring about the passage of two laws. One would prohibit smoking in public places and the other would fine people large amounts of money for letting their dogs crap in the streets. Let me tell you my reasons for saying this. I, personally, find cigarette smoking disgusting. I'm not saying this because smoking causes cancer of the lungs. I'd say this even if smoking cured cancer of the lungs. I'm just saying it because I find smoking nauseating. I think that if anyone is stupid enough to smoke, that person should be required to do it privately, in his or her own home. Many people who smoke don't care about other people's feelings. As far as they're concerned, other people can choke or even croak on their smoke. They don't think about the feelings of the people who are suffering because of their smoking. Unfortunately, a lot of people don't speak up and say how the smoke bothers them. But more and more people are doing this.

The other law, about there being big fines for people who let their dogs crap on the streets, would be for the same purposes. People who let their dogs do this don't think about how disgusted others feel when they step in the dog sh-t. It's really a disgusting thing to have to wipe dog sh-t off your shoes. It's too bad there are so many people in this world who don't think about other people's feelings. What do you think about people who smoke and people who let their dogs crap on the streets?

The major thrust of my responses here is to help an insensitive child appreciate how one's acts can affect others and that those who don't think about how they are affecting others are generally scorned. Included also in my response was a message about self-assertion regarding nonsmokers in their relationships with smokers.

Question: What was the worst punishment you ever got in your whole life? What had you done wrong?

Response: I remember my worst punishment quite well. I was about seven or eight years old at the time. My brother and I had gone off and were playing in an empty lot a couple of blocks from my home. I lived in an apartment house in the Bronx, in New York City. One of the things we liked to do was to make bonfires. We would gather some wood and papers and build a fire. We built them in safe places, not in buildings. We didn't want to burn anything, we just wanted to have some fun building the fire and then throwing garbage and other things into it and watch the stuff burn. Anyway, on this day, we got so involved with the fun of the fire that we didn't realize how late it was. In fact, it was getting dark and we thought that was even greater fun because we could then watch the fire during the night. We were having so much fun that we completely forgot about our parents and how worried and upset they might be because we hadn't come home.

Well, anyway, at about 8 o'clock at night we finally got home. We were supposed to be home about 5:30 or 6 o'clock.

Although our parents were very happy to see us, they were also very angry. They were very worried, so much so that they had already called the police to look for us. The police hadn't started to look for us yet; they just said wait a little while longer.

Anyway, my father hit us both with a strap to help us remember never to do such a terrible thing again. They were not only upset about our building fires—which was more dangerous than we had realized—but about our not having thought about their feelings and about how worried they were when we didn't come home. They were scared that we might have wandered off and gotten lost. They were also scared that we might have been kidnapped or even been killed. And they were extremely upset that we hadn't thought about their feelings. Do you know what lessons I learned from that experience?

My hope here is that the story will engender some appreciation in the child of the effects of antisocial behavior on other people, how other people might feel who suffer from or who are otherwise inconvenienced by the child's antisocial behavior. In addition, it emphasizes the point that there were personal repercussions for my behavior. I received a severe spanking that I remember to this day and I also risked being burned by the fire.

Question: What do you think about a boy who curses at his father?

Response: It's perfectly normal to think curse words about a father. In fact, practically every child I have ever seen will, at times, have such thoughts in mind—especially after something happens that gets the child angry at his or her father. However, if instead you politely talk about the things that are getting you angry, then your father is more likely to listen and maybe then you'll be able to solve the problem. Maybe your speaking politely will help, and maybe it won't. However, there's a greater chance it will help solve the problem if you don't use curse words than if you do. And the worst thing is to say nothing at all when you're angry. Then, you won't solve anything and things will probably get worse.

Question: What do you think about a boy who sometimes wished that his brother were dead?

Response: It's perfectly normal to have thoughts once in a while, and even wishes, that one's brother were dead. This is especially the case in the middle of a fight. But having a thought once in a while and having a wish once in a while and really wanting the brother to be dead are two separate things. Most children are comfortable with the idea that they could think it and wish it once in a while and that there is nothing wrong with them. They know that there is a big difference between having a wish once in a while and really wanting it to happen.

There are some children who have such thoughts once in a while who believe that they are terrible to have such thoughts. They believe that only the worst kinds of children would have such thoughts about a brother. They feel terrible about themselves for having such thoughts and try to blot them out of their minds when they start thinking about such things. If such children knew that these thoughts, once in a while, are perfectly normal they might feel better about themselves. They might not feel so guilty about these thoughts and then they would be happier people.

There are some children who have these thoughts once in a while who become very frightened of them. They think that the thought can actually make the brother die. That's silly. A thought can't make anything happen. In fact, no matter how hard a child thinks something, the thought itself can't make the thing happen. Even if the brother wished very hard that the other brother would die, that wouldn't make it happen. If such children changed their minds and realized that thoughts can't make things happen, they would become less afraid of the death wishes. They would then become more comfortable with themselves over them.

My aim here is to reduce guilt in children who believe that occasional hostile thoughts and feelings, especially death wishes, are terrible to have. I inform the child that such thoughts and feelings are commonplace. Many children with such guilt harbor the notion that they are alone in the world or that only the most lowly individuals would harbor such heinous thoughts and feelings. I also attempt to dispel the notion that a thought has magic powers and can bring about an event. This notion is often intrinsically associated with excessive guilt over such thoughts and feelings.

Question: A girl was very angry at her father and wished that he would be hit by a car. Later that day he was hit by a car. How did she feel? What did she think?

Response: The girl felt very sad. She was not only sad because her father was hit by a car and had to go to the hospital, but she was also sad because she thought that her thoughts had actually caused the car to hit her father. She thought that an angry idea could actually make a thing happen. This of course, isn't true. That would be magic and there is no such thing as magic. A thought cannot make anything happen. Things happen by people doing things. The man who drove the car that hit her father was the one who was responsible for the father's being hurt. Probably it was an accident. If anyone was at fault it was he, not the girl who had the thought and wished that her father would get hit by a car.

The girl didn't realize that everyone has thoughts like that once in a while. She was very angry at her father and, at that time, she had the wish that he would die. It isn't that she really wanted her father dead. It's just that when she was very angry, such wishes came into her mind. Fortunately, this girl discussed the whole thing with her father after he came out of the hospital. He told her that he wasn't angry at her for the accident. He told her that her thoughts were normal and to have them once in a while, when a person is angry, is normal. He told her that he didn't blame her for his having been hit by the car. He didn't even blame the man who drove the car.

He did blame the man who fixed the car, because he had done a poor job. Her father had gotten a lawyer and he was going to sue the mechanic, the man who fixed the car, for the hospital bills as well as the money he lost from work when he was in the hospital. Her father discussed with her her feelings that her thoughts might have made the man in the car drive into her father. He told her that this was not the case. He told her that her thoughts could not make the thing happen. It was the car mechanic's fault and not hers. He told her also that her thoughts could not make the car mechanic make his mistake. After that, she didn't feel so bad. After that she realized that thoughts can't make things happen. Then she felt better about herself.

I deal here in detail with the issue of thoughts having magic power as a central element in guilt over anger. It is important to note that this factor is much more likely to be operative in children under the age of five or six. Prior to that time it is normal for children to believe in the magic of their thoughts. The sicker the child the greater the likelihood this notion will persist beyond the age when it should no longer be believed.

Sometimes I will enhance the efficacy of this message by bringing out the play dolls. I may take the little girl doll and the father doll and playact that the little girl is wishing very hard that her father will die. The dialogue may go something like this:

> And the little girl wished very, very hard that her father would die. But no matter how hard she wished, her father just didn't die. She was very angry at him because he had done such terrible things to her. She hoped that if he would die then he would no longer abuse and hurt her. So she kept wishing and wishing that he would die. But it just didn't work. He just went on living. (I then move the father doll around as if he was carrying out various activities—demonstrating thereby that he is still alive.) No matter how hard she wished, he just didn't die.

I might then bring into the story a teenage brother (or some other powerful authority figure) who asks the little girl what she's wishing for. In the ensuing discussion the teenager also emphasizes the theme that her wishes cannot bring about her father's death. He may, however, enter into a discussion with her about what else she might do to improve her situation.

> *Question:* If a fly followed you around for a day and could then talk about you, what would it say?
>
> *Response:* I followed Dr. Gardner around all day and I noticed that the people he is with hardly ever have any doubt in their minds about what he thinks. He's not afraid to tell people what's on his mind and to express his thoughts and feelings. He avoids a lot of trouble this way. If people had to wonder what he thought, there would be a lot of confusion and trouble. He also gets many things accomplished that he wouldn't have if he didn't speak up.
>
> For example, during his lunch break one day, he went to a restaurant with a friend. He asked to be seated in the *No Smoking* section. After they were there awhile, a man sat down at the next table and started to smoke. Dr. Gardner immediately complained

to the waiter and the man was asked to either put out the cigarette or sit in the *Smoking* section. He quickly apologized and put out the cigarette. Some people probably would have sat there and said nothing. However, Dr. Gardner didn't. By speaking up, he stopped a person from doing something that was making him uncomfortable.

During the evening he went to the movies with his wife. The sound was on much too loud and lots of people were bothered. However, no one was doing anything about it. Dr. Gardner got up, went out to the lobby, and asked for the manager. He asked the manager to lower the volume of the sound. At first, the manager didn't believe him, so he asked the manager to go into the theater and hear for himself. The manager did so and realized that Dr. Gardner was right. He then lowered the volume and then everyone was more comfortable. Again, he saved himself and other people a lot of trouble by politely and firmly expressing his thoughts and feelings. Of course, every once in a while, he may not express his thoughts and feelings and this usually causes some trouble. This helps him remember that the best thing, most often, is to tell people about things that bother you—but to do so in a polite way.

This is another example of my view that it is useful for therapy to help the patient learn important principles in living which can be applied to specific situations as they arise. Clearly, my hope here is that this description will impress upon the child the value of self-assertion. My hope also is that my own ways of dealing with these problems will serve as a model for the child.

Feeling Cards

The Feeling Cards, as their name indicates, encourage primarily the expression of feelings. Many therapists view such expression to be the primary goal of the therapeutic process. These therapists will frequently ask such questions as: "How did you feel about that?" and "That must have made you feel very angry (sad, happy, etc.)." Others speak of therapy primarily as a place where the child can let out or get in touch with his or her feelings. Some pride themselves on their skill when a boy, for example, expresses the anger he feels toward his father by hitting the head of the father doll with a toy hammer. I believe that this view of therapy is naive. I consider the expression of feelings to be a first step toward the alleviation of difficulties. Feelings serve in part to enhance one's efficiency in reaching a goal. When we are frightened, we run faster; when we are angry, we fight harder and more effectively. When sexually excited, we make love more ardently. When hungry we eat, sometimes voraciously. And when tired, we sleep more deeply.

The therapist's goals should be that of helping patients express their thoughts and feelings at the earliest possible time that is reasonable and appropriate. At such times, the feelings are generally at a low level and can be used most effectively. When feelings build up to high levels they are likely to interfere with their effective utilization. When we are irritated, we can use our irritation to attempt to remove the noxious stimulus that is evoking our frustration. If, however, we do not express ourselves early, the angry feelings build up to levels of rage and even fury. When expressed under these circumstances the anger is not likely to be focused on the particular source of frustration. When expressed in a wild and even chaotic fashion, we are not likely to remove expediently the source of irritation. Furthermore, when feelings reach an extremely high level their gratification may become an end in itself, with little further purpose. A murderer, for example, will generally accomplish his or her goal with one or two stabs in the chest. The murderer who continues to stab the victim is no longer using the anger in the service of killing the victim. The same phenomenon applies to sexual gratification, eating, sleeping, and drinking.

As is true of the other cards, the child's reactions should serve as a point of departure for therapeutic interchanges. The examples given here do not present such discussions. Later in this chapter I will provide clinical examples in which sample interchanges are presented. Again, there are no "right" answers to the questions and instructions on the Feeling Cards. Rather, my responses presented here may serve as guidelines for the therapist's responses when playing the game.

Question: What do you think happens to people after they die?
Response: No one knows for sure. Some people think that there is some kind of life or existence after death. Some believe that there is a soul or ghost that remains after we die. Some people believe that we actually come back to life in another form. And some people believe that there is absolutely nothing that happens after you're dead. They believe that your body just rots away in the ground and that there is no such thing as a soul or ghost or spirit or anything else. They believe that that's just the end of it all forever. That's my personal opinion as well. I don't believe that there

is any kind of life or existence after you die. I'm not 100 percent sure, but it's the theory that seems most reasonable to me.

Therefore, because I believe that I only have one life, I try to make it the best life possible. I try not to do things that will foul me up. I work hard so that I'll be able to get the things I want in life. This doesn't mean that I don't take out time to have fun. I do that as well. I try to balance them out and spend time both at work and at fun. However, some of my work is also fun. And some of my fun is also work. The two tend to get mixed up at times. For example, writing books is work, but it's also fun for me. Hiking is fun for me, but it also involves some effort and work.

I think one of the worst things that can happen to a person is to reach the end of his or her life and look back and realize that most of it has been wasted. To avoid this, it is important for people to do those things each day that make life as good as possible. No matter what people believe about what happens after death, most of them agree that it's important to make the one life they have the best possible one. Do you think you're doing this for yourself?

Like many of the questions, the brighter the child, the greater the likelihood the post-response discussion will be rich and meaningful. Although we may enter into a somewhat philosophical discussion, my main purpose here is to help the child gain a sense of the sanctity of life and the importance of doing the best one can for oneself at any point along the way. I believe that people who have a greater appreciation of this unhappy fact are more likely to be motivated to make the most of the relatively short time we have here.

Question: What's the happiest thing that ever happened to you?

Response: I've had many happy days in my life. Three of the happiest were the three days on which each of my children was born. Of course, that happened many years ago, but I still remember the days clearly. I was so happy on each of those days that I cried. They were tears of joy. I still have those warm feelings when I see little babies. It's hard for me not to touch them and sometimes I'll even ask the mother to let me hold the baby so I can cuddle and kiss the child. Although my children, like all children, may give me trouble at times, they also give me great pleasures. And the pleasures are certainly greater than the pains.

We speak often of the importance of the therapist-patient relationship in therapy. However, the factors that contribute to the development of a good relationship in this area have not been well delineated. This question can be used to help foster a good patient-therapist relationship. My hope here is that the child's relationship with me might improve (admittedly in a small way) by the recognition that children produce warm responses in me. The response conveys the notion that I have the capacity for such pleasure with children in general and this response is not simply confined to my own children.

Question: What's something you could say that could make a person feel good?

Response: One thing you could say that could make a person feel good is to compliment the person on an accomplishment, that is, on something he or she did very well. For example, if a boy worked very hard making a model airplane, and it turned out very well and looked very good, then I'd say to him, "That's a beautiful job you did!" That would make him feel very good about himself. Or, for example, if a girl started the school year as a very poor student and then improved significantly, she would also feel very good if someone complimented her on her accomplishment. If, for example, she was spending a lot of time in the early part of the year goofing off and fooling around, then she wouldn't feel very good about herself. Let's say that she then begins to study much harder. After a lot of work over a period of time, the teacher might say on her report card: "Congratulations, Sarah, you have really improved. Whereas you were once a pain in the neck because you never tried or did your homework, now it's a pleasure to have you in the classroom. It's a pleasure to be your teacher. You've really come a long way. Keep up the good work." Now that's the kind of thing that would make the girl feel good about herself. What do you think about what I've said?

When I congratulate a child on an accomplishment, I generally focus my attention primarily on the deed or the act and direct the child's attention to the good feeling he or she must experience over the accomplishment. I secondarily mention other people who may be pleased over the child's accomplishment and/or external rewards, such as high grades, certificates, awards, and so on. Also included here is the notion that hard work is necessary if one is to enjoy these benefits.

Question: Say three curse words. What do you think of people who use these words?

Response: Sh-t. Crap. F-ck. I think these words are okay to use if you're having a fight with someone outside your home. They serve a useful purpose. They get out anger without actually hurting the other person. However, it's a bad idea to use these words in front of parents, teachers, and other adults. They usually get very upset and angry and will tell you that it's not proper to use these words in front of others. So, it's often best to use words that are more polite than these if you want to get something accomplished, especially with an adult. There are times when these words are the best words to use. If another kid speaks to you with such words, it can often be useful to use similar words back. There's an old saying, "Sticks and stones may break my bones, but names will never hurt me." This tells very well what I said before about dirty words helping you use anger without actually hurting anyone.

This card is designed for the child who is inhibited in the proper use of profanity in socially acceptable ways and situations. The child may be initially astounded to hear me use such words—believing that it is inappropriate for a doctor to utilize profanity. Obviously, this is not the response I would provide for the child who has an antisocial behavior disorder and uses such words indiscriminately. Rather, I would provide a response that attempts to induce guilt and/or embarrassment over the use of such words.

Question: What is the best kind of job a person can have? Why? Make believe you're doing that job.

Response: I think the best job a person can have is one in which that person earns money doing something that he or she finds enjoyable. Normally, the more education a person has, the greater the likelihood he or she will have such a job. People who don't have much education, or who drop out of school early, are not likely to have such jobs. It's more likely that they'll have a miserable or lousy job that they hate.

Less important than the fact that they'll earn less money than the more educated person, is the fact that they hate what they're doing. And this is a bad way to spend one's life. It's much better to get education and training. Then, it's more likely that the person will be able to earn money doing something that he or she enjoys.

Therefore, my answer to this question is that there is no one best job. My answer then is that it's any job that the person enjoys doing. And there are hundreds of different kinds of jobs different people can enjoy doing. What kind of thing would you like to do when you grow up?

My hope is that my response will contribute to the child's appreciation that what he or she is doing now is going to play an important role in his or her future life. In addition, my hope is that the response will contribute (admittedly in a small way) to the child's motivation to think about the future and be willing to spend some effort toward gaining greater knowledge and skill.

> *Question:* What do you think is the most beautiful thing in the whole world?
> *Response:* Watching a beautiful sunset, whether it be from the top of a mountain or at the seashore, is to me one of the most beautiful things in the world. It makes me feel relaxed and happy to be alive. Sometimes I read poetry while watching such a scene. And the poems also make me think of beautiful things that help me appreciate how beautiful the world can be if one is willing to stop and enjoy them. Sometimes I will bring along a tape recorder and play a tape of some calm, beautiful music while watching such a scene. This is indeed one of the great pleasures of life.

Healthy pleasure is well viewed to be a general antidote for just about all forms of psychogenic psychopathology. When one is enjoying oneself in a healthy way, one is at that time not suffering the psychological pain attendant to psychiatric disorder. In addition, the pleasurable feelings are esteem enhancing. Because feelings of low self-worth are often involved in bringing about psychopathological reactions, any experience that can enhance self-worth can be salutary. And aesthetic pleasures are in this category. Accordingly, anything a therapist can do to enhance a child's appreciation of beauty is likely to be therapeutic.

> *Question:* What do you think about a boy who sometimes plays with his penis when he's alone?
> *Response:* I think that it's perfectly normal—as long as he does it when he's alone. Of course, there would be something

wrong with him if he did that in the open, in public; but as a private thing I think it's normal. In fact most teenage boys do it a lot, and many kids play with their penises when they're younger as well. There are some kids, however, who think that playing with their penises is a terrible thing. They think it's sinful, or wrong, or dirty. I completely disagree. Those kids are the ones that have a problem, and not the ones who play with their penises once in a while in private. What's your opinion on what I've just said?

Question: What do you think about a girl who sometimes plays with or rubs her vagina when she's alone?
Response: I think it's perfectly normal for her to do that when she's alone. Of course, that's not the kind of thing that one would generally do in front of other people. It's a private matter. What do you think?

For the sexually inhibited child these responses enable the examiner to approach a forbidden subject in a noncontrived way. Discussing the subject is in itself therapeutic in that it provides the child with the living experience that such discussions do not result in dire consequences. That which is unmentionable is far more anxiety and guilt provoking than that which is spoken about. The child whose parents never speak about sex will generally become far more inhibited than the parent who preaches often about the sins and evils of sex. Of course, the latter approach is likely to produce guilt as well, but probably not as much as the guilt produced by the situation in which the subject is unmentionable. For the child who is excessively guilty, I might add:

There are some children who think that touching themselves is a terrible sin or crime. They think it's the worst thing a person can do. This is a strange idea because touching oneself is perfectly natural and normal. It only becomes a problem if the person does it most of the time and then doesn't do other things, or if the person feels very bad or guilty about it. Feeling that it's a terrible sin or crime is then the problem, not doing it. What are your opinions on this subject?

Question: A boy's friend leaves him to play with someone else. How does the boy feel? Why did the friend leave?

Response: Bob invited Frank to play with him at his house. But Bob was selfish. He wouldn't share. Frank was his guest. He should have known that it's important to be courteous to a guest. He should have known that it's important to be nice to a guest. Anyway, Frank wanted to share Bob's toys with him and Bob refused. Also, Bob always wanted to decide which game they would play. Finally, Frank said that if Bob wouldn't play nicely with him and share, he would leave and go play with someone else. Bob's mother overheard the boys talking and took Bob aside into another room. She didn't want to embarrass Bob in front of his friend Frank. She told Bob, while they were alone, that he wasn't playing nicely with his friend and that he wasn't thinking about how his friend felt. She told him that Frank would go home soon if he didn't start to share with him. She told him that Frank had another good friend, George, whom he could go play with if he wanted. What do you think happened? Do you think that Bob listened to his mother? Do you think that his mother was right or wrong in this case?

Some children have great difficulty sharing. They have difficulty putting themselves in the position of their peers and fail to recognize that the child with whom they refuse to share is likely to be alienated. Some of these children have neurologically based learning disabilities that interfere, on a cognitive level, with their capacity to project themselves into other people's positions. Other children may have reached the developmental level where this is possible, but have psychological problems in the realm of egocentricism and narcissism that interfere with healthy functioning in this realm. For children in both of these categories, certain Talking, Feeling, and Doing Cards can be useful.

Question: Make believe you're reading a magazine showing pictures of nude ladies. What do you think about such magazines?

Response: Boy, there really are some exciting looking women in some of those magazines. I think they're great to look at once in a while. They have some of the most beautiful and luscious women in those magazines. Some people are ashamed to admit that they're interested in looking at those women. I don't think there's anything wrong, bad, or sinful to look at those pictures. I don't agree with those people. I think it's natural and healthy. It's only a problem if the person doesn't want to have anything to do with real people and wants to spend a lot of time looking at those pictures. What is your opinion on the subject?

This response is the one I provide for boys who are uncomfortable expressing sexual interest. Obviously, I attempt here to convey some of the excitement that most boys and men have when looking at pictures of nude women. I also attempt to lessen any guilt the child may have over such interest. My hope is that the child will be receptive to my opinions on the subject and will identify with my attitude.

Question: A boy was laughing. What was he laughing about?
Response: This boy was not only laughing, but he was cheering. He was just jumping up and down with joy. He had just gotten his eighth-grade report card and learned that he had gotten into three honors classes in the ninth grade. He was very happy. He had worked very hard in order to make the honor classes and had hoped that he might make one or two of them. But he didn't think that he would get into all three. He was very proud of himself and couldn't wait to get home and tell his parents. His teacher had written a note on the report card that said, "Robert, I am very proud of you. Good luck in high school." He was also very happy because he knew that, when he applied to college, having been in three honors classes would look very good on his record and this would help him get into the college of his choice. And so he ran home from school laughing and singing all the way. It was really a happy day for him. What do you think about what I said about that boy?

This is the kind of response I provide for children with low academic motivation. My purpose here is to enhance their school interest by demonstrating the joys and ego-enhancement that are the potential benefits of such commitment to the educational process.

Question: Tell about an act of kindness.
Response: A good example of an act of kindness would be visiting someone who is sick in the hospital and giving up a fun thing that you'd prefer to do. Let's say that a boy in a class was in an automobile accident, injured his leg, and had to be in the hospital for six weeks. Even though his mother and father visited him often, he was still very lonely. His really good friends were those

who were willing to give up fun things like playing baseball, or watching their favorite television programs, or just hanging around and relaxing, and instead went to visit him in the hospital. He was very grateful when they came to see him. And they felt good about themselves for their sacrifices. Visiting the friend was an act of kindness. Do you know what the word *sacrifice* means?

This is the type of response I provide self-centered children, those who have difficulty putting themselves in the position of others. In the ensuing discussion, I would try to help the egocentric child appreciate the feelings of loneliness suffered by the hospitalized child. I would also try to engender in the child the feelings of self-satisfaction and enhanced self-worth that comes from benevolent acts.

Question: Was there ever a person whom you wished to be dead? If so, who was that person? Why did you wish that person to be dead?

Response: During my childhood and early teens there lived a man in Germany named Adolf Hitler. He was a madman. He was insane. He was the leader of Germany during World War II and was personally responsible for the deaths of millions of people. He was one of the greatest criminals in the history of the world. He used to murder people whose opinions, skin color, or religion differed from his. He not only had them shot but he gassed them to death and burned their bodies in ovens. Millions of people died this way. When I was a boy, I used to wish that he would die. I wished that someone would kill him. I hoped then that maybe all this crazy murdering would stop. To this day, I and many other people in the world feel sorry for the millions of people he killed and all the millions of friends and relatives that also suffered because of his murders. Even though the war ended in 1945, there are still millions of people who are suffering because of the terrible things Adolf Hitler did. These are the people who were put in his prisons and concentration camps and escaped, or were fortunate enough not to have been killed. And these are also the people who are the friends, relatives, children, and grandchildren of those who died there. He was a very cruel man. I really hated him, and I often wished he would die or be killed. Finally, in 1945, he committed suicide. If he hadn't killed himself he would have been captured and executed for his terrible crimes.

This question can be particularly useful for children with antisocial behavior disorders who have little sensitivity to the pains they inflict on others. My hope here, by elaborating on Hitler's atrocities, is to engender in the antisocial child a feeling for the pain that criminal behavior causes others. It is important for the reader to appreciate that when responding to Feeling Cards the therapist does well to try to dramatize as much as possible his or her responses in order to bring about a kind of resonating emotional response in the patient. To engender these feelings in the child who is out of touch with them or who has not experienced them to a significant degree is one of the goals of treatment.

Question: Say something funny.
Response: Okay, I heard a funny riddle. "What's invisible and smells like worms?" (Generally, the patient does not know the answer. In such cases I will give it.) "A bird's fart!" (This joke generally goes over quite well, except among the most inhibited. Incidentally, it is a statement of the low levels to which the child's therapist may have to stoop in the service of his or her calling.)

The joke may he useful for the child with sexual-inhibition problems as an icebreaker. Sexual and scatological issues often get fused and inhibitions in the sexual area often extend to this area as well. By telling the joke the therapist serves as a model for what I consider to be healthy, normal sublimation. It may contribute to the lessening of sexual inhibitions. The child may reason: "If it's okay for him to talk this way, it's okay for me." In addition, the introduction of some levity into the therapeutic experience is also useful. It lightens the session, makes the therapist more human, and increases the likelihood that the child will become involved. It is part of the seductive process, so important in child therapy.

Doing Cards
The Doing Cards involve physical activity in association with the child's responses. These cards, more than the Talking Cards and Feeling Cards, involve a fun element, and this serves to make the session more enjoyable. My purpose here is to counterbalance some of the less pleasurable aspects of treatment that are likely to reduce the motivation for treatment of even the most highly involved child. Some of the Doing Cards involve modeling and this can also be therapeutic.

There are some therapists who consider role modeling and physical activity to be a central part of therapeutic process. I am not in agreement. Often, there is an artificial quality to role modeling, and this makes it less therapeutic than actual experiences or imitations that are spontaneously derived from a situation. Accordingly, I most often use the Doing Cards as a point of departure for direct discussion. My hope is that in the course of such discussions the child will have emotional reactions and experiences that will contribute directly to therapeutic change.

Question: What is the most selfish thing you ever did? Make believe you're doing that thing now.

Response: Well, the most selfish thing I ever did was a long time ago—it was right after the Second World War—it was in 1946 or 1947. I was looking for a way to earn money to pay for my education in college. It was very hard to get jobs after the Second World War. All the war factories were closing down, and people were fired from their jobs. They didn't need them anymore to make tanks, and guns, and things like that. And all the soldiers were getting out of the Army. And everybody was also getting out of the Navy and Air Force. There were millions of people trying to get jobs. And I finally got a job selling magazines to the wives and mothers of the soldiers who had been in the war. I told the people how important it was to buy the magazine because it would help the veterans, the people who fought in the war. After working a few days I found out that this magazine was kind of phony. A lot of people weren't getting the subscriptions they were paying for, and I felt very guilty about what I was doing.

I was preying on people's sympathy. I was saying that this was very important for the parents and the wives of the soldiers who were killed or who had fought in the war, and it was a kind of phony organization. I didn't realize it when I got the job, but after I started working I realized it, and I soon quit. But I felt very guilty, and I think I worked a day or two too much because I needed the money. Do you know what I mean? I should have quit as soon as I realized it. There was so much money to be made, and I needed the money so badly that I stuck with it awhile, but then my guilt overcame me and I quit the job. It was a selfish thing to do. Sometimes when people are hungry, when they need money a lot, then they do things that they would never want to do. I was ashamed of myself when I did that. Do you want to say anything about that?

As mentioned, *The Talking, Feeling, & Doing Game* provides therapists with the opportunity to reveal their own deficiencies in a noncontrived and natural way. This lessens the likelihood that the patient will idealize the therapist. It makes the therapist a more real human being. It lessens the likelihood of the development of the unfavorable comparison in which the patient views the therapist as perfect, and views him- or herself as a bundle of psychopathology. The particular incident was chosen because it demonstrates how guilt can be useful in preventing a person from engaging in antisocial behavior. This is the kind of response I provide for patients who do not have enough guilt over their antisocial behavior. My hope is that the vignette will contribute to the development of a slightly stronger superego.

Question: You're standing in line to buy something and a child pushes in front of you. Show what you would do.
Response: Let's say I'm a kid and I'm standing here in line and some kid pushes himself in front of me. A part of me might want to push him away and even hit him. But another part of me knows that that wouldn't be such a good idea. I might get into trouble or he might hit me back and then I might get hurt. So the first thing I would do would be to say something to him like, "Hey, I was here first. Why don't you go back to the end of the line and wait your turn like everybody else." If that didn't work I might threaten to call some person like a parent, teacher, or someone else around who is in charge. But sometimes there are no other people around to call, so I might just say that it's not worth all the trouble and that all it's causing me is the loss of another minute or two. If, however, the person starts to push me, then I might fight back. But that would be the last thing I would try. Some people might think that I'm "chicken" for not hitting him in the first place. I don't agree with them. I think that hitting should be the last thing you should do, not the first. I don't think that people who hit first are particularly wise or brave; rather, I think they're kind of stupid.

This is the type of response I am likely to provide the antisocial child. As is obvious here, I am trying to educate the antisocial child to the more civilized option that individuals have learned to use in order to bring about a more relaxed and less threatening society. These options may not have been part of the antisocial child's repertoire. Whatever the underlying factors there are in such a child's antisocial behavior (and these, of course, must be dealt with in the treatment), such education is also a part of the therapy.

Question: You're standing in line to buy something and an adult pushes in front of you. Show what you would do.

Response: I would tell the person that this is my place in line and that I would appreciate his going to the back of the line and waiting his turn like everyone else. If the person looks like he's crazy, someone who might do dangerous things, I wouldn't make a big deal out of it. There are times when it's smart not to speak up and fight for your rights, but most often it's wise to do so. The important thing is to size up the situation and get a lot more information before acting. Otherwise, you may find yourself in a lot of trouble.

Obviously, the response to this card should be different from the previous one. It is unreasonable and even injudicious to encourage a child to respond in the same manner to both a child and an adult who pushes him- or herself in line in front of a child. My main point here is that there are times when it is appropriate to assert oneself and other times when it is judicious not to.

Question: Make believe you're doing something that makes you feel good about yourself. Why does that thing make you feel so good?

Response: As you know, I like to write books. I have already given you one of the children's books that I've written. As I'm sure you can appreciate, writing a book takes a lot of work. It's a very hard job. Sometimes I may work over many years on one single book. However, when I finally finish, I really feel good about myself. I feel that I've accomplished a lot. Although I may be very tired over all the work I've put in to it, I'm very proud of what I've done. And then, when the final printed book comes out, that really makes me feel good about myself. I have what is called a "sense of achievement." Do you know what I mean when I say "sense of achievement"?

I use this response for children who are academic underachievers. After clarification of the meaning of the term "sense of achievement," I might ask the child to tell me things that he or she has done that have provided him or her with similar feelings of accomplishment. My hope here, obviously, is to provide the child with some appreciation of the ego-enhancing feelings that one can enjoy after diligent commitment to a task.

Question: Make believe you're smoking a cigarette. What do you think about people who smoke?

Response: First of all, I want to say that I have not once in my whole life ever smoked a single cigarette. I remember when I was about 14 years old I went to a party. Some of the kids there were smoking. One kid gave me a cigarette. I really didn't want to smoke it, but I felt that if I didn't take it, all the kids would think that I was "chicken." So I took the cigarette, and I lit it, and I took one puff. I then gasped and started to choke. It really made me sick to my stomach. I then put out the cigarette and said to the guy that had given it to me, "I can't really believe that anybody can like this sh-t. The only reason that you guys are smoking is because you want to look like big shots. It must take a long time to get used to smoking this filthy weed." And that was the first and last time I smoked a cigarette in my whole life.

Now, if I'm to get a chip, I've got to make believe that I'm smoking a cigarette. Okay, here I go! (imitates cigarette smoking) Egh, is this terrible. (starts coughing heavily) This is disgusting. This is nauseating. (more heavy coughing) Egh, I can't stand this any longer. I hope I've done enough of this to get my chip. It's a heavy price to pay for a chip. People who smoke cigarettes must be crazy. Not only is it a disgusting habit but it can give you all kinds of terrible diseases like lung cancer, heart disease, and diseases of your blood vessels.

I think kids start to smoke because they want to act like big shots. It makes them feel like adults. Then they get hooked on cigarettes and they can't stop. When they get older and begin to appreciate how really terrible it is, they still can't stop. It's a heavy price to pay for looking like a big shot. Also, it's no great stunt to smoke. If you really want to feel big you have to do things, over a period, that make you feel good about yourself. Thinking that you're going to feel good about yourself by putting a cigarette in your mouth is simpleminded. It just doesn't work that way. What do you think about what I've just said?

The response, of course, touches on the most common pathological mechanisms that contribute to children's beginning to smoke. It is quite likely that the antisocial child subscribes strongly and somewhat blindly to these sick values. Not having basic competence in meaningful areas, he or she is likely to embrace quick and superficial methods for enhancing self-esteem. Of course, the utilization of smoking in this regard is strongly promulgated by the advertising of the cigarette industry. Cigarette manufacturers know well that they will increase sales if they associate cigarette smoking with sexual attractiveness and adult "maturity." My response also directs itself to the peer pressure element in the initiation of cigarette smoking. As mentioned, I do not create stories when responding to the cards in *The Talking, Feeling, & Doing Game*. The experiences I relate in my response actually occurred and my reasons for not smoking are those that I genuinely hold.

Question: Make believe someone grabbed something of yours. Show what you would do.

Response: I would first try to use talk before using action. I'd tell the child to give it back and threaten to grab it back if he or she doesn't return it. If the child was my size or a little taller, I'd try to grab it back, providing it wasn't something that could break. If it was something that could break and/or the person was bigger, I would threaten to call the teacher or my parent(s) if it wasn't given back immediately. I might ask a friend or two to help me get it back. But I wouldn't just stand there, say nothing, and let the person get away with it.

Question: Make believe you've just met a bully. Show what you would do.

Response: If he were my size I'd let him know that I'm not going to let him get away with taking advantage of me. Even though I might be a little scared, I would fight back. If he called me names, I would call him names back. And if he threatened to hit me, I would threaten to report him to the teacher or to his parents. Or, I would tell him that I'll hit him back twice as hard.

Most bullies are usually frightened kids, and they usually try to pick on kids who won't fight back. The best way to get rid of a bully is to fight back. If you keep letting him take advantage of you then he'll keep picking on you.

These cards are especially useful for children with self-assertion problems. My response provides advice regarding the sequence of steps one does well to follow when one's rights are being infringed upon.

Question: Make believe you're speaking to someone on the phone. Whom are you speaking to? What are you saying?

Response: I'm speaking to the principal of a school. He's asking me whether I think that a certain girl, let's call her Ruthie, should be promoted. He's telling me that she got Fs in most of her subjects, but that he fears that she'll feel very bad about herself if she's left back, that is, if she has to repeat the grade. He fears that she'll be very embarrassed and humiliated. He's telling me that if she has to repeat the grade, she'll be the oldest one in the class and bigger than anybody else in the class and this will make her feel very bad about herself. He's calling to ask my advice regarding what he should do.

Now this is the answer I'm going to give him. "I think that she should be left back. She really isn't ready to go on to the next grade. She's failed most of her subjects. She'll feel embarrassed if you leave her back. But if you promote her, she'll feel embarrassed in her new class anyway. If you leave her back, she'll be ashamed for a few days or for a few weeks and then she'll probably get over it and get used to her new class. If you promote her, she'll not only be embarrassed all year but will continue to be ashamed as long as you continue to promote her. In addition, she might end up a dropout, because she'll get so far behind that she'll never be able to catch up. It's a choice between feeling bad now for a short period or feeling bad for many years, or possibly even the rest of her life. That's why I'm telling you that I think she should be left back." What do you think about the advice I gave the principal?

There are schools that give the parents veto power over a decision to have a child repeat a grade. This is a terrible disservice to the child. The reasons for my saying this are basically presented to the child in the aforementioned response. The advantage of retention far outweigh its disadvantages, the embarrassed feelings the child suffers notwithstanding. My main purpose here, of course, is to help the child appreciate that there can be consequences if one does not fulfill one's academic obligations, and one of these consequences is being required to repeat the grade and suffer the attendant embarrassment associated with such repeat. In addition, I point out that even if the child does not repeat the grade, there will be humiliations associated with continually being in a classroom where he or she is behind the other students.

Question: Make believe you're playing a dirty trick on someone.

Response: I don't think I'm going to get a chip on this one. I don't like playing dirty tricks on people. I remember when I was a kid how badly I felt if someone played a dirty trick on me. And I used to feel sorry for those kids who had dirty tricks played on them. I remember once a kid in my class used to like stealing other children's books and hiding them. He thought it was very funny. Actually, it was cruel. Then the kid whose book was stolen would go home and not have a book to do his or her homework. He or she would have to go to a lot of trouble to borrow someone else's book or go over to someone else's house. Sometimes the kid wouldn't even find the book and then he or she would have to pay for it.

Sometimes, dirty tricks can be dangerous. I remember once a boy in my class thought it was funny to trip another kid in the classroom. Well, the boy that was tripped fell down and banged his head against the desk. He hit his head right above his eye and his eye almost got knocked out. He got a big cut over his eye and it was bleeding terribly. I really felt sorry for him and everybody was angry at the kid who tripped him. That kid, of course, got into a lot of trouble. The kid who got hurt had to go to the hospital for stitches and for treatment of his eye. His parents threatened to sue the parents of the kid who tripped their son. However, the parents of the boy who tripped the kid agreed to pay for all the medical expenses. So at least they both didn't have to pay for lawyers. These are just some of the reasons why I don't like playing dirty tricks on anyone. How do you feel about playing dirty tricks on people?"

In the attempt to strengthen the antisocial child's superego I elaborate upon the pains that can be caused by those who hurt others.

Children with superego deficiencies, who act out hostilely, generally do not think about the discomforts and pains they cause others.

EXAMPLES OF THERAPIST-PATIENT INTERCHANGES

The examples given above are sample responses to individual cards that I provide when playing *The Talking, Feeling, & Doing Game*. Patient responses have thus far not been provided. In this section I present therapist-patient interchanges in which both the patients' and my own responses are provided. In addition, I comment throughout the transcripts on many aspects of the therapy that emerge from the interchanges.

The Case of Frank: Dealing with a Psychopathic Partner

Frank, an eleven-year-old boy, was brought to treatment because of moderately severe antisocial behavior. He was disruptive in the classroom, a constant thorn in his teacher's side, and had little appreciation of the fact that he was interfering with the education of his classmates. His general sensitivity to the feelings of those who suffered because of his psychopathic tendencies was practically nil. In addition, he suffered with a severe impulsivity problem. He basically lived by the dictum: "I'll do what I want when I want it." Frank's parents were divorced. However, five years after the separation they were still litigating over a wide variety of issues. Often, Frank was embroiled in the divorce conflicts. Some of his psychopathic behavior was derived from identification with his warring parents, both of whom had little sympathy or respect for one another's feelings. In addition, the anger he felt toward them was being displaced onto school authorities. During his third month of treatment, we had this interchange:

> *Therapist:* My question says, "If you could live your life all over again, what things would you do differently?" Well, one thing I would do differently was I made a big mistake about 12 or 13 years ago. You see this building we are in right now?
>
> *Patient:* Uh huh.
>
> *Therapist:* I like this office very much. This is an office building that my wife and I built with a third person. That person became our partner.
>
> *Patient:* You built this whole building?
>
> *Therapist:* Not myself. An architect built it, but I worked

with the architect in planning it, and told him exactly what I wanted in the various parts of the building. I am not an architect and I don't know how to build a building, but I can tell him what kinds of things I want.

Patient: Uh huh.

Therapist: And he was the one who actually designed it, and, of course, builders then came and built it.

Patient: What was the mistake?

Therapist: The mistake was that the man I became a partner with was someone I hardly knew. I knew him a little bit. He was a psychiatrist, and doing that was a big mistake because he turned out to be the kind of person who had many qualities that I didn't like. He wasn't honest. He didn't want to do his share of the work. And he didn't pay his money when it was due. He wasn't a true partner. He didn't think he had to keep promises that he had made or do the things he promised to do in contracts he had signed. And because we had signed papers and because we were locked in here together in the ownership of this building, I couldn't get rid of him so easily. It was a very messy situation.

And I was partly to blame—not that I was doing anything wrong, in my opinion, and nobody was critical of me—because I didn't get to know the man better before I became his partner. I didn't think in advance of the consequences of what I was doing, and I acted so impulsively and quickly. Had I taken time and gotten to know the person better, I might have been able to avoid the trouble. I might have learned things about his personality which would have warned me that this would be a bad idea, that he was a bad-news person.

And for seven years he was my partner, and it was a lot of grief until finally I gave him—it was worth it—and I gave him a lot of money and bought him out. We bought him out, and he left the building, and I was glad to get rid of him. Then my wife and I sold the building afterwards to other people and I am a tenant here now. But that is not the point. The main point is that I shouldn't have acted so quickly. I should have thought in advance about the consequences of what I was doing.

Patient: You were partners?

Therapist: Yeah, right. So then when the guy left, my wife and I were 50/50 partners. What's my main point in saying this? What's the main point I am trying...

Patient: Think before you act.

Therapist: Right! Think before you act. And the second point is: If a person is dishonest, if a person doesn't pull his share of the load, then he's disliked by everybody around him. My wife and I had no respect for him. We couldn't stand him, but we were kind of locked in for a number of years until it became possible for us to get up enough money to buy him out and get rid of him. And so that's the other...

Patient: You got all that money back?

Therapist: Well, we sold the building to another person, and now we just rent it like any other tenant. But, no. It was a loss of money to buy him out, but it was worth it to us. Although it was painful to give him all that money, it was so bad being with him that it was worth it to buy him out. Understand?

Patient: Yeah.

Therapist: He was such an obnoxious individual, and people who do those things really turn others off and produce a lot of resentment in others. Do you want to say anything else about that?

Patient: Yes.

Therapist: Yeah. What do you want to say?

Patient: You made a mistake to take him as a partner in the first place, but you got rid of him so that's really what counts.

Therapist: Right. Let me tell you an interesting story. You've heard of Japan, haven't you?

Patient: Yeah.

Therapist: Well, let me tell you something.

Patient: Okay. (mumbles)...

Therapist: Pardon me?

Patient: The Wall of China.

Therapist: Well, Japan is not China. They are two different countries. They are both in Asia.

Patient: Oh, yeah. That's right.

Therapist: Japan is closer to us, but it's off the coast of Asia. It's part of Asia. Anyway, what I want to tell you is that different people have different customs, and the Japanese are very good businessmen, and Americans...

Patient: They are?

Therapist: Oh, yeah. Very good businessmen.

Patient: Wow!

Therapist: Yeah. They're one of the richest countries in the world. Even though they are small. They are very good business-men, very smart. Anyway, uh, years ago when Americans first went to Japan, American businessmen did not know their customs, and they wanted to make business arrangements with them. They sent some Americans to Japan to talk to the Japanese about busi-ness, and the men would come there and they'd say to the Japanese, "Okay, let's start talking about this deal. We want to buy. You want to sell."

And they would say, "No. Let's hold off for a while." And they'd say, "Let's go to dinner." They would go out to dinner, and the next day the Japanese would say, "How about playing golf tomorrow?" And they'd play golf. And then the third day they'd say, "Oh, let's, go sailing, or let's go boating, or let's go to some restaurants."

And the people back in the United States would call, or wire, or write to their friends, you know, their associates and say: "Hey, what are you guys doing over there? Why don't you start signing a contract there and working out business arrangements?"

And the Americans in Japan would say, "We can't talk to them about business. All they want to do is sit around and talk, relax, recreation, golf, and they won't talk business yet. They keep holding off." Anyway, this would go on for five, six, seven days, and the Americans would get upset. And finally one day the Japanese would sit down and they'd say one of two things. Are you listening?

Patient: Yeah.

Therapist: They would say, "Okay, let's talk business," and they would very quickly negotiate and very quickly come to a decision. Or they would say, "We're very sorry. We've decided we don't want to sell you anything, or buy anything from you, or work out some business arrangement." And they would very politely say, "Goodbye."

Now the Americans couldn't understand that kind of a prac-tice, this custom. And if they did make an arrangement, they'd have a very small contract. They wouldn't have a lot of lawyers, and it would only be a very small contract. In the United States contracts might be almost a book or two with many pages. Do you know why the Japanese did that?

Patient: Why?

Therapist: They felt that the most important thing in a business relationship is the people that you're working with—whether they are honest, whether they are friendly, whether they're nice, whether you can trust them. They felt if they were trustworthy, then they would enter into a business arrangement. And if they didn't like...

Patient: Why, weren't the Americans trustworthy?

Therapist: Sometimes they were. Sometimes they weren't. Some Japanese businessmen are trustworthy and some aren't. But you don't want to have a contract or a business arrangement with someone you don't like. Someone you can't trust. Someone who lies. Someone who is going to steal. You know?

Patient: Yeah.

Therapist: So they decided that since these people came from the United States, and they were in Japan, it was so far away, it was the other side of the earth, they figured let's get to know the person better, and let's see if we like him, if we can trust him, and if we can, then we will sign, and if we can't, we'll say goodbye. What's my main point?

Patient: American don't trust. I mean to trust people.

Therapist: Good try. You're on the right track.

Patient: To, uh, work with the people you know and trust.

Therapist: Yeah. And if you don't know them too well?

Patient: Forget it.

Therapist: Yeah. Or wait. Don't forget it so quickly. Give them a chance, you know. Get to know them well. See if they are trustworthy and honest, and if they are, then you become friendly with them and then you can become friends with them and then you can become business partners or something like that. Okay. Anything else you want to say?

Patient: No.

As the reader can see, I got a lot of mileage out of this card. I first focused on my own impulsivity in making what soon turned out to be an ill-conceived partnership arrangement. My purpose here was to demonstrate to the patient the untoward consequences of impulsivity. My hope was that it would help him become less impulsive. In addition, in the process I was revealing a deficit, and I have discussed the therapeutic benefits to be derived from such revelations. Then, I pointed out how psychopathic individuals invite the ridicule and scorn of those about them. My hope here was that the patient would consider this repercussion with regard to his own antisocial behavior. As mentioned, I do not consider it necessary to switch to a discussion of the patient's behavior in such circumstances. I believe that getting the principle across may be all that is necessary.

The patient was interested in the story and so I decided to get even further mileage out of the card. I then discussed the situation that American businessmen faced when they first started doing business with the Japanese after World War II. My main point, of course, was that honorable and ethical individuals are more likely to be successful in life than those who are dishonorable. Had this message been given in a straightforward manner, it is not likely that it would have "sunk in." However, presented in the format of the Japanese businessmen, the message was more likely to be palatable.

The patient was absorbed in what I was saying. I believe that he got the general gist of my message. I believe that relating stories and experiences in this way is one of the most efficacious mediums for transmitting important therapeutic messages. As mentioned, it is an ancient tradition and the therapist does well to utilize it whenever possible.

> *Therapist:* Okay. Okay. What does your card say?
>
> *Patient:* "Make believe you are giving a gift to someone. What's that gift?" Here. (Patient makes believe he is giving the therapist a gift.)
>
> *Therapist:* Uh huh. Thank you. What is the gift?
>
> *Patient:* It's a thing you put on your desk, and it says, it's your name, Dr. Richard A. Gardner, M.D.
>
> *Therapist:* What is it? Something for my desk? You mean a desk sign? It gives my name? Okay. Thank you very much. That's very nice. I'll put this on my desk, and when I see it, it will make me think of you. You know? It's not just something that's there. When you give someone a gift, and they like you, your gift will remind them of you when they look at the gift and it will give them a nice feeling. It makes you feel good about the person who gave you the gift. And it makes the giver feel good when he knows that the person who got the gift thinks of him nicely and likes him. Okay. Now your chip. You take a chip.

One of Frank's problems was that he did not put himself into the position of those who were victims of his antisocial behavior. My hope here was to help him appreciate other people's feelings via a description of my reactions to a benevolent act on his part. In addition, I hoped that the interchange might contribute to the strengthening of our relationship. It was a description of pleasant and benevolent feelings that can transpire between people, and my hope was that it would contribute to such benevolent feelings between him and me. My basic feeling at the end of the session was that it did contribute to a strengthening of our relationship.

The Case of Andy: The Boy with Hypospadias

Andy entered treatment at the age of nine when he was in the fourth grade. The presenting problems were temper outbursts in school, low frustration tolerance, and a significant degree of self-denigration. Andy was an extremely bright boy who was so advanced in mathematics that he was receiving special tutoring at the ninth-and tenth-grade levels in that subject. In spite of his advanced mathematical competence, he was getting B and C grades because of his temper outbursts in the classroom.

Andy was born with hypospadias, a congenital abnormality in which the urethral opening is to be found at some point along the ventral aspect of the penis, rather than at the tip of the glans. During the first five years of his life he was hospitalized on four occasions for operative repair of his congenital defect. During these hospitalizations it was necessary to tie his hands to the bed rails in order to prevent him from tampering with the dressings. Accordingly, Andy not only suffered with the physical pain associated with his operations but with the psychological stress related to his lack of understanding as to why he was suffering.

Andy had an identical twin brother who was completely normal physically. Furthermore, the brother was also extremely bright and the two of them took their math tutoring together. The brother, however, did not exhibit any of the psychological problems with which Andy suffered and was getting extremely high grades. Nor did he exhibit the self-denigration problem and feelings of low self-worth. The boys had a younger sister who did not manifest any difficulties either. The parents had an excellent relationship both between themselves and among the members of the family. I believed that Andy's symptoms were related to the traumas he had experienced in the first four years of his life and that had he been born physically normal he would not have needed psychiatric attention.

Andy's therapy went quite well. From the outset, we had an excellent relationship. I was immediately attracted to him, mainly because of the warmth of his personality and his strong desire to be helped. His high intelligence, I believe, also contributed to his therapeutic progress. There are some who hold that brighter people do not necessarily do better in treatment. Although it is certainly true that there are many highly intelligent people who are also so sick that they cannot profit significantly from therapy, I believe it is also true that the more intelligent the person is the greater the likelihood he or she will be successful in whatever endeavor the person chooses to be involved in—and therapy is one such endeavor. In the course of his treatment, Andy learned to handle his anger more effectively and to deal with issues very early, before he suffered significant frustrations and pent-up anger—that would ultimately result in temper outbursts. He learned to become more respectful of himself, and this was associated with a reduction in his tendency to berate himself for the most minor errors. The vignettes from *The Talking, Feeling, & Doing Game* that are presented here are from a session that occurred in his sixth month of treatment, about a month before it terminated.

Therapist: Good afternoon, boys and girls, ladies and gentlemen. Today is Tuesday, December 2nd, 1980, and I'm happy to welcome you once again to Dr. Gardner's program. Our guest and I are playing *The Talking, Feeling, & Doing Game* and we'll be back with you when it's time for someone to answer a question. Okay, you go.

Patient: My card says, "A girl was listening through the keyhole of the closed door of her parents' bedroom. They didn't know she was listening. What did she hear them saying?" Now she heard them saying that she, she had a temper tantrum, and they were talking about how to punish her.

Therapist: What were they saying exactly?

Patient: The father said to cut off her allowance for a week, but her mother said not to go to the skating rink Saturday.

Therapist: Uh huh. So it was decided...

Patient: It was decided, uh, to cut off her allowance for a week.

Therapist: Uh huh. Did that help? Did that help her to remember not to have temper tantrums?

Patient: Yes.

Therapist: But the big question is what did she have a temper tantrum about?

Patient: Well, she, she wanted to ride her two-wheeler, but the fender was all broken up. And her father said, "Yeah, we'll have to fix it, but it will be at least a week."

Therapist: Oh, so she was...

Patient: She wanted, she wanted to ride it badly.

Therapist: So she was upset that she had to wait so long. Was that it?

Patient: Yes.

Therapist: What could she have done instead of having a temper tantrum?

Patient: She could just have accepted it.

Therapist: Okay. Any other things she could have done? I think that's part of it.

Patient: ...(big sighs)...I don't know.

Therapist: Anything else? There she was...She wanted to go bike riding...and her bike was broken...and it would take her father a week to fix it...What else could she have done?

Patient: She could...she could have just forgot about it.

Therapist: Well, that's also accepting it. Another thing she could have done is to think about another way she could have some fun. For instance, maybe she could borrow a bicycle from somebody.

Patient: Yeah.

Therapist: Like a neighbor. Or if she had a brother or sister. Then let's say she couldn't borrow a bike from somebody. What else could she have done?

Patient: She could have roller-skated.

Therapist: Roller-skated. She could have done something else that would be fun. Right? Okay, you get a chip for that. Okay. Now I go.

When answering the card about what the girl heard through the closed door of her parent's bedroom, Andy immediately spoke about his temper tantrums. This is an excellent example of how the cards in *The Talking, Feeling, & Doing Game* will often result in the child's focusing on the basic symptoms for which he or she has come to therapy. The parents are arguing about how to punish a girl who had a temper tantrum. The father suggests cutting off her allowance and the mother prefers that she not be allowed to go to the skating rink the following Saturday. The parents are basically utilizing behavior therapy techniques, that is, negative reinforcement. Of course, there is a place for such disciplinary measures, but they do not get to the heart of the problem. As a therapist, I want to go beyond that and not merely foster a method of dealing with temper tantrums that involves suppression and conscious control of them because of the threat of negative reinforcement.

Accordingly, as a point of departure for more extensive psychotherapeutic inquiry, I asked the patient what the girl had the temper tantrums *about*. In this way, I hoped to obtain a specific example which would serve as a point of departure for a discussion into the causes of the temper tantrum. As mentioned earlier in this book, the therapist does well to use concrete examples rather than abstractions when discussing therapeutic issues. In response, the patient gave as an example the girl's broken bike. She was not only upset that she could not ride it but that it would take a week to have it fixed. At this point, I ask the patient, "What could she have done instead of having a temper tantrum?" In this way I introduce an alternative mode of adaptation to the problem. As mentioned, one of the purposes of therapy is to expand the patient's repertoire of options available for utilization when dealing with life's problems. A broken bicycle presents most children with one of the basic problems of life. In this case, the girl was dealing with it with a temper tantrum, clearly an inappropriate and maladaptive way of responding to the situation. Rather than suggesting immediately to the patient what I would consider to be a preferable mode of adaptation, I tried to elicit his contribution to the solution of this problem.

His response was "She could just have accepted it." This is certainly a mode of adaptation that can be useful. However, I would not consider it high on the hierarchy of solutions. Rather, I would only recommend such resignation after all others have failed. There are certainly times in life when we have to resign ourselves to the fact that there is nothing we can do about a problem. However, I do not generally recommend that solution as the first. Rather, it should be the last, after all others have failed. Accordingly, I asked the patient if there were any other things she could have done. The patient had difficulty coming up with another solution. Accordingly, in order to facilitate his coming up with another solution I slowly repeated the problem: "There she was…She wanted to go bike riding…and her bike was broken…and it would take her father a week to fix it…What else could she have done?" My hope here was that my restatement of the problem might catalyze the formulation of another solution by the patient.

Finally, Andy said, "She could…she could have just forgot about it." This response, although somewhat different from the resignation response, is still low on the hierarchy of optimal adaptations. Relegating a problem to the unconscious is certainly a way of adjusting to it. However, it is not a solution that generally involves any gratification, and so the frustrations that generate the forgetting reaction are likely still to be operative. At this point, I considered the patient to have exhausted all of his possibilities and therefore considered it proper for me to suggest an adaptation myself. And this, too, is an important therapeutic principle: It is only after the therapist has given the patient every opportunity to find solutions him- or herself that he or she should suggest modes of adaptation. Accordingly, I suggested that the girl might borrow a bicycle from someone (introducing thereby the principle of substitute gratification). The patient immediately responded well to this suggestion. However, I did not stop there and again invited the patient to consider what options the girl might have if she could not borrow a bike from someone. He responded, "She could have roller-skated." This is certainly a reasonable alternative and allowed the patient himself to contribute to a solution to the problem.

> *Patient:* "What's the best kind of job a person can have? Why? Make believe you are doing that job." I think the best job a person can have is working for a charity drive, like UNICEF, or the American Cancer Society or something like that.
> *Therapist:* Okay. Why is that?
> *Patient:* Because it can help other people who need the help.
> *Therapist:* Uh huh. Right! Right! So you can help other people through the Cancer Society and UNICEF.
> *Patient:* Uh. Try to raise money for treatment for cancer.
> *Therapist:* Right. And UNICEF?
> *Patient:* To raise money for poor people around the world.
> *Therapist:* Uh huh.
> *Patient:* For people who don't have enough food.
> *Therapist:* Do you know what that answer tells me about you?
> *Patient:* What?
> *Therapist:* It tells me that you're the kind of person who's very sensitive to other people's suffering, and who cares a lot about people who are sick, or who are starving, and that's a fine

quality to have. And that tells me something about you that's a very admirable trait. Do you know what an admirable trait is?

Patient: No. I don't know what it is.

Therapist: Admirable is something you admire in somebody. You know?

Patient: Yeah.

Therapist: It shows me that you're a thoughtful person who thinks about other people and feels sorry for those who are sick or in pain, and those who are hungry. That's what it tells me about you. Anything you want to say about that?

Patient: I...Thank you.

Therapist: You're welcome. Okay. You get a chip for that.

The patient's response was clearly an unusual one for a child of nine and a half. In fact, I cannot recall having had a response to that card which demonstrated so much sensitivity to and sympathy for the sick and the starving. I considered the response to reflect very healthy values, values that can only enhance the self-esteem of the person who has them. Furthermore, I praised Andy for his sensitivity, and he was genuinely touched by my comment. I believe this was an esteem-enhancing experience for him also.

Therapist: My card says, "Say something about your mother that gets you angry." Well, I remember when I was a kid, about nine years old or so. Those were the days that we had radios, but no TV, if you can imagine such a world. There was absolutely no television, which they had invented already, but it wasn't around in everybody's house. And I used to listen to the radio.

My favorite program was *The Lone Ranger*. Have you ever heard of *The Lone Ranger*? (The patient nods affirmatively.) The Lone Ranger and his Indian friend, Tonto. And I used to love listening to that at night. And I remember on a few occasions that my mother would say to me that I couldn't listen to it until I had finished my job. I had some jobs to do around the house, and I had this homework, and then after I finished that I'd be able to listen to *The Lone Ranger*, and I used to get angry at her for that because...

Patient: (interrupting)...because it was your favorite program.

Therapist: It was my favorite program. Right. And then once

I got very angry and I remember, uh, screaming and yelling and using had language at her, and really having a fit, and then she punished me. She wouldn't let me watch it (sic) at all for a couple of days, and I really felt bad about that, and was very angry...

Patient: Did you have TV in your home?

Therapist: No, I said there was no TV in most people's homes then.

Patient: Then how come you said you "watch it"?

Therapist: Did I say "watch it"?

Patient: Yeah.

Therapist: Yeah? Did I say "watch it"?

Patient: Yeah.

Therapist: No, I listened to it.

Patient: Oh.

Therapist: That was my mistake. I guess I would have wished that I could have watched it, in my thinking back now as a kid, seeing it was really...

Patient: Did you have that when you finally got a TV? Or did you never get one?

Therapist: Oh, we have TVs now when I got older. But TV sets didn't come, weren't in people's homes, I believe, until the late 1940s, the early 1950s I think. It was after the Second World War. Then they had lots of TV sets around. At any rate, that was one of the things that I was angry at my mother about, her not letting me watch *The Lone Ranger*. But I guess it taught me some lessons about being angry about something. That you don't accomplish much by having a fit. That just makes it...

Patient: I know.

Therapist: That just makes it worse.

Patient: I know. I usually have a...before I came here, I usually had a lot of them.

Therapist: Uh huh. Do you...

Patient: And I got punished for them.

Therapist: Uh huh.

Patient: Usually I got sent up to my room, but I got really angry just for that.

Therapist: Uh huh.

Patient: I wanted to play with my brother and sister and I couldn't because I was upstairs.

Therapist: Oh, I see. You were being punished for a fit?

Patient: Uh huh.

Therapist: And what have you learned here about those fits?

Patient: They couldn't help anything!

Therapist: Uh huh. What's a better way? What's a better thing to do when you're angry?

Patient: Just to, just to...

Therapist: What's a better thing to do if you are angry about something?

Patient: Just to think about...like...I could be angry. I could watch what I want to watch afterwards, after the punishment.

Therapist: Uh huh.

Patient: Besides, it would be on again.

Therapist: Uh huh. But what if you are angry about something, before you get the punishment, before you have the fit? What's a good way to handle something that bothers you?

Patient: Don't handle it in that way.

Therapist: Uh huh. What's a better way?

Patient: Uh...a better way is to talk about why you are angry.

Therapist: Right. Right! And by talking about it, what do you try to do?

Patient: You...you try to let out your anger but by not having any fits and talking about it.

Therapist: Right! And then what's the purpose in talking, besides letting out your anger? What else does it do?

Patient: It helps you understand...

Therapist: It helps you understand, and anything else?

Patient: Let's see...

Therapist: It helps you solve the problem. It helps you do something about the problem without having a fit.

Patient: That's right.

As mentioned, I always give an honest answer to the cards in *The Talking, Feeling, & Doing Game*. I usually have some ambivalence when I get a card that instructs me to make comments about members of my family. I believe that the therapist has an obligation to selectively and judiciously reveal things about him- or herself for the purposes of the therapy. However, one has an obligation to one's family members not to reveal things to others (patients or nonpatients) that are private family matters. What one decides to reveal about oneself is a personal decision; what one reveals about one's family members must take into consideration their needs and right to privacy as well. I have also mentioned how useful I have found the response that relates to some childhood event of mine—an event that occurred when I was at approximately the age of my patient at the time of therapy. This helps strengthen the relationship and can enhance the likelihood that the child will become involved in the therapist's response.

Both of these principles were applied in response to the card. My "criticism" of my mother here really said nothing particularly critical about her. Rather, it describes a "deficiency" within me. In addition, I related an event that occurred during my childhood, an event that I suspected the patient could relate to. And he definitely did. He was interested in hearing about my childhood experience. Just as children's hearing about their parents' experiences strengthens the parent-child bond, a child's hearing about a therapist's childhood experiences (when appropriate) can strengthen the therapist-patient relationship.

Andy picked up my error regarding "watching" *The Lone Ranger* on radio and this in itself can be therapeutic. It makes me human and lessens the likelihood that the patient will idealize me. It can be ego-enhancing for him to benevolently correct an error of mine. It is important for the reader to appreciate that something very important happened here when the patient corrected me. My responding to it in a nonchalant manner provided the patient with a therapeutically beneficial experience. Were he to have been in my position he would have reacted with self-denigration ("How stupid can I be"). By my responding in a relaxed and nonself-deprecatory way, I served as a model for such behavior for the patient. He was also provided with the living experience that one can make a mistake and not necessarily castigate oneself for it.

The patient then spontaneously began talking about his own fits. This switch provided an opportunity to discuss what he learned about dealing with his anger. We spoke about the measures to take that would reduce the likelihood of his anger building up to such a level that he would have a temper outburst. We spoke about dealing with problems in the earliest phase by expressing one's resentment at the outset. As mentioned, the patient was very bright and was able to learn these lessons well. He clearly was able to use his intelligence therapeutically.

> *Patient:* My card says, "What is the worst thing a person can do? Show someone doing that thing." Waste their life away. That's what I think.

Therapist: Uh huh. Give me an example, like somebody who would be wasting his or her life away.

Patient: Let's say there were two boys. Their father died, and each got half the will. One boy...

Therapist: (interrupts) What's a will?

Patient: The will.

Therapist: The will...the will. Oh, the will when someone dies? Yeah. Yeah.

Patient: (nods affirmatively) Each got a thousand dollars.

Therapist: This is a made-up story of yours?

Patient: Yes.

Therapist: Right.

Patient: One person, actually it's a different version of a story from the Bible.

Therapist: Okay.

Patient: The one that Jesus told.

Therapist: Okay.

Patient: Well, one person used it wisely and went and got a job, but the other one just wasted his life away with it, and wasted most of the money having a good time.

Therapist: Uh huh. Then what happened?

Patient: He did a lot of things. But when the money was gone, he lost his friends and had no more friends.

Therapist: Uh huh.

Patient: So he had to turn to be a bad guy.

Therapist: That was a real waste of his life.

Patient: But the other one continued, continued to prosper, and he still used his money wisely.

Therapist: Uh huh.

Patient: To get food.

Therapist: Uh huh.

Patient: Clothing.

Therapist: How did he get all that money?

Patient: Put it in a bank, and got interest on it.

Therapist: Is that how he...? That was in the Bible?

Patient: No, it wasn't in the Bible.

Therapist: (smiling) What was the interest rate in those days?

Patient: (laughs) No, I said this is sort of like a modern-day fable.

Therapist: All right. I see. But besides putting the money in the bank and getting interest, did he do anything else?

Patient: Yes, he continued his job.

Therapist: Continued his job. That sounds more like the Bible to me. (Therapist laughs.)

Patient: Yes. (Patient laughs.)

Therapist: Uh, anyway, uh, now, so what do we learn from that story?

Patient: That you have only one life to live, and if you waste it, that's it!

Therapist: But some people would say that the second guy really had a great time. He just spent the money and really enjoyed himself while the first guy went to work. And what's so great about going to work? Some would say that this guy was the wise one. What would you say about that?

Patient: I think they're wrong.

Therapist: Why do you say they're wrong?

Patient: Because if you lose all your money, how can you have a good time when you lose all your money?

Therapist: Let's compare the two guys when they got older. See there was one guy, the first guy, he put his money in the bank—at a good interest we assume—and therefore didn't have much fun when he was young because he wanted to work and he put all his extra money in the bank. Then when he was old, he had a lot of money but was too old to enjoy it. The second guy, the one who pissed all his money away when he was younger, ends up badly, but so does the first. What about those two guys? During that period of their lives?

Patient: They both were not living their lives wisely. Well, you put it that way I'm not really sure now.

Therapist: Uh huh.

Patient: Think it was about equal because...

Therapist: Why?

Patient: Because that person, the one who saved his money and stuff had a lot of fun when he retired and stuff.

Therapist: I see. So the one who worked was planning for the future. Was that it?

Patient: That's it.

Therapist: Okay. So that he was the smarter guy.

Patient: Uh huh.

Therapist: That's what you are saying?

Patient: Yes.

Therapist: Because he was taking care of his future. He just wasn't only thinking of the present. Is that what you are saying?

Patient: Yes.

Therapist: I would say that there is something else too. Depends upon the kind of job he had. Some people like their work, and some people don't. What about the guy in your story?

Patient: That guy liked his work.

Therapist: Uh huh. What kind of work did he do? What was he doing?

Patient: He was a founder for the ASPCA.

Therapist: A founder? What's a founder? Oh, you mean he started the organization?

Patient: Yes.

Therapist: I assume that this was not what happened in the Bible.

Patient: (laughs)

Therapist: Very good. So he was involved in an organization that took care of animals?

Patient: Yes.

Therapist: I see. Well, that's a very nice thing...

Patient: The American Society for the Prevention of Cruelty to Animals.

Therapist: Right. So he did a very noble thing.

Patient: Yes.

Therapist: Do you know what noble means?

Patient: I know what it means but I can't put it into words.

Therapist: Okay. It's very good and kind, and things like that.

Patient: That's what it usually means. Usually I know what it means, but I just can't put it into words.

Therapist: Yes. Sometimes it is hard to define the word that you know what it means. So, actually, though you are comparing the lives of these two guys in different phases of their lives. The guy who was working was still enjoying himself in a different way from the guy who was just splurging his money. Right? What happened to the guy who splurged his money?

Patient: He was dead in a couple of years.

Therapist: What about your guy who's working? Did he have any fun at all?

Patient: Yes he had fun.

Therapist: What did he do for fun?

Patient: Well, he had a pet of his own.

Therapist: Uh huh.

Patient: And, and he wanted a dog.

Therapist: Uh huh.

Patient: And since he took pretty good care of it, in the hunting season the dog returned his gratefulness.

Therapist: By?

Patient: Digging out rabbits out of his hole in the ground so he could shoot them.

Therapist: I see. So he was very helpful. But he had a good time with his dog? Is that what you are saying?

Patient: Yes.

Therapist: I see. So he wasn't just an all work kind of guy. He recognized that life required a balance of having fun and working at the same time. Is that right?

Patient: He was very smart.

Therapist: It sounds like that. Okay. Very good. You get a chip. That was a good one. Here's a chip for you.

The patient's response to the question about the worst thing a person could do revealed healthy values on the one hand and, in my opinion, a somewhat stringent value system on the other. His story, obviously based on biblical themes, revealed his appreciation that there is a price to be paid for the self-indulgent life. However, I considered his values to be somewhat rigid and self-abnegating. Accordingly, I introduced a little more flexibility in our conversation about his story. I helped the patient appreciate that a more balanced lifestyle might be the more judicious—a lifestyle in which there was room for both work and play. I also reinforced the patient's selection of a benevolent career for the wise brother, namely, the ASPCA. This is another example of the patient's healthy values with regard to giving.

Therapist: Okay, now it's my turn. Mine says, "Make believe you're drinking a glass of water." Glugh, glugh, glugh, glugh. You know what?

Patient: What?

Therapist: I have to drink a lot of water.

Patient: How come?

Therapist: A couple of years ago, I had a very painful illness.

Patient: What is it?

Therapist: It's called a kidney stone. Do you know what a kidney is?

Patient: No.

Therapist: Well, I'll tell you. I was in the office here with a patient, with a boy and his mother really. In the middle of the session I started to get terrible cramps. And they were so bad that I had to interrupt the session, and I told the people that I can't go on, I had such pain. And we would have to stop the session, and I became...

Patient: Did they understand?

Therapist: Yes. They saw that I couldn't work. It was too painful for me. I was in such pain, and I didn't know what was going on. I had never had any pain like that before, and it was really terrible. And then finally, after about two hours, I thought about the various possibilities what it was. And I punched myself lightly over here (Therapist points to his back over the kidney area.) and I really leaped. And I knew then that I probably had a kidney stone.

Patient: How did you know?

Therapist: You see I'm a psychiatrist and I'm also a doctor. A regular doctor. And I figured when that happened...I remember from medical school that that means that I probably had a kidney stone. I didn't know. But certainly it sounded like it. Anyway, I called my doctor and went to the hospital and it was a very painful experience. Uh...but it finally passed out. And...

Patient: What is a kidney stone anyway?

Therapist: Well, you know the kidneys are up here? (Therapist points to kidney area on his back.)

Patient: Yes.

Therapist: Kidneys. And what the kidney does is take the waste from the blood.

Patient: What...it's all blocked up?

Therapist: It filters out waste. You know, your kidney makes your urine.

Patient: Yes.

Therapist: Urine is waste.

Patient: Yes.

Therapist: And waste goes out of your body in your urine when you urinate and go to the bathroom for a bowel movement.

That's waste products. The things your body doesn't need.

Patient: Yes.

Therapist: Okay. Now the kidney manufactures the urine, and look what it does. It goes from here in the kidney, which is a round thing like that. (Therapist points to his fist.) And the urine goes down this tube called the ureter. (Therapist draws line with finger over anterior surface of his abdomen which follows the path of the ureter.) Then it goes into this thing called the bladder, which is like a ball or sac.

Patient: It's concentrated.

Therapist: Yes, it's concentrated. Very good! The kidney stores it there. It concentrates it and passes it down into the bladder.

Patient: You know what is done with it? When the bladder gets too full, you have to let it out.

Therapist: You let it out. Right! Now the kidney stone is from the kidney. The urine stagnates—it stands there—in certain little places in the kidney. And when that happens it forms stones, which are like little rocks. And then when that rock has to come out, it's very, very painful. It has to go down through the tube called the ureter. And that is very painful. Then the stone goes into the bladder.

Patient: Will I have to have those stones some day?

Therapist: I don't see any reason why.

Patient: Does everyone get them?

Therapist: No. No. I have a special problem with my kidney that makes my kidney make the stones. I mean it's more likely that I'm going to get them than other people. I have that problem. One of the things I have to do is to drink a lot of water, because if I drink a lot of water, then it will lessen the chances that I will get a stone.

Patient: Oh. That's why you have to drink a lot of water.

Therapist: Yeah. Right. That's for me. That's for my kidney. Now let's see. You had a problem too in that same area. Right?

Patient: Yes.

Therapist: Yep.

Patient: I know what it is.

Therapist: Well, what am I talking about?

Patient: Well, my kidneys...

Therapist: Not your kidney. Where was your problem?

Patient: In the bladder, I think.

Therapist: No...no...what are you saying?

Patient: I am saying...ask my mom.

Therapist: You know. You know what you had.

Patient: No, I don't.

Therapist: You had a problem in that your urine wouldn't come out the right way?

Patient: Uhm.

Therapist: Do you remember that problem?

Patient: Yes.

Therapist: Uh huh. How do things stand with that problem now?

Patient: I didn't like it one bit!

Therapist: What happened with that problem?

Patient: Well, after the operation, they got it back to normal.

Therapist: How is it now?

Patient: Okay.

Therapist: Uh huh. What do you remember about those operations?

Patient: (big sigh) The four of them I had in Englewood. The fifth one, the last one, I was in New York.

Therapist: Uh hmm. And what do you remember about the operations?

Patient: What do I remember of it?

Therapist: Uh huh.

Patient: Not much because they were four years ago.

Therapist: Uh huh. How old were you then?

Patient: Five.

Therapist: Uh huh. I see. Do you remember anything about them?

Patient: Uh...hmm.

Therapist: Do you remember anything about them?

Patient: Yes, it was really painful.

Therapist: Uh huh. Very upsetting, huh?

Patient: Yes.

Therapist: Do you still think you are upset about that now?

Patient: No.

Therapist: Do you think about it anymore?

Patient: No.

Therapist: Did we talk about...did we talk about those operations here?

Patient: Yes.

Therapist: Did you learn anything here about them that was useful? Here? About those operations?

Patient: I don't really think so.

Therapist: You don't really think so. Uh huh. Did you feel worse about it before you came?

Patient: I felt worse about it before I came.

Therapist: Uh huh. Is there anything about anything that happened here to you that made you feel less worse about the operations?

Patient: Yes. When it was over.

Therapist: What?

Patient: When it was over.

Therapist: I don't know what you mean.

Patient: The operations were...

Therapist: No, no. I mean about coming here that made you feel less bad about the operations.

Patient: Yes. I remember everybody has to get sick once in a while, so I don't feel so bad about my operations.

Therapist: That's one thing. Right! Another thing is to talk about it. You know, not to be ashamed about it. It's no sin. It's no crime. You know?

Patient: I know.

Therapist: It's not...but you're right. I agree with you. Everybody has something. Everybody has some kind of sickness and things that happen to them, but it doesn't make you a terrible person or anything else. You know?

Patient: I know.

Therapist: Do you think less of me because I had this kidney stone? Do you think I was a terrible person for having it?

Patient: No.

Therapist: No? Anything to laugh about, or people to think it's funny or something?

Patient: No.

Therapist: Uh huh. Do you think I think less of you because you had that trouble?

Patient: No.

Therapist: No. Not at all. In fact, I admire you very much. I think you're a very fine young man.

Patient: Thank you.

Therapist: And I always think well of and respect you.

Patient: (smiling) Thank you.

Therapist: Okay, I'll tell you. Our time is almost up. We want to watch a little bit of this. Okay?

Patient: Okay.

Therapist: So let's see who wins the game. Let's see. How many chips do you have?

Patient: Five.

Therapist: Five? I have three, so you are the winner. Congratulations. (Therapist and patient shake hands.) Okay. Let's watch this.

I used the relatively innocuous card "Make believe you're drinking a glass of water" as a point of departure for talking about a problem of mine that was similar to a problem of the patient's. I suspected that this was a good way of getting him to talk about his hypospadias, and my suspicion proved to be true. Talking about my kidney stone provided me with the opportunity to reveal a physical problem of my own and this, I believe, served the patient well. He and I had something in common. I too knew about pains in that area of the body. I had suffered, as had he.

I believe that a factor in the patient's presenting complaint of self-denigration related to his feelings that he was less worthy an individual than others because of his hypospadias and the operative procedures he had suffered in association with its repair. The patient had the experience that I did not look upon him as less worthy a human being because of this problem. Furthermore, my telling him about my kidney stone provided him with the opportunity to see that he himself did not look down upon me for having had this disorder. And this added to my credibility when I said that I did not look down upon him and that others were not likely to disparage him because of his hypospadias.

Andy's treatment progressed quite well. The interchange transcribed here took place about one month prior to termination. He enjoyed a marked reduction of his temper outbursts as well as significant alleviation of his tendency to deprecate himself. His grades improved and he became much more acceptable to friends. I believe the primary factors in his therapeutic improvement were his high intelligence and his winning personality. These attracted me to him and this resulted in his liking me. I also admired his healthy values and I believe my reinforcement of them served to enhance his self-esteem.

This enhancement of his feelings of self-worth was another significant factor in his improvement.

The Case of Morton: Therapists Also Get Rejected

Morton entered treatment at the age of nine because of disruptive behavior in the classroom. Although there was a mild neurological problem present (he was hyperactive, impulsive, and distractible), his primary problem centered on his relationship with his father. Morton's parents were separated and his father often did not show up for planned visits, or when he did he was often late. In addition, he was not the kind of man who basically enjoyed being with his children. Morton's anger was intense, but it was displaced onto his mother, teacher, and peers because he was fearful of revealing it to his father. While playing *The Talking, Feeling, & Doing Game*, the following conversation took place.

Therapist: My question is "What's the worst thing that ever happened to you?"

Well, I would say that one of the worst things that ever happened to me occurred when I was a teenager. There was a girl in my class in high school who I liked very much. I guess at that time I would say that I loved her. And I thought about nothing else but this girl, and I kept thinking about her and I stopped studying. All I could do was walk around and think about her and I don't think she cared for me too much. She wanted to be friendly with me, but she didn't like me anywhere near as much as I liked her. And I met her around June or so or May. I really got hooked on her and started thinking about her all the time, and she didn't treat me very nicely. And it wasn't until the end of August when she sent me a very painful letter in which she spoke about how much she didn't like me. And I discussed this with a friend of mine and he kind of knocked sense into my head and told me that I was crazy if I answered that letter. And after that, it was hard, but I didn't answer it and I stopped seeing her and I gradually got over it. But it was very painful to me and it was too bad that I didn't realize that it was a foolish thing...

Patient: (interrupting) I got the message.

Therapist: What's the message?

Patient: Like you loved the girl so much, but she didn't love you!

Therapist: Right. And so what do you do in such a situation?

Patient: Just ignore her. That's all I can think of. Other things? I don't know.

Therapist: Well, what should you do?

Patient: Don't let it bother you.

Therapist: Uh huh. Try to get wise, not trying to get something...

Patient: (interrupts) Yeah, yeah, yeah, yeah, yeah! (throws dice)

Therapist: Okay. Good.

I believe that my responding revelation about the incident that occurred when I was a teenager was of therapeutic benefit to the patient. While talking about my own experience, I was really encouraging him to take a more realistic attitude toward his father. By my relating the course of events that led to my own resolution to discontinue trying to get affection from someone who was not going to provide it, I was encouraging him to act similarly with his father. At the same time, I revealed to him that I too am susceptible to similar rejections and I hoped thereby to lessen the antitherapeutic idolization that so often occurs in treatment.

Some readers may have wondered at this point whether I was really being candid with the patient when I stated that being jilted by a teenage girl was the "worst thing that ever happened to me in my whole life." I can easily envision a reader saying, "Is that really true, Gardner? That was the worst thing that ever happened to you in your whole life?" My response is simply that 20 years ago, when this interchange took place, I still recalled the incident as one of the most painful of my life. It was selected because it lent itself well to therapeutic utilization. Had I to answer that question now, I would select from some more recent and certainly more formidable tragedies (such as the murder of my brother in 1985) that would more reasonably qualify for being considered the worst.

A subsequent interchange:

Therapist: Okay, my card says, "Make believe a piece of paper just blew in the window. Something is written on it. Make up what is said on the paper."

It says on the paper, "If at first you don't succeed, try, try again. If after that you still don't succeed, forget it. Don't make a big fool of yourself." That's what it says on the paper. What do you think of that?

Patient: (laughing) That's a good one.
Therapist: Okay.

My response is a quote from W. C. Fields who is alleged to have made the statement. In my *The Boys and Girls Book About Divorce* (1970a, 1971b) I have elaborated on this message and made it into a chapter entitled "Fields' Rule." The message here is essentially a reiteration of my previously described experience with my teenage girlfriend. This time, however, the patient did not resist the message and stated with enthusiasm, "That's a good one."

The Case Of Harry: Getting Therapeutic Mileage From An Auto Mechanic

Harry's background history was presented in Chapter One (*Valentine's Day Candy from a Loving Mother*). The interchange recorded below took place while playing *The Talking, Feeling, & Doing Game.*

Patient: "What do you think about a boy who lets his dog make a mess in the house? What should his parents do?" His parents should not let him do what he wants and tell him that if he wants a dog, he's going to have to take care of his messes and everything.
Therapist: And suppose he still doesn't listen?
Patient: Then if he doesn't listen, he's not going to have a dog.
Therapist: Right. And that would be a sad thing. Do you know any other way to do it?
Patient: No.
Therapist: I can't think of one. If he wants to have the fun of a dog, he has to have...what's the word?
Patient:...The fun of the dog, then he has to take care of the dog.
Therapist: Right!
Patient: If he does not want the fun of the dog, then he is not going to get it.
Therapist: Right! He has to have the responsibility, and he has to do things sometimes he doesn't like. That's how most things are in life. They're a mixture. If you want to get a certain amount of fun, you have to do certain things you don't like sometimes. Do you know anything that's not like that?
Patient: (nods negatively)
Therapist: Well, it's hard to think of something that isn't like

that. There's always a mixture of these things.

Okay, my card says, "Of all the things you learn in school, what do you like learning about least? Why?" Well, I don't go to school anymore, but I remember when I was in school the subject that I didn't like very much was economics. Do you know what economics is? What is economics?

Patient: Sort of like a job.

Therapist: Well, it's something like that. It's about money, and buying, and selling, and prices, and things like that. It didn't interest me very much, but I knew I had to take that subject if I wanted to pass in high school and in college. You know?

Patient: Yeah.

Therapist: They just required it. Because I wanted to get my diploma and finish up and because I wanted to take the other courses, I knew I had to take it. I had to take the bad with the good. Do you understand?

Patient: Yes.

Therapist: That's something like we were talking about before, that nothing is perfect and everything is a mixture. What do you think about that?

Patient: (nods negatively)

Therapist: You don't like that idea too much?

Patient: (without much conviction) It's okay.

Therapist: It's okay. Is there anything like that in your life? Accepting the bad with the good? Do you know of anything in your life that's like that? I do. Do you have to accept bad things with the good things in any part of your life?

Patient: Yeah, I do.

Therapist: Can you give an example from your life of that?

Patient: No.

Therapist: I can think of one.

Patient: What?

Therapist: Your parents' divorce. There are things there where you have to accept the bad with the good. There are things with your parents' divorce that has to do with accepting the bad with the good.

Patient: No.

Therapist: Oh come on, you can think of something.

Patient: I don't want to say it.

Therapist: You don't want to say it. Well, okay. That's too bad. In this game you get chips for answering. Right? Do you feel like playing this game? Okay, because part of the game is to answer the questions. So if you want to get a chip, you have to say something about your parents'...

Patient: (interrupts) Well, you've got to answer your questions, I don't.

Therapist: I answered already. I answered with economics. But I'm giving you a chance to get an extra chip if you can say something about your parents.

Patient: No, I don't want an extra chip.

Therapist: You don't want it. Okay.

One of Harry's problems was that he refused to accept responsibility. He did not want to suffer any discomfort or inconvenience. He fit well into the category of the boy whom I described earlier—the deprived child who lives by the pleasure principle because he was never rewarded with love and affection for self-restraint. I tried to use the examples of the dog and the subject of economics to get across the point that toleration of discomfort is often necessary if one is to enjoy certain benefits. On an intellectual basis, the patient appeared to be somewhat receptive. I then tried to shift into a discussion of the advantages and disadvantages of parental divorce. However, Harry would have no part of the discussion. The lure of the chip reward did not serve as an incentive. Accordingly, I did not pressure him any further and we proceeded with the game.

The interchange with Harry here raises an important technical point in the treatment of patients. Some therapists take a very passive position regarding any pressures on the patient to speak about a specific subject. They consider this not only respectful of the patient's wishes, but believe that to do otherwise is to invite further resistance to the treatment. They also believe that such urging can be anxiety provoking and that it is per se antitherapeutic. I generally do not pull back so quickly when a patient exhibits manifestations of resistance and/or anxiety when discussing a "touchy subject." I believe to do so might deprive the patient of an important therapeutic experience. Some patients need a little urging and are better off afterwards for having experienced the thoughts and feelings attendant to dwelling on the sensitive subject. The therapist cannot know beforehand how much anxiety and resistance will be engendered by suggesting further inquiry into a given area. He or she should be exquisitely sensitive to whether or not the therapist's pressure is producing undue anxiety and/or resistance. If such appears to be the case, it is time to "pull back." Here, I believed that Harry was approaching that point when he adamantly refused to pursue this subject—even after being informed that he would thereby deprive himself of a further chip. He firmly stated, "No, I don't want an extra chip." I got the message, and we proceeded with the game.

Therapist: Let's go on then. (throws dice) My question is, "What do you think your life will be like 20 years from now?" Well, 20 years from now I will...

Patient: (interrupts) You might be dead in 20 years.

Therapist: Well, how old do you think I am?

Patient: Forty-two.

Therapist: Thank you very much. I appreciate the compliment. No, I'm going to be 50 next month. What do you think of that?

Patient: I thought you were 40-something.

Therapist: I am 40-something. I am 49, I am 49 and 11/12. So 20 years from now I will be 50. (Therapist laughs as he immediately recognizes the slip and its obvious significance.) I really wish I would be 50. Twenty years from now I will be 70. Do you think I'll be dead?

Patient: Yes.

Therapist: You think so?

Patient: Yes, because my uncle was in the hospital and he died.

Therapist: There are a lot of people who die before 70, and there are a lot of people who don't. I certainly hope that I'm still alive.

Patient: (speaking with warmth and conviction) So do I.

Therapist: Anyway, if I am alive, and I think I probably will be, I can't be 100 percent sure, I will probably still be a psychiatrist and will be trying to help kids.

Patient: But you will not have me as a subject (sic) because I will be 30 years old.

Therapist: You will be 30 years old? What will you be doing then? I will be doing psychiatry.

Patient: I will be an auto mechanic.

Therapist: An auto mechanic.

Patient: Do I get a chip for that?

Therapist: Okay, you get a chip for that. I hope you will be a good auto mechanic, and I hope you have a very good business.

Patient: Yeah, so do I. Lots of money!

Therapist: But you have to work very hard at it, you know. Whatever you do, if you're going to goof off, if you're an auto mechanic and you goof off, you're not going to have any customers. People are not going to come back. But if you do a good job, then you'll have many customers. Right?

Patient: (nods affirmatively)

Therapist: Okay. Very good.

One could argue that Harry's thinking I might be dead 20 years from now was definitely a manifestation of hostility. Although I admit this is certainly a possibility (especially because it was preceded by my strongly encouraging him to talk about the touchy subject of his parents' divorce), his comment may have had nothing to do with hostility. It is important to appreciate that Harry was 10 years old, and I was mid-to late-middle-aged. Children's appreciation of adult's ages is often limited. Furthermore, his appreciation of the significance of a 20-year advance in my age is also likely to be somewhat distorted. I did not automatically assume that his interjected response reflected hostility. (I do not doubt the possibility either; I only consider it unlikely.)

I did, in the true analytic spirit, ask Harry to guess my age rather than blurt it out. However, in Harry's case, I did not consider it a fruitful area of inquiry to delve into his erroneous speculation any further. His guess that I was 42 instead of 49 was not, in my opinion, conclusive evidence for some kind of psychodynamically determined error. To have done so, in my opinion, could have been antitherapeutic in that it would have involved us in an inquiry into a subject that might or might not have had psychological significance. I was content to leave the issue alone and reveal my actual age. As mentioned, I believe there is often an important benefit to be derived in treatment from such revelations. They bring the patient and therapist closer, and this may be more important than an analytic inquiry. Even though the therapist may be depriving the patient of some important psychoanalytic insight, this may be more than compensated for by the strengthening of the therapist-patient relationship that such divulgences bring about.

I answered the question by informing Harry that I fully intended to be continuing to do psychiatry in 20 years. I wanted to get across the notion that I find my work interesting and enjoyable, and that the prospect of retiring completely is not only distasteful to me, but would be completely out of character for me. My hope was that some of this attitude toward productive endeavors might filter down to Harry.

Harry then answered the question and offered that he would be an auto mechanic. I generally follow through with such interruptions because they often provide useful therapeutic material. Unless the interruption is obviously a resistance maneuver, I "milk it for all it's worth." It would be completely outside of the philosophy of the game for me to say to the patient: "Hey, wait a minute now. This is my question. You wait your turn." Such a response would totally defeat the purpose of the game—which is to elicit psychodynamically meaningful material from the patient.

The patient emphasized the material benefits to be derived from being an auto mechanic. I took this opportunity to introduce a comment about the work ethic and the importance of doing a good job and establishing a good reputation. I do not believe at that point that the statement "hit him in the guts." However, it behooves the therapist to transmit his or her therapeutically important messages and hope that they will ultimately be received. In no way did I consider Harry's switching the subject to his future life as an auto mechanic to be a resistance maneuver. Rather, I welcomed it from the realization that school and work are analogous and that anything I could say about his work as an auto mechanic would be likely to have applicability to his schoolwork. Furthermore, because Harry was extremely unreceptive to discussing his schoolwork directly, I viewed discussions about the principles of being an auto mechanic to be a potential vehicle for talking symbolically about Harry's school difficulties in a way that Harry would welcome.

> *Patient:* My card says, "What would you do if you found $10,000?" If I found $10,000, first I would return it to the police station to see if it is anybody's. Then, if it is not anybody's, I would know in 30 days that I would get to keep it. If I get to keep it, then I am going to buy my own auto mechanic shop.
>
> *Therapist:* That's a good purpose.
>
> *Patient:* So my store will be nice, and many people will come. So it will be a nice clean place to get your car fixed, and washed, and everything, and take every bit of advice to make people's cars look nice. It will be a real, nice, clean place.
>
> *Therapist:* To create a good impression. Right?

Patient: Yeah, to create a good impression.

Therapist: That's important. It's important to create a good impression. It shows you have pride in your place; but it's also important that you do good work, you know. There are some places that look flashy and nice, but the work is no good.

Patient: Mine is going to look flashy and do the best work.

Therapist: Okay. I think that the important thing is the work. The second important thing is how it looks.

Here, the patient again focused on external appearances and made no mention of the quality of work that his auto mechanic shop would provide. I praised him on his interest in a clean shop that made a good appearance, but I also emphasized the importance of high-quality work. This was especially important for this boy whose commitment to the work ethic in school left much to be desired.

These interchanges on the subject of the auto mechanic shop represent what I consider to be among the most efficacious forms of child psychotherapeutic interchange. To the casual observer, the patient and I are involved in a relaxed discussion on the somewhat neutral and even banal subject of auto mechanic shops. There is almost a "folksy" quality to the conversation. From the patient's point of view it is probably just that: simply a conversation. From my point of view, however, much more is going on. At every point, I am actively concerned with two processes: 1) the ostensible conversation and 2) the underlying psychodynamic meaning of what is going on. What may appear to be a relaxed conversation is, for me, almost a façade. The wheels are ever going around in my head. I am ever concerned with both of these processes simultaneously. I am ever trying to relate my comments to the patient's basic difficulties and how they are reflecting themselves in what he is saying. This is the way I transmit my most important therapeutic communications. I cannot emphasize this point strongly enough.

Freud referred to dreams as "the royal road to the unconscious." I am in full agreement. And I would consider stories and conversations of this kind to be the royal road to therapeutic change in children. And even with adults the process has merit. Quite often, I will in the course of the session with an adult patient relate an anecdote or an event that has relevance to his or her problems. It is a way of getting home a point with a vehicle that is extremely powerful; far more powerful, I believe, than a therapeutic approach that relies upon gaining insight into unconscious processes. Lastly, it is an approach that has history to recommend it. It is an ancient method that has survived to the present day because of the universal recognition of its efficacy.

> *Therapist:* "Of all the things you own, what do you enjoy the most? Make believe you are doing something with that thing." I would say that one of the most important things I own is my typewriter. (Therapist imitates typing.)
> *Patient:* (interrupts) Isn't that your favorite thing? What about that? (Patient points to mounted video camera.)
> *Therapist:* You like that too?
> *Patient:* Yeah!
> *Therapist:* Why do you think I would choose that?
> *Patient:* Because you could make movies.
> *Therapist:* That is a lot of fun. I think that's a good answer too. That is also one of my favorite things. I like the TV because I can see myself on television anytime I want.
> *Patient:* You can say hello, and you can look at the television, and see yourself say hello.
> *Therapist:* Yes, but more important than that it helps me be a better psychiatrist.
> *Patient:* It does?
> *Therapist:* Yeah, because we are playing this game here and people see themselves on television, and it helps them see themselves better, and it helps me be a better psychiatrist in this way.
> *Patient:* Uh-oh!
> *Therapist:* What is uh-oh?
> *Patient:* You're supposed to have two of these chips.
> *Therapist:* Oh, did I forget? Okay, I guess I forgot. (Therapist takes chip.) Okay. Let's get back to the question. You were close when you guessed the TV camera, but I was not going to say that. I was going to say *typewriter* because with the typewriter I write books, and stories, and things like that. It makes me feel very good because when I write a book—and especially when it comes out—it makes me feel good that I created something.

I began responding to the question about my favorite possession by mentioning the typewriter. I planned to use it as a point of departure for discussing the gratifications I enjoy from writing. My hope was that this would engender in Harry greater motivation in his academic pursuits. However, he interrupted me and pointed to the video camera that was recording the program that we were making. As mentioned, I generally welcome such interruptions because they usually relate to issues that may be more relevant to the child than those that I may be focusing on at that point. (Of course, when the interruption is a reflection of resistance, then I do not permit it and insist upon my right to return to my card and answer my question.)

I allowed the digression and got as much mileage as I could out of a discussion of the video camera and the closed-circuit television system. I got in the message that it was useful for helping people see themselves and this, of course, is a crucial aspect of treatment. I did not get very far with this explanation when the patient noted that I had failed to collect one of my reward chips. When the game is being played at its best, both the therapist and the patient may forget whose turn it is and may forget to collect the reward chips. Following the rectification of this error, I returned to the typewriter theme and focused on the good feeling I have when a book of mine comes out. At that point Harry interrupted me, and the following interchange took place.

> *Patient:* (interrupts) What's that over there? (Patient points to a pile of just-published books, *Dr. Gardner's Fables for Our Times* [1981b].)
> *Therapist:* That's my new book. It just came out.
> *Patient:* When?
> *Therapist:* The book came out yesterday. Would you like to borrow a copy?
> *Patient:* (very enthusiastically) Yeah!

The psychological significance of this interchange concerning the new book, as well as the subsequent conversation, will be more meaningful with the following background information. I routinely give a complimentary copy of my book *Stories About the Real World* (1972a) to every new patient. These stories cover a wide variety of conflict situations of childhood, and it is a rare patient who does not relate to at least one of the stories. I use the child's reactions as a point of departure for therapeutic interchanges. Accordingly, Harry had been given a copy of this book during my initial consultation. Subsequently, I lent him a copy of my *Dorothy and the Lizard of Oz* (1980d). Unfortunately, he lost the book. When he told me of the loss, it was with a complete absence of embarrassment, guilt, remorse, or a desire to make restitution. Because of this, I told him that I would lend him another book with the understanding that if he lost this one, he would have to pay for it. I considered this requirement to provide Harry with a useful therapeutic experience. Not to have made some attempt to require responsibility on his part would have been, in my opinion, antitherapeutic. This is just the kind of living experience that I consider important in therapy. The therapist should seize upon every opportunity he or she can to provide patients with such experiences. The interchange over the lost book is an excellent example. Harry absolutely refused to accept the book with that proviso. We discussed it for a few minutes at that time, and I tried to impress upon him that I felt bad that the book was lost and that I wanted to protect myself from further losses. I also tried to help him appreciate his own lack of remorse over the loss, but this fell on deaf ears. In the conversation I knew that he wished to borrow the book, but I knew also that he did not wish to assume responsibility for its loss. I believed that my refusal to lend him the book without "protecting myself" might have been a more valuable therapeutic experience than any discussions we did have or might have had on the subject.

This is what I was thinking when Harry pointed to the new book. It was not placed there to attract his attention. (I do not set up artificial situations like this in therapy. No matter what items are present in the therapist's office, the pressure of the unconscious is going to invest them with special meaning in accordance with the psychological processes of the patient.) Harry immediately expressed interest in the book, and I thought this would be a wonderful opportunity to offer to lend him a copy. He responded with enthusiasm.

> *Therapist:* I'll let you borrow a copy, but let me ask you something. If you were in my place, would you be hesitant to lend the book? Should I be hesitant to lend you a book?
>
> *Patient:* I think you should give me the book just like you gave the *The Real World Stories*.
>
> *Therapist:* Okay, but what about lending you a book? You don't think I should lend you the book?
>
> *Patient:* No.
>
> *Therapist:* Why not?
>
> *Patient:* I don't know.
>
> *Therapist:* I had an experience with you that made me hesitate to lend you a book. Do you remember that experience? What

was the experience?

Patient: The last...book you lent me I lost.

Therapist: Yeah, I lent you a book and you lost it.

Patient: (angrily) So don't give me the book; I don't really care.

Therapist: But if I just give it to you, that won't help you remember not to lose things.

Patient: Ah, I don't want your book...just forget it!

Therapist: It's a new book of fables called *Dr. Gardner's Fables for Our Times*.

Patient: I don't really care about it; you can keep it for yourself.

Therapist: I just want to say something. If I lend it to you now...I would like to lend it to you and give you a second chance. I never condemn a person for one mistake. Do you know what I mean? You're entitled to a mistake; everybody makes mistakes. But it makes me hesitant; it makes me a little concerned. How about this? I'll lend you the book?

Patient: (interrupts) No, I don't want it!

Therapist: Let me tell you what I'm suggesting.

Patient: I don't want it!

Therapist: I'll tell you what. I'll lend you the book, but if you lose it, you have to pay for it.

Patient: No, I'm not going to do it.

Therapist: Why not?

Patient: Because I don't need the book.

Therapist: Okay, that's up to you, but I would have liked you to have borrowed it, but I'm not going to lend it to you just like that, because I'm afraid you might lose it or not take good care of it. But maybe you'll change your mind. If you change your mind, let me know.

Patient: Okay. Did you answer your question?

Therapist: I think I did.

Patient: Wait...what was that question?

Therapist: "What are my favorite things?" I said my typewriter because it makes me feel good when I write books and the books help other people. Books help other people with their problems. They teach them things and lots of people say they learn a lot from them. And that makes me feel good too. You feel good when you do something that helps other people. Do you do things that make you feel good? What do you do that makes you feel good?

Patient: I'm nice to people.

Therapist: That's right, it makes you feel good when you're nice to people, right?

Patient: Yeah.

Therapist: Right. You get a chip for that answer, because it was a very good answer. And I get a chip for my answer.

It was quite clear that Harry really wanted to borrow the book. However, he absolutely refused to assume any responsibility for its loss. I tried to seduce him into making a commitment by continuing the conversation in the hope that it would intensify his craving for the book. Although I was unsuccessful in getting him to make the commitment to provide restitution if the book were lost, I do believe that he had a therapeutic experience. There were indeed repercussions for his casual attitude over the loss of my book, and he had the living experience that book owners under such circumstances are likely to be reluctant to lend him additional books. He suffered the frustration of not being able to borrow the book. This, I hoped, would be a useful therapeutic experience. There was no analytic inquiry here; there was little if any insight gained by Harry. However, something therapeutic was accomplished—the lack of insight on Harry's part notwithstanding.

Many therapists are far less enthusiastic than I about interchanges such as these. They are deeply committed to the notion that without insight there cannot be therapeutic change. They subscribe deeply to Freud's dictum: "Where there was unconscious, there let conscious be." I am not as enthusiastic as Freud was over the therapeutic benefit of insight. I am much more impressed with the therapeutic changes that occur from experiences as well as messages that are imparted at the symbolic level. For therapists who are deeply committed to the insight route to change, I often provide the analogy of my scuba-diving experience. My instructor repeatedly advised the class that it was vital for all of us to learn ways of dealing with emergency situations while under water. The worst thing that one can do in such situations is to hold one's breath and get to the top as rapidly as possible. It is one of the quickest ways of killing oneself. It is one of the quickest ways of bursting one's lungs. Accordingly, we were repeatedly advised to fight the impulse to rise to the top when we were in trouble. We were meticulously taught the various ways of dealing with underwater emergencies. I can tell the reader from personal experience that the urge to hold one's breath and rise to the top under such circumstances is immense. It seemed that every force and reflex in my body was dictating such a course of action. It was only with formidable self-control that I fought these urges on two occasions when I had difficulty. Of course, my knowledge of the consequences of submitting to them was of help in my suppressing them.

I mention the scuba experience because it relates directly to those therapists who are deeply committed to insight as the primary mode for helping their patients. Just as my scuba instructor urged me to fight my impulse to hold my breath and rise to the top, I suggest that therapists fight their impulses to pursue the insight route. I suggest that they consider the alternatives discussed in this book. I do not view insight as totally meaningless in the therapeutic process, but I generally view it as less significant for children than it is for adults, and even for adults it is a low-priority therapeutic modality. It is frosting on the cake. I am in agreement with Frieda Fromm-Reichmann who said, "The patient needs an experience far more than an insight."

CONCLUDING COMMENTS

The popularity of *The Talking, Feeling, & Doing Game* has been a great source of gratification. It has become standard equipment for the child psychotherapist, and many therapists consider it vital in their work with children. Over the years, I have received many letters in which the therapist has expressed gratitude for my introduction of the game. I have even had the dubious compliment on a few occasions of plagiarized versions being introduced. These, to the best of my knowledge, have never enjoyed similar popularity. (One such plagiarizer lost motivation to continue marketing the game after a letter from my attorney "reminding him" of the consequences if he did not cease and desist.)

Although the game was originally devised in an attempt to engage children who were not free enough to provide self-created stories when utilizing the mutual storytelling technique and its derivative games, it has proven useful for more cooperative and insightful children as well. In fact, I would say that it is a rare child who will not get involved in the game.

I have also found it useful in the therapy of small groups of children in the five-to-twelve age range. Children in this age bracket are traditionally poor candidates for group therapy because of their age-appropriate rambunctiousness. Often, the therapist finds him-or herself serving more as a disciplinarian than a therapist. *The Talking, Feeling, & Doing Game* provides an organization and a structure that is often so powerful that children of this age are diverted from the horseplay that often compromises significantly the group therapy. One can use it for this purpose in a number of ways. One way I have found useful is to have the first child respond to a card and then get input from each of the other players on the first player's response. Each of the other participants, of course, receives a chip for his or her contribution. The second child may now answer the same question or choose one of his or her own. In this way I go around the board, engaging each child in the responses of the others. When utilizing the game in this manner, the therapist can choose whether or not to participate as a player. I generally prefer to play as one who takes the card him- or herself for the sake of "egalitarianism" as well as the desire to gain the therapeutic benefits to be derived from my revelations about myself.

The game can also be useful in selected family therapy situations. Generally, unsophisticated and/or uneducated parents may welcome the game as a catalyst for family discussion; more sophisticated and/or educated parents will generally not need such assistance in their family therapy work.

The Talking, Feeling, & Doing Game is not without its disadvantages. All good drugs have their side effects. In fact, it is often the case that the more powerful the drug the greater the side effects. One of the main drawbacks of *The Talking, Feeling, & Doing Game* is that it may be too enticing to both the patient and the therapist. It is seemingly an easy therapeutic modality. Many therapists, I am certain, play it without fully appreciating its complexities and how difficult it can often be to utilize it properly for therapeutic purposes. The child, too, may find it attractive because it seemingly protects him or her from talking about more painful subjects directly. It should not be used as the only therapeutic modality because it will deprive the therapist of some of the deeper unconscious material that can more readily be obtained from projective play and storytelling. In short, therapists should not be tempted into using the game throughout every session; they should do their utmost to balance the therapeutic activities with other modalities.

I have also found the game particularly useful in the treatment of children with neurologically based learning disabilities. Its utilization for this purpose is described elsewhere (1973b; 1974a; 1975c,d,e; 1979b; 1980b,c). For further articles on the game's general utilization I refer the reader to book chapters of mine on the subject (1983b, 1986).

References

Bellak, L. and Bellak, S.S. (1949), *Children's Apperception Test.* Larchmont, New York: C.P.S. Co.

Conn, J.H. (1939), The child reveals himself through play. *Mental Hygiene*, 23(1):1-21.

___ (1941a), The timid, dependent child. *Journal of Pediatrics*, 19(1):1-2.

___ (1941b), The treatment of fearful children. *American Journal of Orthopsychiatry*, 11(4):744-751.

___ (1948), The play-interview as an investigative and therapeutic procedure. *The Nervous Child*, 7(3):257-286.

___ (1954), Play interview therapy of castration fears. *American Journal of Orthopsychiatry*, 25(4):747-754.

Freud, S. (1909), A phobia in a five-year-old boy. In *Collected Papers*, Vol. III, pp. 149-209. New York: Basic Books, Inc., 1959.

___ (1924), The passing of the Oedipus complex. In *Collected Papers*, Vol. II, pp. 269-276. New York: Basic Books, Inc., 1959.

Gardner, R.A. (1968), The mutual storytelling technique: Use in alleviating childhood oedipal problems. *Contemporary Psychoanalysis*, 4:161-177.

___ (1969), Mutual storytelling as a technique in child psychotherapy and psychoanalysis. In *Science and Psychoanalysis*, ed. J. Masserman, Vol. XIV, pp. 123-135. New York: Grune & Stratton.

___ (1970a), *The Boys and Girls Book about Divorce.* New York: Jason Aronson, Inc.

___ (1970b), Die Technik des wechselseitigen Geschichtenerzahlens bei der Behandlung eines Kindes mit psychogenem Husten. In *Fortschritte der Weiterenwicklung der Psychoanalyse*, ed. C.J. Hogrefe, Vol. IV, pp. 159-173. Göttingen: Verlag für Psychologie.

___ (1970c), The mutual storytelling technique: Use in the treatment of a child with post-traumatic neurosis. *American Journal of Psychotherapy*, 24:419-439.

___ (1971a), *Therapeutic Communication with Children: The Mutual Storytelling Technique.* New York: Jason Aronson, Inc.

___ (1971b), *The Boys and Girls Book about Divorce* (Paperback edition). New York: Bantam Books, Inc.

___ (1971c), Mutual storytelling: A technique in child psychotherapy. *Acta Paedopsychiatrica*, 38(9):253-262.

___ (1972a), *Dr. Gardner's Stories about the Real World. Vol. I.* Cresskill, New Jersey: Creative Therapeutics.

___ (1972b), Little Hans–the most famous boy in the child psychotherapy literature. *International Journal of Child Psychotherapy*, 1(4):27-32.

____ (1972c), "Once upon a time there was a doorknob and everybody used to make him all dirty with fingerprints..." *Psychology Today*, 5(10):67-92.

____ (1972d), The mutual storytelling technique in the treatment of anger inhibition problems. *International Journal of Child Psychotherapy*, 1(1):34-64.

____ (1973a), *The Talking, Feeling, & Doing Game*. Cresskill, New Jersey: Creative Therapeutics.

____ (1973b), Psychotherapy of the psychogenic problems secondary to minimal brain dysfunction. *International Journal of Child Psychotherapy*, 2(2):224-256.

____ (1973c), *Understanding Children–A Parents' Guide to Child Rearing*. Cresskill, New Jersey: Creative Therapeutics.

____ (1973d),*The Mutual Storytelling Technique* (12 one-hour audiocassettes). Cresskill, New Jersey: Creative Therapeutics

____ (1974a), Psychotherapy of minimal brain dysfunction. In *Current Psychiatric Therapies*, ed. J. Masserman, Vol. XIV, pp. 15-21. New York: Grune & Stratton.

____ (1974b), La technique de la narration mutuelle d'historettes. *Médecine et Hygiène* (Geneva), 32:1180-1181.

____ (1974c), Dramatized storytelling in child psychotherapy. *Acta Paedopsychiatrica*, 41(3):110-116.

____ (1974d) The mutual storytelling technique in the treatment of psychogenic problems secondary to minimal brain dysfunction. *Journal of Learning Disabilities*, 7:135-143.

____ (1975a), *Psychotherapeutic Approaches to the Resistant Child* (2 one-hour audiocassettes). Cresskill, New Jersey: Creative Therapeutics.

____ (1975b) Techniques for involving the child with MBD in meaningful psychotherapy. *Journal of Learning Disabilities*, 8(5):16-26.

____ (1975c), Psychotherapy of minimal brain dysfunction. In *Current Psychiatric Therapies*, ed. J. Masserman, Vol. XV, pp. 25-38. New York: Grune & Stratton.

____ (1975d), Dr. Gardner talks to children with minimal brain dysfunction (one-hour audiocassette). Cresskill, New Jersey: Creative Therapeutics.

____ (1975e), Dr. Gardner talks to parents of children with MBD (one-hour audiocassette). Cresskill, New Jersey: Creative Therapeutics.

____ (1976), *Psychotherapy with Children of Divorce*. New York: Jason Aronson, Inc.

____ (1979a), Helping children cooperate in therapy. In *Basic Handbook of Child Psychiatry*, ed. J. Noshpitz, Vol. III, pp. 414-433. New York: Basic Books, Inc.

____ (1979b), Psychogenic difficulties secondary to MBD. In *Basic

Handbook of Child Psychiatry, ed. J. Noshpitz, Vol. III, pp. 614-628. New York: Basic Books, Inc.

___ (1980a), The mutual storytelling technique. In *The Psychotherapy Handbook*, ed. R. Herink, pp. 408-411. New York: New American Library.

___ (1980b), Minimal brain dysfunction. In *Child Normality and Psychopathology*, ed. J. Bemporad, pp. 269-304. New York: Brunner/Mazel, Inc.

___ (1980c), What every psychoanalyst should know about minimal brain dysfunction. *Journal of the American Academy of Psychoanalysis*, 8(3):403-426.

___ (1980d), *Dorothy and the Lizard of Oz*. Cresskill, New Jersey: Creative Therapeutics.

___ (1981a), The mutual storytelling technique and dramatization of the therapeutic communication. In *Drama in Therapy*, ed. G. Schattner and R. Courtney, pp. 211-235. New York: Drama Book Specialists.

___ (1981b), *Dr. Gardner's Fables for Our Times*. Cresskill, New Jersey: Creative Therapeutics.

___ (1983a), Treating oedipal problems with the mutual storytelling technique. In *Handbook of Play Therapy*, ed. C.E. Schaefer and K.J. O'Connor, pp. 355-368. New York: John Wiley & Sons, Inc.

___ (1983b), The Talking, Feeling, & Doing Game. In *Handbook of Play Therapy*, ed. C.E. Schaefer and K.J. O'Connor, pp. 259-273. New York: John Wiley & Sons., Inc.

___ (1986), The Talking, Feeling, & Doing Game. In *Game Play: Therapeutic Uses of Childhood Games*, ed. C.E. Schaefer and S. Reid. New York: John Wiley & Sons.

Hug-Hellmuth, H. von (1921), On the technique of child analysis, *International Journal of Psychoanalysis*, 2(3/4):287-305.

Murray, H. (1936), *The Thematic Apperception Test*. New York: The Psychological Corp.

Schneidman, E.J. (1947), *The Make-A-Picture Story Test*. New York: The Psychological Corp.

Solomon, J.C. (1938), Active play therapy. *American Journal of Orthopsychiatry* 8(3):479-498.

___ (1940), Active play therapy: further experiences. *American Journal of Orthopsychiatry*, 10(4):763-781.

___ (1951), Therapeutic use of play. In *An Introduction to Projective Techniques*, ed. H.H. Anderson and G.L. Anderson, pp. 639-661. Englewood Cliffs, New Jersey: Prentice-Hall, Inc.

___ (1955), Play technique and the integrative process. *American Journal of Orthopsychiatry*, 25(3):591-600.